SUBHAS CHANDRA BOSE

Subhas Chandra Bose

A Biography

MARSHALL J. GETZ

McFarland & Company, Inc., Publishers
Jefferson, North Carolina, and London

Frontispiece: Subhas Chandra Bose, about to become President of the All-India National Congress, 1938. From *The New York Times* (Paris Bureau). Courtesy of the US National Archives, photo no. 306-NT-122205.

Library of Congress Cataloguing-in-Publication Data

Getz, Marshall J.
   Subhas Chandra Bose : a biography / Marshall J. Getz.
      p.   cm.
   Includes bibliographical references and index.

   ISBN-13: 978-0-7864-1265-5
   (softcover : 55# alkaline paper) ∞

   1. Bose, Subhas Chandra, 1897–1945.   2. India — History —
20th century.   3. Nationalists — India — Biography.   I. Title.
   DS481.B6G37   2002
   954.03'5'092 — dc21   2002000753

British Library cataloguing data are available

Cover artwork ©2002 Art Today and PhotoSpin

Manufactured in the United States of America

McFarland & Company, Inc., Publishers
   Box 611, Jefferson, North Carolina 28640
   www.mcfarlandpub.com

To my parents, Judy and Lowell Getz, with all my love.

ACKNOWLEDGMENTS

First and foremost, I would like to thank my parents, Judy and Lowell Getz, who have always supported and encouraged me throughout my many educational endeavors. They have made everything possible for me.

No one attempting scholarly pursuits could find a more enriching and supportive environment than the Department of History at Texas A & M University. The late Dr. Shirley J. Black sparked my interest in history and became my mentor. Dr. Betty M. Unterberger taught me how to write, and for this, I will forever by grateful.

I began my research into Bose's life while still a student at TAMU, and three people played a special role in my project. They are Dr. Kwang Ro from the Department of Political Science and Dr. R.J.Q. Adams and Dr. Arnold Krammer from the Department of History. Dr. Krammer's classes inspired me, and he taught me how to teach. He took an active role in my Bose research, and he remained encouraging throughout. He has also been a dear friend for 25 years.

As I did the background work on the Netaji, the late Dr. Sisir K. Bose of the Netaji Research Bureau, Calcutta, and the late Ranjan Borra of the U.S. Library of Congress proved most helpful.

This work could never have been completed without the assistance of the Interlibrary Loan Department of the Sterling Evans Library at Texas A & M University.

When my project developed into a book, two mentors gave me invaluable advice: Drs. Ruth and Al Schaffer of the Department of Sociology, Texas A & M University. They helped prepare me for the publishing stage.

It is obvious that I have been blessed with great parents and fine mentors.

CONTENTS

INTRODUCTION

There are three kinds of friends:
Your friend, the friend of your friend,
And the enemy of your enemy, who is also your friend.
—Old Arab Proverb

Subhas Chandra Bose made world headlines as the extremist leader of the Provisional Government of Free India after its establishment by the Axis during World War II. Though Bose's organization was based in Singapore, many hopeful Indians regarded it as the legitimate government of their homeland. From 1943 to 1945, Netaji Bose, with his colorful fascist trappings, caused anxiety throughout the Allied world, since he seemed poised to claim India for the Axis. His apparently imminent takeover meant that an entire subcontinent would fall into enemy hands. When the Allies smashed Bose's Indian National Army in April 1945, the world breathed a sigh of relief, and quickly forgot one of Asia's most curious personages.

Although Bose died mysteriously two years before his country achieved its independence in 1947, his political activities profoundly altered India's fate. The Netaji, or Revered Leader, alerted the West to his country's plight, in terms that Europeans easily understood. For over two decades, he unified India's multiethnic population while enlisting the support of overseas Indians on two continents. His methods, however, were clouded by controversy and left the man with the most checkered of reputations.

In contrast to Bose, Mahatma Gandhi practiced a pristine, almost holy nonviolence that brought him international admiration, even from his political enemies. The Occidental mind rarely fathomed Gandhi's philosophy, but the gentle nationalist generated warmth and changed the indifferent into

1

followers. Bose's message, on the other hand, came across in terrifying, simple words, and journalists featured him in their articles as an Asian hybrid of Hitler and Quisling. To the British, he epitomized the treacherous revolutionary, and seemed even more intractable than the Mahatma.

After Indians discovered the radical politics of Subhas Bose, some gave their ardent support, while others cursed his aggression and impatience. As in the case of Gandhi, even those Indian congressmen and reporters who reviled Bose never questioned the desires and integrity of this angry young man of Calcutta.

Scholarly treatment of Bose as a figure of history varies as widely as the editorial coverage he earned in life. Some Western sources dedicate no more than a passage to Bose; in the vast majority, he receives no mention at all. Within the last half-century, a few studies, such as Hugh Toye's *The Springing Tiger* (1959), and Gerard H. Corr's *The War of the Springing Tigers* (1975), have concentrated on that brief folly known as the Indian National Army. By citing the misadventures of the INA, they hope to prove that Bose's armed struggle made little impact on the Indian independence movement as a whole. They frequently portray Bose and his soldiers as armed clowns, devoid of the barest instincts for the conduct of war. On the other hand, some British historians express a slight undertone of uneasiness regarding the army's unfulfilled potential.

Private recollections and national pride continue to influence many Indian academics, who have elevated Bose to near-sainthood. They rank him with Gandhi as one of India's martyred founding fathers, describing his life as a challenge met. The INA still lingers in their memories as heroic, as the Indians of today relate the story of what *could have* happened had the INA won the key Battle of Imphal. Occasionally, they will deal with Bose's early years as an outspoken Bengali politician, but most, like the British, merely cover his later years in Southeast Asia, as he rallied his forces for that final — and futile — push to Delhi.

While scholars study the glitter and tarnish of a ragtag army, they unanimously neglect Bose's most effective tactics. The Netaji worked best in the conference rooms, not the battlefields. The British-educated Bose practiced statesmanship in the European tradition: understanding him therefore requires an in-depth examination of his politics, and how events in Europe shaped his views.

Like many intellectuals growing up after World War I, Bose put his faith in socialism as a system to govern undeveloped countries. Throughout his career, he found inspiration in European revolutionary history and contemporary activism. His education in history and political affairs taught him the art and science of revolution, which he intended to apply to India. He assumed that the centralized aspects of a socialist government would save India from the postrevolutionary unrest that occurred in France.

By 1935, the focus of Bose's attention shifted from revolution in general to fascism in particular. He believed that a worldwide *Zeitgeist*— not only India's — called for the adoption of fascism. His enthusiasm for Nazi militarism and the shared resentment of the European establishment led many historians to claim that Bose personally adhered to fascist values. This conclusion clearly shows how misleading the available literature is. Throughout his life, Bose hoped that India would thrive as a free *socialist* nation — economically and politically. Although his sympathy with fascism and his own Netaji persona became pronounced after his return to the East in 1943, he never abandoned his socialist values.

The precedent for an alliance between the Indian Left and the German Right dated back to World War I. Authoritarian Kaiser Wilhelm II sponsored a cell of Indian radicals who plotted to overthrow the British colonial government, known as the Raj. In principle, the Kaiser abhorred the idea of colonial subjects fighting for their independence, yet he had to weaken Great Britain. Wartime demands forced German ministers to deal with Indians who vowed to establish the world's first socialist nation. Various agencies in Berlin assisted them in several ways. Some specialized in relocating Indian "students" throughout Western Europe, Russia and the Middle East, while others sent money and arms to rebel leaders in India. The Germans taught Indians sophisticated techniques of sabotage, and briefly considered re-educating captive soldiers from Indian Army units for use against the Crown. The Kaiser's interest in the early Indian liberation movement abruptly ended with Germany's defeat in the First World War.

In a move not unlike that of the Indians who approached the Kaiser, in 1941, Bose chose Nazi Germany as a potential sponsor of an Indian independence program. Hitler's admiration of the British Empire and virulent German racism made Berlin an unlikely choice, but Bose held a narrow-minded view of the nature of fascism. Bose mistook the fascists' struggle for political and military supremacy in Europe for anti-imperialism. This misunderstanding led Bose to conclude that the oppressed peoples of the world would naturally turn to revolutionary fascism. He assumed that the adoption of fascism as an international movement, as well as the resulting alliances, would force the Nazis to downplay their racism. The Netaji predicted Germany to be the victor in any impending conflicts, particularly against imperialist powers such as England and France. Obviously, Hitler's military strength attracted Bose. While Mussolini seemed more favorable to helping Bose, who established good relations with Rome in 1941, Il Duce lacked Der Führer's weaponry and manpower.

Bose's initial experiences in Germany proved disappointing. During his various European tours of 1933–38, he tried to contact leading Nazi officials. Claiming neutrality toward British colonial issues, the Germans rejected him.

Some Indologists in the German diplomatic corps and dissident Nazis took passing interest in Bose, yet he returned to Bengal empty-handed. By 1941, however, Germany had become embroiled in World War II, and Bose developed a concrete proposal describing India's value to the Axis.

Hitler's desire to destroy the United Kingdom forced him to set aside his esteem for its Empire. Berlin discovered Bose's potential as a propaganda weapon, and established him in the Free India Center. Despite the fact that the Nazis never officially committed themselves to the Indian cause, Bose made broadcasts promising his countrymen that the Axis would promote Free India. Berlin expanded Bose's role in August 1942 by appointing him Commandant of the Indian Legion, a unit of rehabilitated Indian prisoners of war. However, numerous Indian mutinies and confusion over the Legion's purpose severely damaged Bose's relationship with the Nazis, and his deteriorating credibility and German military defeats in 1942 forced the Nazis to reconsider their interest in him.

Throughout 1942, Bose expressed his desire to return to Asia and assist the Japanese. Again, Bose mistook a fascist crusade for anti-imperialism; in fact, Tokyo merely planned to replace the European colonial powers in the Orient. Part of Premier Tojo Hideki's deception included a program of carefully choosing local nationalists and helping them succeed. The Japanese needed a new man for India, since by December 1942, their choice, an obscure army officer named Mohan Singh, had proved to be too rambunctious. Bose willingly returned to Asia, but soon discovered that his abilities as a statesman could be retired. Tokyo wanted a figurehead while it engineered India's break from the British Empire and entrance into the magnificent scheme of the Rising Sun.

In a gust of exhilaration, the Netaji condemned the British in speeches and editorials. To Japan's satisfaction, Hindus, Muslims, Sikhs and other religious and ethnic minorities from Mother Hind set aside their differences and proclaimed themselves *united Indians*. With an Indian National Army consisting of reformed Indian prisoners of war, Bose marched across Southeast Asia to India in March 1944. As they crossed the border from Burma, the Japanese war machine buckled. Japan could no longer bear the military effort and the expenses of foreign nationalistic struggles any more than her European counterparts could. To guarantee her own national commitments, Japan suddenly curtailed her international program. Subhas Chandra Bose and his version of Azad Hind, or Free India, were lost.

Bose ended his campaign on a mysterious mission, probably to the Soviet Union. With the Axis powers in their death throes, he hoped to salvage his movement by establishing an alliance between Moscow and Tokyo. Ironically, Bose had considered the USSR a potential backer when the Nazis initially rejected him in 1941. At that time, the Kremlin shunned Bose like a demon, while in August 1945, fate determined the outcome of the Netaji's second overture.

Much of the work published on Bose focuses on his tragic cooperation with the Japanese military government. As indicated earlier, such treatment fails to analyze his skills as a diplomat in dealing with European and Asian leaders. To ignore his successes in recruiting European aid and unifying his diverse people is to leave a major gap in the literature of India's revolution and East-West relations. Merely branding him a fascist fails to account for his left-wing political philosophy. Bose fulfilled his role of statesman, misguided and flawed as he proved in its execution.

To explore the career of Subhas Bose, one must consider German and Japanese historical concerns for an Indian revolution, dating back to the early 1900s. Was Bose's Azad Hind campaign the last in a series of unsuccessful internationally funded insurrections? If Bose's movement appeared to be essentially non–Indian, and even Western in outlook and style, how did he make it acceptable to Hindu and Muslim ideologies?

If few secondary sources cover Bose's diplomatic relations with the Axis, primary material proves more enlightening. Excluding the ominous and sometimes inaccurate magazine accounts, the history of Bose's negotiations with the fascist powers can be viewed through the detailed memoirs of the participants and the available documents. In 1978, Washington declassified numerous United States War Department documents summarizing data obtained through Project MAGIC. The MAGIC operation intercepted Japanese diplomatic messages during World War II. These reports often gave insight into Bose's tense dealings with the Axis, and revealed facts that Bose's colleagues either never knew about, or were too embarrassed to describe. Bose's own writings, biased to be sure, described his career as he shifted from politician to diplomat to military leader. Comprehensive research into his works may explain the goals of this unusual man; yet with the exception of certain oft-cited quotes, the bulk of his literature remains untouched.

Concentrating on Bose's diplomatic missions to the Axis nations may shed some light on this fascinating revolutionary, and dispel persistent myths that Gandhi and Nehru were the only active Indian nationalists. The Netaji took his place in a sporadic program of foreign support of Indian insurrection, and he had an essential role in making an Occidental type of violent revolution palatable to India.

The majority of proper names in this book are Indian, and like Westerners, Hindus, Muslims and Sikhs put their given names first, then their surnames. Traditionally, all Sikh males have "Singh" for their surname.

Thais also put their surnames last, but by convention, they are referred to by their given names. The Chinese put their surnames first. Today, most writers use Pinyin spellings for historical names, which encourages more accurate pronunciation. Pinyin spellings also exist for the names of places, but as most writers lean toward the older Wade-Giles system, I have followed that. I use "Nanking" rather than "Nanjing."

The Japanese used to follow the Chinese custom about putting family names first, but writers typically Westernize Japanese names. In my text, I put surnames first. When citing authors, I used their names as found in their publications.

JANAKINATH'S SON

A Sixth Son

Subhas Chandra Bose was born on January 23, 1897, the sixth son of a prominent family of Cuttack, Orissa, a small town in an eastern province of India. His father, Janakinath Bose, enjoyed an outstanding reputation as a lawyer among the local population of 20,000. He never spent much time with his children, but his career fed his large family. Over the next few years, Janakinath and his wife, Prabhavati, had five more youngsters.[1]

According to one theory of modern psychology, Subhas should have been the most likely candidate for anonymity. As a middle child, he never held the distinction and respect bestowed on the elder siblings, and the novelty of being "the baby" quickly moved on to the subsequent Bose infants. In a home already notable for its reserved parents, the middle boy grew up with emotional insecurities. Subhas remembered feeling "awed" by his parents, and he always desired a closer relationship with them. The lack of parental love in his large family taught Subhas the importance of compatibility, although that lack limited both his development as an individual, and any sense of confidence. "I used to feel like a thoroughly insignificant being," he wrote as an adult.[2]

The quiet youngster attended a European-style elementary school, run by Protestant missionaries. He found grade school quite difficult, since he never spoke English as a child. In those years, English colonial schools emphasized tedious Bible study, at the expense of Indian culture and language. As his schooling progressed, Subhas discovered the inherent bigotry in the British Raj. Not only did British educators avoid dealing with the social problems of Indian children living under colonial rule, but also they created smoldering discontent by whippings and slaps for misbehavior. Such measures, the standard forms of corporal punishment in England, constituted the gravest of insults to Asians. The school system mirrored society in general — a society quite destructive to the Indians.[3]

In certain elite circles, sophisticated Indians regarded Oriental culture and Hindu religious practices as repugnant and socially inhibiting. These people, such as the Babus of Bengal, imitated British manners and customs in an attempt to position themselves as members of an upper class. They embraced foreign rule, and in hope of bettering their social status, insisted that their children forsake the Indian languages, Hindu gods and even dietary laws. In the minds of many upwardly mobile Indian families, the English schoolmasters were right. Organizations such as the Brahmo Samaj, Satya-Shodhak Samaj, and the British Indian Association of Calcutta encouraged Indians to gain political power by adopting European ways. Some even believed that eating meat, sacrilegious and distasteful to devout Hindus, supposedly gave the British their strength. Even Mahatma Gandhi succumbed to this fad; for a brief period during his adolescence, he lunched daily on beef and lamb.[4]

Considering Bose's later fame as a westernized politician of Asia, one might think that the British assimilated him during his school years. Such was not the case. Subhas endured his structured British education as his personal trial. While viewing himself as an insignificant individual, he never forgot that he belonged to the Bose clan, a *khatriya*, or warrior-caste family, that he traced back 26 generations. Over the centuries, the Boses of Mahinagar occupied offices of high importance, first in the military, later as politicians and writers. Bose expressed his sense of obligation to his ancestors in the autobiographical study *An Indian Pilgrim*. "I started life with a sense of diffidence — with a feeling that I should live up to the level already attained by those who had preceded me."[5]

For Subhas, excelling in school meant the avoidance of failure, rather than a compromise of his Hindu culture or for social mobility. Proving to be a fine student, he wanted to attend a preparatory school to give him the necessary background for entrance to a university. When he learned that the Raj barred Indians from taking the scholarship examination for a European gymnasium, he enrolled at Ravenshaw Collegiate School in 1909. At this undistinguished academy in his hometown, the shy, chubby boy ignored athletics and puerile roughhousing, and instead turned to austere books of Hindu philosophy and poetry. He spent long hours practicing yoga and transcendental meditation, or reading obscure and mystic volumes. Subhas claimed that he reached a true religious insight, which, in turn, fostered a social consciousness. High grades enabled him to enter Calcutta's Presidency College in 1913. He was only 16 years old.[6]

External Influences and India's Search for Identity

As Subhas entered college, his adolescence closely paralleled the growing pains of India's revolutionary movement. Indian nationalism jelled in the early 1900s, with the Bengalis in the vanguard. By 1947, revolutionary leadership came from many parts of India; however, Bengal's significant and continuous role can be explained by several factors. The initiating factor — the proverbial spark — was the devastating Partition of Bengal in 1905. The underlying causes for this partition can be found in a historical analysis of the British Raj in general, and its special relationship with Bengal.

The Hindu population of India had long endured a history of foreign influence by 1757, the year that the British East India Company claimed its trading territory as a Crown Colony. As early as the eighth century, Arab explorers monopolized the seas from the Persian Gulf to the China coast. From India's shores, they took ivory, aromatic wood, gold and rare spices, but left a new religion. The Hindus reeled upon hearing that the miracles of Shiva, Kali, Krishna and all the other deities had been performed by the Hands of Allah. The concept of one supreme being and His prophet, Mohammed, gained a permanent foothold in India, particularly in the coastal regions. Muslims eventually became India's largest minority group, and their political influence has remained to the present.[7]

The tough, sword-swinging Afghans were the first followers of Mohammed to rule India. Around 1000 A.D., the Mughals, Islamic invaders from what is now Iran, conquered India and founded a dynasty that lasted for 700 years. Extravagances such as the Taj Mahal and herds of bejeweled elephants cost money, so the greedy kings of India showed keen interest in Portuguese, French, Dutch and British traders, who, in turn, cast hungry glances at Mughal treasures. The Europeans, and in particular, the English, combined foresight with avarice; they planned their futures as they watched the Mughals decline. The agents of the British East India Company saw that the Hindus traditionally accepted fate, but Muslim zealots frequently revolted, often at the slightest provocation.[8]

From that fateful moment when the British raised the Union Jack over India in 1757, the Raj viewed the Muslims as the naughty boys of India. The colonial administration assumed that any dissent would come from India's pockets of Islam, and, like their Mughal predecessors, began a general policy of oppressing and alienating the Muslims. Like the Arabs who gave them their faith, Indian Muslims reacted with fanatical prejudice toward anything foreign — including ethnically different Muslims. In 1863, British soldiers halted a vicious Islamic insurrection called the Wahabi Revolt. After they were crushed, the Muslims retreated into their private communities and avoided the British. As a consequence, they rarely participated in the Indian military or held government jobs. They never exposed their children to British schools, but sent them to study under the learned mullahs, or holy men.[9]

The British and Hindus forged closer ties. The Hindus seemed open-minded about their Occidental rulers. This apparent passivity resulted from their previous exposure to foreign occupation. Before the Muslims arrived, the Hindus viewed themselves as totally unique and pure in relation to the barbarity of the outside world. This doctrine of elitism, relatively common amongst Asian people, *could* have been the heart of a nationalist movement. However, that sense of unity, so necessary for any patriotic revolution, never existed in traditional India. Feudalism, great geographical distances, and the caste system, which gave society order, all prevented nationalism from taking root. Left without any feelings of patriotism, Hindus remained highly susceptible to British influence.[10]

As the Hindus watched the English build India into a mercantile-political-industrial complex, they discovered how these western foreigners succeeded where the Mughals had blundered. From Raj headquarters to the highest suites of London's Foreign Office, the powerbrokers realized that the nation which owned India as a colony insured their eternal hold over her by incorporating the Hindus into the Raj. Throughout the mid-1800s, the Raj found itself isolated from the Muslims, as they introduced the Hindus into the colonial establishment. To state their intentions bluntly, the British hoped to transform Asians into Occidentals, as alchemists attempted to work lead into gold.[11]

At the urging of Lord Thomas Macaulay of the Governor-General's Executive Council, all Indians would be forced to learn English. The council used local Indian intellectual leaders, such as Rajah Ram Mohan Roy, to promote their educational policies. Beyond the educational sphere, the British Army offered food, shelter, clothing and a chance to serve the Empire as an enlisted soldier. The Raj reserved commissions for whites only. For the Hindus, joining the Indian Civil Service became the quickest method to gain security and social status. According to Subhas Bose, a position in the so-called "heaven-born service" signified the pinnacle of success for Indians during the colonial years. These three outlets — education, the military and the Civil Service — gave large numbers of Hindus the opportunity to cooperate with the British, and learn European characteristics.[12]

Despite this amiable relationship, Hindu traditionalists found certain changes in their society disturbing. By 1850, the eons-old village system — the basic social unit in the Orient beyond the family — had been shattered, with an unnatural program initiated as its replacement. Governor-General Charles Cornwallis pioneered the establishment of the zamindars, or local Indian tax collectors working for the Raj. Although tax-farming occupied an essential niche in some traditional economies, especially in China, such an activity, along with land renting, violated Hindu tenets. Nonetheless, Indians prized the position of tax collector, since the Raj expected only a certain amount and anything more became pure profit.[13]

Being a zamindar had one major disadvantage. If tax-farmers failed to collect the money by nightfall of the deadline date, they immediately lost their position, and the government put their licenses up for auction. To avoid the Sunset Law, many zamindars went into debt and eventually lost their property to creditors. Tax-farming caused an increase in crime, as the collectors extorted higher sums from their subjects, and resorted to desperate measures to keep their offices. The average Hindu attributed his higher taxes to British colonization.[14]

A second factor for Hindu discontent stemmed from the general lack of achievement experienced by Indians working for the Raj. While the first law of mercantilism dictates that a colony must exist for the benefit of the mother country, the British overexploited India's economic sphere by strangling village industries and imposing a cruel tax system that promoted corruption. At the political level, only the British held positions of power. The Indian Civil Service provided Indians with white-collar jobs, but the British still made the decisions over India's affairs. The British Army was an alternative to poverty, but it offered a miserable life for its native enlisted men. Indian soldiers suffered the abuses of British officers, and performed menial tasks with no hope of promotion.

The military routinely ignored cultural mores, especially in its administrative disregard for caste. The barracks style of housing of higher Brahman and warrior-caste men with their cultural inferiors created additional tensions. By 1857, grievances against the army had festered and they erupted in that year with the Sepoy Mutiny. The enraged Hindu soldiers literally tasted their final humiliation; their bullet cartridges, usually opened with the teeth, were allegedly greased with lard, the fat of hogs and cows. Simply having this in their mouths would have rendered them ritually unclean.[15]

The Sepoy Mutiny of 1857 revealed a crisis in Hindu society that ran far deeper than tainted ammunition or even the vile conditions in the military. Foreign ways thoroughly polluted India, and her people reacted as any group would upon discovering its vulnerability. Indians tolerated British businesses operated by Englishmen, and accepted the fortresses manned by British soldiers. Even the new religion — Christianity — was introduced to India without the raising of Hindu eyebrows. British historian Percival Spear theorized that "the import of western ideas and their spread through western education, foreign officials, and administrative methods was a different matter…. From this concern with the new ideological invasion which could not be evaded arose the phenomenon which we call Indian nationalism."[16]

Spear's implications are astounding. European rule came to India at a time when mainstream Hindus doubted their faith, leaving them quite susceptible to new outlooks. The traditionalists immediately resorted to fundamentalism and xenophobia. Such a mindset led to the disastrous Sepoy Mutiny, and, like the futile 17th century Hindu guerrilla wars occasionally waged against the Mughals, again proved that prejudice and religious jingoism alone never fostered viable nationalistic movements. Where would India's revolution come from? Spear believed that "India was not herself going to produce nationalism; it would require some sort of stimulus from outside."[17]

Interestingly, it was the British themselves who unwittingly seeded the liberation of their colony. England's fear of losing the crown jewel of her Empire motivated her use of bureaucracy and the British style of schooling to Westernize Indians. While offending Indian conservatives, such developments introduced modern governmental and social techniques to a select group of Hindus. These elites possessed the required skills to create an independent India. Out of this corps stepped Subhas Chandra Bose.[18]

Awareness

Like so many young people from upper or middle-class families, Subhas Bose grew up in a sheltered atmosphere. His conservative British schoolteachers adamantly refused to discuss Indian current events, while Janakinath Bose prohibited political discussions in his home. The whispered debates among his elder brothers never meant much to Subhas, nor did witnessing a special parade in protest of the 1905 Partition of Bengal. Cuttack was a small town in relatively quiet Orissa Province, but the Partition bombing wave of 1908 made the Boses "momentarily interested" in Bengali affairs. In the classroom, these terrorist acts received terse condemnation without further mention.[19]

Still, the word trickled down to Subhas and his peers that the so-called terrorists were evil only in the eyes of adults. Subhas began tacking up newspaper clippings and photographs of radicals throughout his house. This practice stopped after a cousin, who happened to be a policeman, dined one night with the Boses and voiced his dismay at the family's lack of pro–British patriotism. Subhas returned to more conventional projects. At the age of 14, he entered the George V Coronation Essay Contest, and extolled the virtues of His Majesty, the King of England.[20]

Political awareness dawned on Subhas when he entered Presidency College. This son of a lawyer, a member of the provincial gentry, learned the ways of the world in Calcutta, the center of Bengali intellectualism. Living away from home in a big city granted him new freedom. Though he loved his parents, Subhas secretly enjoyed rebelling against them. "I had no hesitation in disobeying them," he wrote, "because by that time I believed ... that revolt is necessary for self-fulfillment — that when a child is born, its very cry is a revolt against the bondage in which it finds itself."[21]

Political activity and association with members of various castes could be the most thrilling ways of doing just that.

Bengali Politics: Swadeshi

The fact that Bengal took the reins of that wild horse called the Indian independence movement should not be a surprise, since Calcutta was — and is — its leading city. The British established their capital in Calcutta in 1773, although only a few thousand inhabited the city then. Throughout the 1800s, the British developed it into a major trade and manufacturing center of the Far East. Most Westerners visualize Calcutta as a fetid sewer crowded with dying humanity, or associate the city with its infamous sweltering dungeon nicknamed the "Black Hole." In contrast to this image, during its heyday, many considered Calcutta the Singapore or Hong Kong of its time. The royal houses of Bengal had long since fallen by the wayside when the British moved in, but the rich Tagores and other merchant dynasties of Calcutta resembled local potentates, in terms of both political strength and lifestyle. Nearly all of these families descended from upper-caste Hindu clans.[22]

Despite Britain's successful ties with local Hindu bluebloods, growing religious unrest throughout Bengal forced the Raj to reconsider its relationship with the Hindus. Muslim leadership, representing 60 percent of the population, felt outrage over the lack of opportunities and legal protection for Indian Muslims. During most of the 19th century, the British tended to ignore their complaints, or blame their continuance on the Islamic tendency to withdraw from contact.[23]

Still, the Raj never expected the support of all religious factions in India. In fact, it depended on intercommunal tension to combat mounting Hindu intolerance, which, by 1900, strained life in Bengal. Hindu parents charged that Western-style schools only corrupted the minds of their children. The students themselves, especially those in the upper forms, wondered if the Raj wanted them to succeed, as most of the scholarship examinations were offered only in the United Kingdom. The whispered fears about the motives of the Raj seemed to become a reality. London appeared to be losing its hold on India, particularly Bengal. Obviously, the British had to strike up new friendships — and quickly.[24]

In private moments, it was evident that the officers of the Raj had shifted their preferences. By 1905, Viceroy George Nathaniel Curzon and his Secretary of State, Lord John Morley, created a plan to woo the Muslims and forcibly teach the Hindus respect for British rule. Curzon and his staff kept the plans shrouded in secrecy, as they plotted the most devastating punishment against the Hindus short of military force. The Curzon Administration predicted that once they divided the giant Province of Bengal into smaller Muslim and Hindu regions, the Bengali Muslims would support the Raj for this token political recognition, and Hindu nationalism would dissolve. The redistricting of East Bengal insured a Muslim majority, destroying the power of the Hindus holding the western sections. London soon regretted its disastrous mistake in appointing Curzon.[25]

On October 16, 1905, or the 30th Day of Aswin on the Bengali calendar, the Partition went into effect. One veteran revolutionary, Arun Chandra Guha, remembered that date as a "day of mourning and animosity." Bengalis still regard October 16th and August 7th — the date Curzon announced the impending Partition — as somber holidays, reminders of the horrid action taken against them. The first Hindu reaction to the redistricting of their homeland was an immediate religious strike called a *hartal*, or observance of an extended Sabbath. From October 16th, devout Hindus stopped cooking and began fasting. Businesses never opened. The faithful even went so far as to link holy rakhi ribbons to their wrists, symbolizing a chain across broken Bengal. The Hindus petitioned Curzon to reverse his policy. He refused. The Hindus then unveiled their secret weapon, aimed at the most vulnerable organ of the Raj.[26]

The vitals of any political unit must center in its purse, and so Hindu leadership called for Swadeshi, the total boycott of all things British. The boycott had a twofold goal: firstly, it was a protest against the British, and secondly, it was designed to encourage native industries. The announcement of Swadeshi arrived at Curzon's office only eight weeks before the textile exporters of Manchester sent their cloth to India for sale. British manufacturing companies, producers of cloth made from Indian cotton and sold to Indians, recognized financial doom when the merchants of Calcutta cancelled their orders. Britain's leading industry suffered unprecedented losses in 1905. Many British officials and Indian civic leaders, as well as the Indian Imperial Assembly and the conservative Bengal Council treated the boycott as a passing phase. In actuality, Swadeshi organizers designed it that way. While British textile magnates made frantic appeals to Downing Street, the Hindus of Bengal piled their English-labeled clothing into bonfires. Moreover, Hindu protest extended to other areas; Indians began to farm their own salt from the sea as an alternative to purchasing the British import.[27]

The Hindus were not alone in 1905. Strike leaders even encouraged the Chinese merchants of Bengal to observe the boycott. Hindus held clandestine meetings with Muslim nationalists, and through these contacts, lured important Muslim businessmen, landowners and civic leaders into the movement. For Hindus and Muslims to forge an alliance, religion could not be the common ground. Swadeshi heralded a new era of social reform for all Bengalis, in addition to the demand for the old provincial boundaries. Swadeshi leaders set three major goals in hopes of altering the Raj through the boycott: a) court procedure revisions, b) improved health care, and c) sanitation and water development programs.[28]

Mahatma Gandhi used the basic principles of Swadeshi — the cloth and salt boycott — as part of his nationwide civil disobedience campaign of the 1920s and 1930s. Subhas Chandra Bose applied several underlying themes of Swadeshi in his Azad Hind Movement. Swadeshi transcended religious barriers, something which Bose always considered essential for the successful unification of India. At the time, the Swadeshi policy of a Hindu-Muslim alliance confounded the British, who viewed the movement as a Hindu scheme, due to its close association with traditional Sabbath practices.[29]

The fact that Muslims followed a religion far different from that of the Hindu majority separated them from the center of Indian life. Muslim alienation created tensions, which plagued India throughout the 20th century, and obviously will continue into the 21st. In 1905, the British authorities resolved to control India by playing one side against the other. In 1947, an anguished Mahatma Gandhi sacrificed the unity of his nation by agreeing to the Islamic State of Pakistan, and lost his life for that compromise five months later. In contrast, Subhas Bose thrived, as one of the few Indian politicians never bedeviled by religious conflicts. As a liberal Hindu from a predominantly Muslim area, he not only sympathized with Muslims, but also concluded that the *Raj* was India's greatest problem, not religion. As a politician —first socialist, and later, fascist — Bose always generated a secular image, unlike the priestly Gandhi.

From 1942 to 1945, Subhas Bose, who was strongly influenced by Swadeshi, took pride in the prominent Muslims who marched under his Springing Tiger flag in three theaters of war. While their sons fought under Bose's command, wealthy Muslims from the Indian communities of Malaya, Burma, Singapore and Thailand made generous donations to his various Free India charities. Like the Muslims who joined pro–Swadeshi Hindus, Bose's supporters saw in him a Hindu working for a greater India.

◆ 2 ◆

MONEY ALWAYS HELPED

From Swadeshi to a National Character

When famed statesman-publisher Dadabhai Naoroji convened the Indian National Congress at Calcutta, as president of its 1906 session, he felt a shocking new mood in the assembly hall. Reversing the Partition and improving social conditions would not move India far enough. Naoroji listened attentively as his colleagues openly discussed ousting the hated Raj. Some of the less extreme delegates expressed the need for step-by-step measures to give Indians power; they hoped that a gradually changing framework would prove acceptable to the colonial administration. The Swaraj, or Self-Rule Movement, began at the 1906 Congress. The concept of self-rule never implied independence, but rather the opportunity for Indians to control the domestic affairs of the colony. However, most nationalists regarded Swaraj as the first step toward freedom. A rather interesting quality emerged as part of the self-rule phenomenon — attention shifted from discontent in Bengal to injustices at the national level.[1]

An effective financial war, centering on the strike, finally gave India what centuries of religious revivals and open revolts had failed to provide — the *national character* of a unified people. Indians who never related to those of other faiths always hesitated to embark on a campaign, which they feared questioned their religions. Realizing that a Bengali strike brought Britain to her knees inspired all Indians — Hindu and Muslim alike — to save themselves. Wallet warfare played only a partial role in the nationalist movement, but its triumph showed Indians their latent strength in collective action. This power became one of the themes of the freedom movement, which reached success on Independence Day, August 15, 1947.[2]

Before Swadeshi turned into a militant movement, nationalists primarily relied on donations from affluent Indians to establish native schools and businesses. The concept of strength in Indian enterprises had always been on the minds of Bengali leaders, and they never forgot that Swadeshi literally translated into "own country." The pragmatic strike organizers of Calcutta noticed the reports of Japan's growing preeminence in Asia, fueled by her skyrocketing economy. They correctly decided that industrialization had to be the soundest basis for political growth. Moneyed clans built Swadeshi stores and factories. Textile mills, match and soap manufacturers, bakeries, yarn-spinners and even banks sprang up overnight — the fertile mushrooms of Swadeshi. When one considers the primitive tradition of India, the emergence of any serious local industrial undertaking must be regarded as an important step toward modernization. Modernization, in turn, led to political education and a growing discontent with the Raj.[3]

Subhas Bose never forgot the small business ideal, and actively promoted it while in Congress. In December 1938, he addressed the first All-India National Planning Committee. The Bengali stressed that a major industrialization program posed no threat to cottage and artisan businesses, as was commonly feared. He promised that heavy industry would not wipe out small-scale operations, such as cloth-weaving. Bose maintained that industrial development automatically assisted all enterprises. He told his colleagues that, "Mother industries ... aim at producing the means of production," especially tools and electricity. He even attributed the economic power of Japan and Germany to a balance between cottage and highly efficient major industries. While Bose obviously overestimated the strength of German and Japanese small businesses and minor industries, Indian radicals respected any ventures that lessened their dependence on Europe.[4]

If Swadeshi industries inspired the ultra nationalists, terror gripped the moderates. They rightly anticipated a severe reaction against any competition to colonial business. Some Swadeshi activists found their business partnerships suddenly dissolved and their memberships in anachronistic but exclusive clubs canceled. Swadeshi leaders and their wealthy backers soon discovered that an economic boycott against Britain risked more than friendships, social status and careers. By 1907, the British refused to tolerate further economic losses or the humiliation of having their schools ignored. Britain's retaliation hurt; as the Raj began to persecute Swadeshi benefactors, local support dwindled. The lack of donations forced the patriots to consider other means of obtaining funds. Had the government silenced the radical chiefs and liquidated their assets a year earlier, the movement would undoubtedly have been strangled. However, by 1907, Swadeshi had extensive manpower, and only needed to explore alternative methods of surviving.[5]

Political Criminality: The Ultimate Commitment

At civic meetings throughout India, political bosses informed young people of the new purpose of Swadeshi: the continued *active* struggle for a national identity. A threatened Swadeshi demanded the ultimate commitment from its members. Since the old nationalist families had either been financially drained or jailed, future funds had to be stolen from rich pro–British Indians. The recruitment of those willing to steal for the movement always prompted controversy, and some left.[6]

The presidents of various Swadeshi promotional unions chided the Anglophiles who abandoned their country, they were told, when it needed them most. The cooler activists suggested that the criminality and the resulting punishments perverted the original philosophy of Swadeshi, while accomplishing nothing. The firebrands reminded their conservative colleagues of those already imprisoned for the cause. The crackdown against the Swadeshi program proved that the British authorities feared the Indian socioeconomic campaign. Armed with that logic, activism prevailed. Whether one merely intended to continue boycotting as before, or planned on indulging in revolutionary violence, supporting Swadeshi now demanded unwavering loyalty.[7]

The strike managers of Bengal explained to their followers that since Swadeshi activities — even overt crimes — had the most honorable of purposes, they were considered morally justified. Burglary, the most common act, seemed far less criminal when labeled as a "loan" from the rich, to be reimbursed after a successful revolution. This style of lawbreaking is known as an act of dacoity, the perpetrator a dacoit. Frequently defined as a highwayman with a particularly swashbuckling reputation, the term dacoit truly has no Western counterpart. Dacoits perhaps filled the niche occupied by the Black Panthers or Weathermen in the United States during the chaotic 1960s.[8] Members of Swadeshi unions and samitis readied themselves for violence in the name of national identity.

Victims of dacoits, most of them from the establishment, naturally regarded them as common thugs or punks, while the dacoits called themselves revolutionaries. Certainly the preparations all Swadeshi dacoits went through would suggest a high degree of planning and organization, but that was not the case. Samitis required all followers to take oaths pledging adherence to Hindu values. While the leaders promoted criminality, they reminded their dacoits that humanitarianism forged the key to revolution. Remembering the ideal stated in the Upanishads, "*tena tyaktena bhunjitha,*" or "enjoy the renunciation," the dacoit trainees proved their total dedication to their communities by engaging in social work.[9]

Initiation into a samiti often included the rite of amabashya, in which the members-to-be demonstrated their fearlessness by staying in a cemetery on the night of a new moon. Amabashya not only tested the initiate's willingness to face ghosts, but their readiness to risk disease. Pledges openly risked horrible maladies by aiding epidemic victims without inoculations or sanitary procedures. Swadeshi tolerated pacifists, but not those who showed any apprehension about consigning their bodies to the cause. Initiates lived a monklike existence, eating Spartan diets, doffing their shoes and never using combs. All dacoits, even married men, heightened their senses through abstinence. When not tending to the ill or destitute, the dacoits relaxed with boxing, martial arts practice, fencing and other sports.[10]

Samiti leaders assigned religious and classical books, such as the Bhagavad Gita, the Chandi Upanishads Ramayana, the works of Vivekananda, and Aurobindo's *Bhawani Mandir* (*Universal Mother India*). Key social and political tracts included Digby's *Prosperous British India?*, Dadabhai Naoroji's *Poverty and Un–British Rule in India*, and historian Rajani Kanta Gupta's pro–Indian interpretation of the Sepoy Mutiny. Some patriots discovered a revolutionary message in American poetry, but most fiction came from Russia and India. Tolstoy enjoyed popularity with the cultured set, while many activists read and reread the novels of Bakun Chandra for his reasoning on the morality of violence.[11]

Newspapers kept the people informed about current events. *The Bengalee* and the *Amrita Bazar Patrika* appealed to older, educated folks, while the young read the *Hitavadi* and *Basumati*. *Sanhya*, the colorful Bengali workers' paper, published stories in a simple style for a mass audience. The Calcutta-based *Bandemataram* reigned as the most famous Swadeshi periodical.[12]

Both the Calcutta activists of the early 1900s and the Netaji of some 40 years later knew that fostering devotion to any cause required a secret educational program and a massive propaganda machine. Union-sponsored instructors linked history with contemporary social issues. Along with Napoleonic France and the story of Holland, the United States provided inspiration to the Indians. Many studied the story of the American Revolution and the Civil War, and they were enthralled by the biographies of Franklin, Washington and Lincoln, along with the fiery essays of Thomas Paine. The Red Shirts, Carbonari and other participants in the Italian liberation movement became heroes in Bengal. India's royal activist, Prince Gaikwad of Baroda, was frequently compared to Victor-Emmanuel II of Piedmont-Sardinia, Italy's original native monarch. Gaikwad, amused at the thought of founding a national ruling dynasty, joked, "Who is going to be [India's] Garibaldi?"[13]

If any one aspect of the Swadeshi movement held Subhas Bose's attention, it was the emphasis on history. Bose found a framework and logic for revolution in history. He knew that history provided the spiritual confidence to challenge the Raj, and a formula to avoid tragedy in a newly liberated nation. While Bose never lived to guide independent India, and so could never prove how well he learned the lessons of the past, he often motivated the soldiers of his outnumbered private army with thrilling tales of India's ancient lions. Bose's followers marched to their deaths in 1945 fueled by his retelling of Mother Hind's golden heritage.[14]

Through the media, foreign affairs became a topic of heated debate among Swadeshi campaigners. The Boer War of 1899–1902 generated further Indian hatred toward British colonial policy. Of course, any event in South Africa gained attention because of the large Indian population there. Indians bragged that Japan's victory in the Russo-Japanese War of 1904–05 was a triumph for all Asian peoples. If tiny Nippon defeated the gigantic Slavic bear, then the secret army of Swadeshi could defeat the Raj. Even the most nonviolent of nationalists, Mahatma Gandhi, felt his political heartbeat quicken at Japan's success, and wrote a number of editorials describing his hopes for Asia.[15]

The Indians identified with the peasants of Russia, and though Westerners may have some difficulty equating the British administration with the barbaric Russian czars, one must never forget who experienced the oppression firsthand. They regarded the dacoits as nihilists, since both aimed at similar targets for similar reasons. News of the March Revolution of 1917, in which Nicholas II abdicated in favor of the Duma, hit India as the paramount event of the 20th century, a superb example of the natural process of liberation. Gandhi compared the Indian boycott to the Russian Revolution, although he abhorred the need for violence. Naturally, Gandhi found the militant trend in Swadeshi disturbing. He condemned the use of what he called "Russian methods" by Bengalis, and erroneously predicted that violence would not assist the Indian independence movement.[16]

Increased Militancy and Revolutionary Violence

Violence in the Swadeshi movement developed in two distinct periods: the first running from about 1907 until 1914, and the second during World War I. Overall, the Indian campaign accomplished very little when it adopted the use of dacoities, or robbery by dacoits. Without organization, equipment and proper training, the early Swadeshi criminals made only a minor impact for their cause. They spent their days in meditation, yet made few if any practical preparations before a crime spree.[17]

Preferring not to attack banks, they generally broke into the homes of

Indian merchants in the middle of the night. They rarely knew exactly what treasure they were looking for when they burglarized a house. They banded together in groups of either too many or insufficient numbers. Some dacoits even rode to the job sites in taxicabs, often donning gaudy masks or uniforms as disguises. If two or three youths carried off a strongbox, they often found the police immediately on their trail. If they managed to escape with a handful of jewelry or rupees, the loot rarely helped their band.[18]

The dacoits emphatically stated that they only used force when necessary, such as when pursued by constables. Such claims were misleading, since nearly all dacoits packed weapons of some kind, and tended to use them with the slightest provocation or threat. Swadeshi supporters accounted for a wave of personal murders in the name of political assassinations. Some even became "hit men" and specialized in killing police officials who investigated their unions. Once again, a lack of planning confounded their impact. Many killings later proved to be the result of mistaken identity. One famous example took place on April 30, 1908, in which terrorists bombed a carriage containing two women instead of a leading magistrate.[19]

Obviously, training for a dacoit was minimal. Arms were difficult to obtain, so building arsenals became a top priority in all samitis. Turkish and Afghan drug dealers, foreign laborers and sailors — men without obvious ties to the Raj — supplied the guns of Swadeshi. Indian employees of the license departments forged papers to facilitate gun purchases, while Hindu civilians working for the army stole rifles and ammunition. Many foremen of large companies discovered their security offices vandalized, with all weapons taken, and the Indian workers smiling in bland innocence. Since policemen were the most common assassination targets, quick dacoits took the pistols from their victims.[20]

Since the sons of Swadeshi needed more weapons than those available, bomb-making became an experimental activity in many unions. Ironically, one of the earliest to suggest this endeavor was a Hindu religious scholar, Brahma Bandhab Upadhyaya, while a nobleman, the Raja of Nazarjole, financed one of the first explosive laboratories. Although the Tagores and other radical elites scraped the bottoms of their coffers to support the factories, most failed due to a lack of materials and trained personnel. Occasionally, the dacoits recruited a chemist into the movement, and purchased quantities of gunpowder and picric acid. In most cases, workers built explosive devices by following contraband European terrorist manuals in their squalid forest hideouts. Of course, many by-the-numbers ordnance men blew themselves up accidentally.[21]

The problem did not confine itself to Bengal. In the Punjab, the northwestern region of India, the cyclone of revolution aroused the Sikhs. The Sikhs, a fanatical Hindu sect established five centuries ago in reaction to Muslim influence in India, historically supported the Raj, and they formed a significant part of the Royal Indian Army. The Punjab's arid weather and sandy earth never provided much for her inhabitants, and with improper land and farming laws imposed by the Raj to protect the gentry, their poverty increased.[22]

By 1911, a depression inflamed the Punjab to the point of insurrection. Lala Hardayal, the Swadeshi leader in the area, condemned the poverty, famines and epidemics, while openly blaming the corrupt colonial administration. When the editor of the *Punjabi* was arrested for writing what was deemed propaganda, Hardayal called for an immediate revolt. One might have predicted a response in Lahore, Amritsar and other cities, but even starving rural communities exploded with a frenzy that amazed Hardayal himself.[23]

After the government heard rumors that Lala Lajpat Rai and Sardar Ajit Singh plotted a mutiny within the army, the Commander in Chief, Lord Horatio Hubert Kitchener, vowed to give up his post if the two famous revolutionaries could not be found. English troops soon quelled a disturbance within the Tenth Jat Regiment, and police apprehended Rai and Singh and jailed them in Burma. Eventually all three Sikh leaders found safety in exile, Singh moving to Iran and Hardayal to the United States. Apparently, Hardayal refused an Oxford scholarship before deciding to move to Berkeley, California. There he made contacts with the overseas Indian community, and started the Ghadr (Revolt) Party. He lectured to Indian immigrant groups, and told them not to forget their enslaved homeland. Hardayal published a journal in several dialects, and sent copies to India. The Sikh made sure that Punjabi and Urdu editions reached would-be comrades among the Tenth Jats and other units. At a 1913 conference in Canada, he urged all overseas Indians to return home, join his fellow Sikhs in the vanguard, and wreak havoc on the Raj.[24]

Although not especially successful, the cult of violence born in Bengal received a great deal of press and government attention, which only furthered its spread across India. The Swadeshi campaign sparked a consciousness extending far beyond Bengal's borders. People fell under the influence of either a philosophy of revolution based on conservative Hindu ideals, or the rough creed of Bengali-style aggression. Numerous political groups opted for the latter. Like their brothers in Bengal, many Indians took secret blood oaths, swearing loyalty to the canons of the Gita. Raising their holy swords to the Goddess Kali, they prayed for the strength to fight for Mother India. While 14-year-old Subhas Bose wrote a wonderful essay lauding King George V, 3,000 citizens of Madras promised to murder His Majesty on his 1911 Coronation Commemorative Tour.[25]

In 1909, Swadeshi violence spread beyond the borders of India. On July 1, Madanlal Dhingra assassinated Sir Curzon Wyllie, an assistant to Lord

Morley, at the National Indian Association Convention in London. The young killer, a stylishly dressed engineering student, turned out to be an active member of the London chapter of the Abhinava Bharat Society. The membership consisted of devotees of violent revolution, who honored the writings of Vinayak Savarkar as their holy scriptures. Savarkar advocated bloodshed to purge the foreign evil from India. Despite the shocking murder in the British capital, Dhingra became something of a cult figure in the United Kingdom. After his execution, the Irish press, David Lloyd George and even Winston Churchill praised him as a misguided hero.[26]

While Europe's fascination with and fear of Indian nationalism increased, the Raj faced growing unrest. The colonial police tried to curtail all radical activities, mainly by hanging several men known to belong to the Maniktola Revolutionary Society, and other subversive groups. Spectacular acts, such as Wyllie's murder or the 1912 attempt on Viceroy Lord Hardinge, did indeed attract attention and certainly upset the authorities, but one must remember the general trends in violence. Most violence stemmed from common dacoities, and many of these acts were foiled or easily solved. The Raj pinned rather ominous-sounding names on rather amateurish deeds — the so-called "conspiracy cases." The Alipore Conspiracy Case, the Howrah Conspiracy Case and the Khulna Conspiracy Case all remain as infamous, if not effective chapters, in the history of British India.[27]

In at least one dacoity, the Muzaffapur Incident, the way in which the police handled the case helped the Indian cause more than the crime itself. When the officers cornered a dacoit in Muzaffapur, Kashmir, the youth shot himself rather than surrender. The government used the surgically decapitated head to exhibit the self-inflicted wound as court evidence. This stirred up a public outcry against the legal authorities. According to Hindu tradition, the whole body must be cremated immediately after death for the soul to be reincarnated. One can imagine the concern Hindus showed for the violated spirit of their young martyr.[28]

Despite the attention, not many of Swadeshi's fighters became martyrs, and their loyalty has been questioned in retrospect. Author and retired activist Arun Chandra Guha recognized this first period of violence as a serious mistake. Betrayal and mistrust within the strike associations hindered the movement as much as the strength of the colonial intelligence officers and police force. Guha once reminisced, "But in those exciting and hectic days, the young men did not have the time to think over an issue calmly and soberly; they were often hustled by the remorseless force of events into acts of violence. If they had not cared for the [lives] and property of others, they were even more reckless about their own [lives] and comforts. History will certainly take this fact into consideration."[29]

Although the 1907–1914 Swadeshi period seemed to end on a futile note, the movement will never be forgotten for two reasons: the concept of Swadeshi alone not only initiated India's first large-scale organized strike, but also planted the seeds of national identity. Indians gained confidence and began a continuous struggle to shatter the British colonial administration. Their labor bore fruit in the figures of Mahatma Gandhi, Jawaharlal Nehru, Subhas Bose and the other nationalists who worked so actively to achieve independence.

When India's patriots saw that armed robberies failed to either bring in money or promote Swadeshi, they recruited students and other would-be dacoits into the world of international terrorism. Some Indians readily accepted the use of extremist methods to overthrow the Raj. Ultraviolence required advanced techniques and costly support. Fortunately for the Indian revolutionaries, Britain had a powerful enemy in 1914. That enemy eventually became the friend of Subhas Chandra Bose.

◆ 3 ◆

THIEVES, SPIES AND SABOTEURS—THE FRIENDS OF WILHELM II

The origins of World War I are rooted in a combination of growing militarism, economic rivalry and entangling alliances. History's first total war had its genesis in the wild ambitions of Wilhelm II, Germany's aggressive young Kaiser. While still a boy, the Prussian Prince saw his grandfather, Wilhelm I, and Chancellor Otto von Bismarck unite the German states through three wars. Growing up in an environment of militarism spawned a belief that Deutschland was destined for glory, and Teutonic iron would crush any of the Fatherland's enemies. Wilhelm II ascended the throne in 1888, at the end of his father's three-month reign. By 1890, he had retired Bismarck and taken full control of German foreign policy.

The Kaiser assessed the European situation, but he lacked the subtle insight of Bismarck. France posed risks, but he paid more attention to her chief ally, Russia. Wilhelm II recognized Russia's potential because of her immense population and resources, but he knew that Nicholas II's empire remained barbaric, a remnant of the Dark Ages in a rapidly changing Europe. The German monarch judged Great Britain as his nation's only threat on the continent.

From 1895 to 1902, Britain existed in a remote world of "splendid isolation," while Germany increased its defense budget and practiced an assertive style of foreign relations. During the Boer War, Berlin eagerly sent arms to the Boers, since the South African Dutch shared cultural links with the

Germans and the war gave the Kaiser a unique opportunity to test new weapons. Britain ended the war an exhausted victor, fully aware that Wilhelm II intended to formally join the Boers. London abandoned isolation and signed a landmark treaty with the Japanese in 1902. The British then forged alliances with Paris and St. Petersburg, which completed the Triple Entente.

The United Kingdom chose these alliances carefully. Being the only major power in the Far East, Japan upheld her part of the treaty by safeguarding British interests in the region. At the onset of World War I, a revised version of this treaty enabled the Allies to concentrate on the European Theater, while Japan attacked German possessions in China and the Pacific. The alliance with Russia clarified some issues dealing with the Middle East. London signed these agreements with China and India in mind. The Kaiser's *Drang nach Osten*, or Drive to the East, included plans for a Berlin-to-Baghdad Railway. Although Berlin canceled the massive project, the idea of German expansion that close to India terrified the British.

Wilhelm II looked toward Asia for several reasons. A fanatically jealous man, the Kaiser felt a need to have precisely what the English had, including an outstanding navy and an empire. The quest for an empire satisfied more than the Kaiser's raging dreams. Under Bismarck, who viewed Germany as a continental power, Britain and France increased their colonial holdings, while Berlin seemingly ignored the imperialist movement. Colonies played a major role in the world economy before 1914. After the 19th century Industrial Revolution paved the way for mass production, small industries suddenly grew into heavy industries. To maximize profits, companies established monopolies and cartels, and there was pressure on them to control the supplies of their raw materials and open new markets. As colonies provided raw materials and markets, they became increasingly important. If Bismarck showed little interest in imperialism, the German ruler did not.

Naturally, Wilhelm II gazed toward India with the eyes of an alpine wolf. Since economic and colonial rivalry partially created the tensions that caused the war, it may be initially surprising that the Kaiser did not attempt to conquer India. In fact, rapidly escalating war commitments in Europe prevented him from attacking England's prized territory. Still, Berlin found an indirect means of hurting Great Britain; Germany befriended the frustrated soldiers of Swadeshi.

Indians in World War I: The Berlin Committee

In the years before World War I, the Swadeshi movement appeared to be on the verge of collapse, due to the disorganization of the programs, duplicity within the ranks, and a general lack of funds. Indians remember the first phase of violence for its exaggerations rather than its reality. World War I threw Great Britain into a crisis, giving Indian nationalists their chance to break the colonial shackles.

During wartime, any mother country expects her colonies to remain loyal and supportive. However, the British acknowledged the discontent within the crown jewel of their empire. In London, Prime Minister Herbert Henry Asquith made vague promises about reconsidering Indian issues after the war. Moved by Woodrow Wilson's dream of self-determination, Indians suggested Swaraj (Self-Government) as a substitute for full independence. Many noblemen and political leaders accepted this arrangement, and left India for the battlefields of Europe, to fight alongside their British comrades in arms. Gandhi, certainly not a soldier himself, heartily believed in the persuasive capacity of a strong Indian war effort. He urged his followers to support the Allies in nonviolent ways, by serving in medical units or by filling clerical positions.[1]

Some Indian extremists, however, found numerous reasons for not supporting Britain. They noted how Irish nationalists, in particular Sir Roger Casement, used the war as an opportunity to rebel against the Crown. The story of Casement, who was hanged for purchasing German military equipment for terrorist purposes, reminded Swadeshi campaigners of their vows to free India. In April 1916, Indian patriots cheered upon hearing the news of Ireland's bloody Sinn Fein Riot. The sons of Swadeshi adapted the Irish catch phrase: "Britain's adversity is Ireland's opportunity."[2]

As the Indian nationalist movement turned towards Europe, the role of overseas Indians suddenly gained importance. Naturally, many politicians who ran afoul of the law went into exile, where the Raj could not stop their work. In addition to the fugitives, Indian students, professionals, laborers and merchants relocated to various parts of the world, but never forgot Mother Hind. Students probably made up the largest group of Indian radicals abroad. Many had been former Bengali terrorists. Their youthfulness and station in life made them a perfect pool for continued extremist activity. They traveled to Europe and the United States to study the sciences, which often provided the formal instruction necessary for designing explosives. Most, however, simply hoped to create the foundation for an all–Indian industrial complex.[3]

Students were the first Indian nationalists to seek German aid. They discussed their ideas with agents in the German Foreign Office soon after the war began. A handful of young socialists calling themselves the Berlin Committee wanted to establish a revolutionary network spanning Europe, North America and the Far East. German officials, thrilled by the idea of striking a flint in England's most vulnerable tinderbox, suggested that select radicals come to Europe. Soon, Berlin Committee members or people they sponsored went to Germany, Italy or Switzerland.[4]

When the Indian nationalists made their first overture to the Germans in 1914, they had not yet developed any clear, long-range plans. They arranged for Bengali students to take lessons in bomb-making from a Berlin dynamite works, while revolutionary leaders created a program worthy of presentation to the German government. By autumn of that year, it seemed as if the Germans had already pledged themselves to the Indian cause. Representatives of the Berlin Committee met with an obscure official simply referred to as Baron Von Oppenheim. Von Oppenheim promised that Germany would finance and arm nationalist cells throughout India, after a number of Berlin Committee members returned home to incite the rebellion.[5]

Both sides agreed on the importance of Germany's role in training Indian saboteurs in Berlin, and smuggling revolutionary propaganda to India. They discussed the possibility of using repatriated Indian prisoners of war for a revolutionary army. This proposal fit in with Berlin's numerous attempts to radicalize its European POWs before returning them to Italy and Russia. Although the Germans never really followed up on the Berlin Committee's offer, Subhas Bose and his sponsors eagerly used a similar "Indian Liberation Army" in another war, some 30 years later.[6]

The Indians showed some reservations about aligning with the Germans, at times suspecting them of ulterior motives, or questioning Berlin's commitment to their movement. Germany had a small colonial empire, and the Kaiser's jealousy of Asian territories under British rule was no secret. In fact, German police held Sikh activist Lala Hardayal during his 1914 visit, after he expressed his own concerns about Wilhelm II's ambitions. Both parties knew that Germany did not care for Mother Hind as much as hurting England. For that reason, the Indians, while admitting the need for German officers to instruct their revolutionary army, rejected any thought of German infantry units landing on Indian soil.[7]

Before the program began, the Indians asked for various guarantees from the German government. Von Oppenheim, probably unsure of how to best utilize his band of revolutionaries, found it easier to appease them rather than dismiss them outright. The apprehensive nationalists warned Von Oppenheim that *Indians* intended to manage the Berlin Committee and guide India's revolution. They reminded their German host of their intentions of bringing about a socialist state. The Baron reassured them that Germany approved of their aims, and would naturally ignore requests for aid made by any other groups, including any insurgent monarchies established by reactionary maharajas. The shady German agent listened indifferently when the Berlin Committee made the preposterous demand that Germany take responsibility for the radicals and their families, in the event of an aborted revolution. Von Oppenheim at least guaranteed that Berlin would deny any extradition requests from Britain and the Allies.[8]

Incredibly, Germany's role in the Indian movement hinged upon using the United States as a field of operations. The United States became the unwitting overseas center for nationalist activity immediately before and during World War I, although the history of the American role has been virtually overlooked in Western sources. Since America remained nonaligned for much of the war, Indian radicals found an easy host and a viable Indian community. In San Francisco, Lala Hardayal's leftist Ghadr (Revolt) Party blossomed into a vibrant unit bent on freeing India. Through many underground newspapers, the Ghadrites urged overseas Indians to pledge their loyalty to Germany in 1914. A second organization, the Indian Independence League, planned to join forces with the Ghadrites.[9]

Until the United States officially joined the Allies in 1917, Indian radicals worked freely with the German embassy in Washington, DC. Uncertain of the practical basis behind the secret Indo-German alliance, some Ghadrites actually petitioned to serve in the Kaiser's Imperial Army, but German diplomats assured them that their effectiveness depended upon their returning to India. When revolutionary leaders in India required the services of certain comrades living in the US, the German ambassador arranged, and in some cases paid for, the return voyage.[10]

Bose's cooperation with the Nazis was somewhat different from the relationship between the Berlin Committee and the Kaiser's government. Adolf Hitler and Wilhelm II both respected the colonial system, but needed to destroy the United Kingdom. Fully understanding the Kaiser's attitudes, the Berlin Committee attempted to maintain autonomy and gain assistance from a reactionary government that essentially opposed its goals. Bose viewed fascism as the catalyst for world revolution and a toxin to empires. While he never actually condoned the horrible excesses of Nazism, and the Germans never softened their racist stand, Bose still moved closer to his hosts than the Berlin Committee did to theirs. At best, the Kaiser's men regarded the Berlin Committee as a secret band of wild-eyed radicals, while Bose eventually earned hard-won diplomatic status. By 1942, Bose had become a public figure with an exaggerated reputation for being favored by ranking Nazis, if not by Hitler himself. He did try to befriend the Führer as a fellow revolutionary, and for this, Bose's notoriety will never be forgotten.

Intrigue in Every Corner

Since the Berlin Committee needed solid communication lines between its European headquarters and activists in America, physician Chandra Kanta Chakravarty received the appointment as official liaison. German Foreign Minister Alfred Zimmermann personally wrote him a letter of introduction to the embassy in Washington. Chakravarty's primary mission was to report on the "different units of Indian revolutionaries" operating in the US. This point is interesting, since sources usually discuss American-based activists in terms of either the Ghadr Party or the Indian Independence League, not multiple cadres. Chakravarty's first report to the German Foreign Office so impressed Zimmermann, that the minister gave the doctor exclusive rights to handle Indo-German policy.[11]

In the United States, the cohesion between the Indian revolutionaries began to dissolve. After Hardayal fled to Europe to avoid US federal agents, Chakravarty chaired the executive committee of the Ghadr Party. He ruined the committee, and his colleagues began to suspect that he functioned as a British spy. While activism in the United States foundered under Chakravarty's leadership, Dr. Sailen Ghose began to seek out influential friends in California. The dedicated professor swayed the most powerful among Randolph Hearst's editors to the Indian side, but management problems within the Ghadr Party limited his effectiveness.[12]

Ghose found his efforts cut short in April 1917, when the US entered the war. In what Indian scholars refer to as either the San Francisco Case or the Hindu Conspiracy Case, law enforcement officials rounded up approximately 50 Indian suspects. To avoid arrest, Ghose escaped to Mexico. Despite the obvious risks, he crossed back over the Rio Grande in 1918. The police caught him and he went on trial with his comrades, along with a handful of Germans accused of aiding traitors to the Allies. Concurrently, there was a similar case involving Germans and Indians in Chicago.[13]

What was the significance of the San Francisco Case? The evidence showed a frightening breach of American security. Attorney General A. Mitchell Palmer and John Lord O'Brien, his Special Assistant for War Work, monitored the trial and investigated the allegations. As in Ireland, the Germans apparently supplied the Indian extremists with arms for shipment to India. The brains of the operation — a combined effort of the Berlin Committee and the German Foreign Office — secured themselves far beyond the reach of the US Department of Justice. Although the smuggling took place in California, the plans were made in Berlin. Whatever its effect on America's concern for security, the Indo-German plot failed. The US State Department alerted the Raj that two ships, the SS *Maverick* and SS *Henry*, were steaming toward India with cargoes of weapons. Colonial police met the ships when they attempted to dock.[14]

The court delivered rather light sentences considering the wartime circumstances — four years' imprisonment for the Ghadr ringleaders; months and weeks for the rest. More notable than the convictions, perhaps, were the dramatic vignettes that took place during the trial. Dr. Chakravarty, Zimmermann's handpicked revolutionary ambassador, proved to be an embarrassment to both the Germans and the Berlin Committee. Although the sources seem to conflict about the exact time frame, Chakravarty defected from the movement — after "borrowing" about $50,000 from the German embassy for a real estate deal in New York — and became a witness for the government. He even met with Robert Lansing, the Secretary of State, and explained the Ghadrite program. Since Chakravarty served as a state's witness, he could act as his own lawyer without any complications. Washington used his testimony to prepare its case, yet declared it "top secret." In this way, the government kept the witness and his evidence out of the courtroom. Despite the ranting of Franz Bopp, the former German consul general, the authorities cleared Chakravarty of all charges.[15]

While the American government short-circuited the Indo-German collaboration's best efforts, some of India's fighters continued their seditious activities in West Asia. A number of prominent revolutionaries hid in Iran, Iraq, Afghanistan and other areas immediately beyond India's borders. Only sparse groups of seminomadic Muslim tribesmen lived in these frontier territories. While not active in World War I, the frontiersmen refused to aid the Allies, since both Britain and Czarist Russia had tried to colonize their homelands. Raja Mahendra Pratap, who later surfaced as a bizarre profascist demagogue during World War II, seemed to be the only important figure to emerge from this ineffective wing of the nationalist movement. Pratap, the son of a well-to-do family from India's United Provinces (now called Uttar Pradesh), declared himself President of the Provisional Government of India on December 1, 1915. Headquartered in Afghanistan, this government in exile established diplomatic relations with Germany, Afghanistan and Ottoman Turkey, although, not unexpectedly, it failed to gain the recognition of neighboring Russia. Like Subhas Bose, Pratap collaborated with the German military to weaken Britain's hold over India and West Asia. Pratap's relations with Berlin began in the days of Wilhelm II and ended with the chaotic nightmare of Nazi Germany.[16]

Berlin's interest in an independence movement inflamed the revolution in India, yet it accomplished very little. Bengali dacoits put on uniforms and armed themselves with any available weapons, including smuggled Mauser pistols and antique muskets. These ragtag militias still behaved like bumbling dacoits. Radicals carried anti–British literature into the barracks of Royal Indian Army units stationed at home, but found little success in converting the soldiers.[17]

The Raj, naturally terrified by even the thought of an Indo-German conspiracy, became determined to stop the revolution. As a first safeguard, the colonial government recruited Muslim Pathans and Nepalese Gurkhas into its police and armed forces, since neither of those Asian tribes identified with the Indian cause. Third-degree tactics became commonplace in Bengal as the police waged their crackdown. Even an associate of a possible radical was apt to be imprisoned without charges, and deprived of food and water until he or she confessed or incriminated that friend. Those detainees who left with their psyches intact told horrible stories of torture and humiliation. Guha recalled a young woman who claimed that after her arrival at the police station, male officers stripped her and, while her thighs were forcibly spread apart, one poured chili powder into her vagina. While German-sponsored activities, such as the Berlin Committee program, died out as the war ended, militant Swadeshi and Swaraj terror did not.[18]

Subhas Chandra Bose grew up with the rise of organized rebellion in India. As the young man searched for identity, his country began to develop its national character. The Bengali mainstream reacted only after the British threatened Hindu influences with the redistricting of Muslim areas in 1905. Once the Swadeshi strikes proved successful, Indians outside of Bengal resorted to violence to safeguard the movement. The militancy that emerged after the Partition of Bengal remained an integral part of the Indian struggle for the next 40 years.

At first, clumsy dacoits achieved little beyond terrorizing the British and those Indians who refused to support Swadeshi. England's entry into World War I saved the revolution from certain death. When Indian radicals appealed to Germany, the Kaiser's foreign ministry explored the possibilities of undermining the enemy's Empire. Using their embassy and consulates in the United States, the Germans agreed to smuggle guns and saboteurs but little else, while the Berlin Committee demanded autonomy in guiding India's future.

Germany's defeat and pressure from the colonial police did not eliminate the clique of diehard rebels, nor did those factors extinguish the Indian revolutionary spirit. British oppression peaked in the 1930s, and a militant new power ruled Germany. Subhas Bose became a bridge between the two forces, after rejecting both his conservative Hindu upbringing and a domestic political career. He revived the untried plans of the old Berlin Committee, and joined the fascists in 1941. Within four years, Bose created an army. His clash with British and American soldiers in Asia will be remembered as the most violent — and the most flawed — chapter of Indian history.

◆ 4

HIS PATH

Education Ends, Politics Begins

At Calcutta's Presidency College, Subhas Chandra Bose met politically minded students who advocated various means of liberating wartime India, including the use of violence. Bose disagreed with all of them and concluded that India's freedom depended upon a "process of natural reconstruction." He thought in terms of an organized movement, using force only as a last resort. Bose took a greater interest in politics than in his studies, and he quickly fell in with a group of reportedly seditious students, including Swadeshi activist Ananga Mohan Dam. The Raj's intelligence and security branch, the Criminal Investigation Department (CID), kept this clique under surveillance.[1]

On occasion, these students even physically attacked their conservative British professors. Bose got involved in one such assault and was expelled from Presidency in 1916. After being rejected by the army, he appealed to the college authorities for readmission, eventually entering Scottish Church College at Calcutta. There he joined the officers' training unit of the Bengali cadets called the India Defense Force. He set politics aside, studied hard, and graduated in 1919 with a Bachelor of Arts degree in philosophy. He began a master's curriculum in experimental psychology, but left it after a short time.[2]

At his father's suggestion, Bose went to study at Cambridge to qualify for a position with the Indian Civil Service. In 1920, he took the Civil Service Examination, and scored high enough to be awarded a coveted bureaucratic post. He soon became bored with his work, especially as he watched the rise of Mahatma Gandhi. His old interest in politics returned with renewed vigor and he left the Civil Service in May 1921.[3]

As Subhas Bose entered the postwar Bengali political scene, he found that while the general population still called for "home rule," organized violence was no longer the vehicle for change. Postwar inflation and European business superiority wreaked havoc on local Indian businessmen, especially the jute traders. Even the most established Indian merchants, who would never have donated one rupee to a Swadeshi union in 1905, suddenly backed the nationalist movement. The workers suffered even more than their employers did, and they reacted with disorganized strikes, particularly in Calcutta. Journalists, clerks and other white-collar workers felt more political consciousness than their blue-collar counterparts, so they developed general labor unions. C.R. Das, a High Court lawyer, Swadeshi advocate and one of Gandhi's lieutenants in the early civil disobedience movement, founded the Bengali Workers' Union. In 1923, Das became president of the increasingly influential All-India Trade Union Congress.[4]

The labor union or *kisan* movement provided India with her first cadre of locally minded socialists. Such thinkers attracted Subhas Bose. He actually met Gandhi for the first time on July 16, 1921, but Gandhi's mystical charisma did not impress him. However, Bose found a soul mate in C.R. Das. Together, they published a liberal paper, the *Forward*, and Das convinced Bose to participate in Gandhian civil disobedience. In 1922–23, they made a promotional tour of India to advertise Das's newly formed Swaraj, or Self-Rule Party.[5]

Mahatma Gandhi desired self-rule, of course, but he took a different path to attain it. Gandhi, who combined Hindu mysticism with Christian teachings, adopted a policy called Satyagraha. The term actually means "persistence in truth," but Indians commonly knew it as passive resistance and civil disobedience. Gandhi first swore to abide by this philosophy on September 11, 1906, at a special meeting in Johannesburg, after the South African government issued the anti–Indian Asiatic Law Amendment Ordinance. In practice, the Mahatma's policies continued many activities quite similar to those of the Swadeshi movement, that dynamic campaign following the 1905 Partition of Bengal. Gandhi's children boycotted British cloth and produced a coarse homespun substitute called khadi. Khadi served as both protest and an economic asset, since almost anyone could be taught to weave. The Great Soul himself believed that such activities would force the British to grant self-rule, while still allowing India to remain in the Empire.[6]

To understand Indian politics of the 1920s and 1930s, one must avoid identifying labels used in India with their meanings in the West. Gandhi and his faction of the Indian National Congress made up the "right wing," which included the "moderates" and "liberals." They believed in adhering to the peaceful restrictions of the Congress constitution and self-government under the Crown (dominion status). The "extremists" and "nationalists" who made up the "left wing" challenged them. The leftists believed in full independence and held that only violent revolution could spawn such freedom.[7]

The socialist Bose, a wiser planner than many of his colleagues, prepared an elaborate course of study that had to be made before the revolution started. First, political leaders needed to methodically analyze the Anglo-Indian relationship, paying careful attention to the pros and cons of living under the British Raj. Bose expected India's patriots to make a general study of empires, considering such examples as the British, Roman and German. Finally, the act of revolution obligated the leadership to fully understand the mechanics of political change, to spare India the chaos suffered by the French in their postrevolutionary period. Bose obviously improved on the educational programs developed by the Swadeshi unions and other related civic organizations of two decades before.[8]

Bose's intelligence and ideas earned him the admiration and support of many, including those, like Gandhi, who did not always agree with him. As a liberal philosopher, Bose easily adopted socialistic beliefs, but how did he accept the role of chieftain of the Congress extremists? Social historian Krishnalal Shridharani, author of *My India, My America*, contends that Subhas Bose virtually fell into place, simply because of a general weakness among his fellow leftists. Bose certainly had character, since the introverted boy had grown into a man of the strongest passions. One of his earliest major political endeavors was the cofounding of the radical Independence for India League with Jawaharlal Nehru in 1928. Nehru, an anti–British socialist like Bose, spoke in much milder tones, however. That year Bose sat on Calcutta's city board and organized the Bengal Students' Conference. Like his friend Das and Sikh activist Lala Lajpat Rai before him, Bose headed the All-India Trade Union Congress in 1929. He also served terms with the Bengal Legislative Council and held the post of Secretary-General of the All-India National Congress.[9]

Having a political career in India had legal ramifications. The British frequently jailed Bose, Gandhi and their compatriots on charges of revolutionary activity. Their widely varying philosophies, especially on the use of force, never mattered to the authorities. The British regarded all independence seekers as equally seditious. The Raj branded Bose a terrorist and he became the subject of widespread controversy. The Legislative Assembly discussed his possible links to bomb-tossing dacoits throughout Bengal, although there is no evidence that he ever directly participated in a violent act outside of warfare, nor did he have strong terrorist contacts in the 1920s and 1930s. In 1926, Bose sued the Anglo-Indian newspaper the *Englishman* for libel. He won an apology and 2,000 rupees. Despite these facts, the colonial government continued to imprison him. In 1930, while in jail in Mandalay, Burma, he compiled the notes of his major opus, *The Indian Struggle*, which he completed while on a 1933 health furlough and published three years later. In his sweltering Mandalay cell, he contracted tuberculosis and developed the gastrointestinal problems that plagued him for the rest of his life. In September 1930, just prior to being released, Bose became Mayor of Calcutta.[10]

Through the 1930s, the tension of increased political activity and renewed oppression from the Raj rocked India. Viceroy Lord Willingdon declared the All-India National Congress illegal in 1932, and seven years later, the government issued a White Paper, revoking the 1935 Constitution and indefinitely postponing any plans for independence. The British arrested the more radical politicos, such as Congress Party boss Sarat Bose, Subhas's brother, and paroled the more conservative ones, in hopes of creating a foundation of Indian leaders amenable to colonial rule. In 1938, Gandhi pushed for Subhas Bose's election to the Presidency of the banned All-India National Congress. He prayed that Bose's strength and dedication would unify the Congress. As President, Bose spoke less of socialism and more of democracy, but moved to the far left during his second term and demanded India's freedom within six months. Bose's ultimatum and his growing interest in European fascism caused further rifts in the Congress. Clashing with Gandhi and Nehru meant certain political suicide, but Bose incorrectly predicted that, "if we come to a parting of the ways a bitter civil war will commence."[11]

Gandhi began to erode Bose's support. As a religious figure, the Mahatma wielded tremendous moral clout among the Hindu masses, so they remained silent as he drove Subhas Bose from the Congress. Bose resigned in April 1939, and Gandhi imposed on him a three-year suspension from political participation. Ironically, not holding a major office gave Bose the freedom to follow his extremist pursuits. At first, he concentrated on organizing the leftists. Bose partially blamed the lack of support from nationalist dons such as Nehru on the fragmentation and squabbling within the left wing. He had the respect of most leftists — they had reelected him to the Congress presidency in the controversial snap election of December 1938. Real organization of the left wing came with Bose's formation of the Forward Bloc Party in 1939. Bose saw the Forward Bloc as a function of the *Zeitgeist*— the spirit of the times. In his 1941 essay, "Forward Bloc — Its Justification," Bose wrote, "when the mainstream of a Movement begins to stagnate, but there is still vitality in the Movement as a whole — a Left Wing invariably appears. The main function of the Left Wing is to stimulate progress when there is danger of it being arrested."[12]

The black sheep of Indian politics created the Forward Bloc from three basic leftist types: Congress Socialists, ultraleftists, Royists (followers of Communist M.N. Roy), and any additional ardent anti-imperialists. Its goals were simple: full independence and the creation of a leftist Indian government. In an interview for the *Daily Worker* of London, Bose said that India needed a socialist regime, which he described as a "synthesis between Communism and Fascism," although he later admitted that he used a poor choice of words. The Congress formally acknowledged the Forward Bloc within a year. Bose toured India to promote his party, making vicious attacks on the "sacred cows" of Gandhi's philosophy: spinning and prohibition. Soon, the Forward Bloc's strength ranked with that of Gandhi's own party, the Seva Sangha.[13]

Bose's party strategy included publishing the weekly *Forward Bloc* magazine, which warned the leftists not to be hindered by the sluggishness of right-wing congressmen who did not represent the Indian people. Bose directed two anti-imperialist conferences at Nagpur: the first in October 1939, and the second in June 1940. At the 1940 conference he reiterated the goals of the movement: "...the capture of political power by the Indian *masses* as early as possible and the reconstruction of India's national economy on a socialist basis.... All power to the Indian people, here and now."[14]

During National Week in early April 1940, Bose shocked the authorities by convening the All-India Anti-Compromise Conference at Ramgarh. The future Netaji bellowed a storm of propaganda advocating strikes and riots unless the British left India immediately. Bose's new ultimatum led to the birth of the Haryan Movement—a radical version of Gandhi's Satyagraha. The conference proved that the majority of Indian leftists fully accepted the Forward Bloc as a new political entity.[15]

Now the Forward Bloc virtually directed the general left, but that did not mean that all extremist factions followed Bose. The Communists would always be Bose's serpentine nemesis. Upon his 1939 resignation from the Congress, Communists condemned him and his colleagues for "playing the role of British agents." The Indian Communists wanted more than independence for their country—they called for the end of the Chamberlain Government in Britain! However, they paid too much attention to their wild theories and rarely got involved in the grass-roots struggle for freedom. Since the disorganized Communists had little clout in India, Bose ignored their accusations that he and his compatriots were pro–British.[16]

Bose's International Experience

While Subhas Chandra Bose was salvaging the shattered left wing in his country, he paid close attention to events in Europe. His numerous trips abroad shaped his opinions regarding the situation there. From 1933 to 1936, he had lengthy sojourns on the continent, during which he avoided arrest warrants at home, and looked for the chance to enlist European support for the Indian struggle. He continuously remembered C.R. Das's prophecy— that making the world conscious of India's problems blazed the path to India's independence. Bose considered himself Das's agent, although he would go farther than Das ever imagined going.[17]

Bose found his first European excursions both successful and informative. By speaking in terms of Western concepts, he convinced the people of Eastern Europe that they shared many hardships. He told his audiences (which mainly comprised academics specializing in Asian history or political affairs) of the common experience whenever powerful outsiders crushed national identities. Poland showed a poignant sympathy for India's plight. Polish scholars impressed Bose with their knowledge of Hindu thought and the Sanskrit language. To his delight, he discovered a thriving Oriental Society in Warsaw, which catered to students of Asian culture. Unfortunately, Bose failed in his attempts to form a Polish-Indian Society, which, he had hoped, would have been a study circle for political and economic issues. He studied Czech political history at Prague, and renewed a friendship with the University's Indologist, Professor Lesny. On Bose's earlier trip in 1934, the pair had created the Czechoslovak-Indian Association, with Lesny as its chief executive officer. While in Prague, Bose delivered a series of formal lectures on Indian politics.[18]

Bose even dared to make a controversial tour of Britain in 1938. His stopover in Ireland went well, especially after he reminded the Irish that, like Indians, they struggled to keep their native language and culture from becoming casualties of British colonization. President Eamon De Valera received Bose as a fellow revolutionary. In contrast to Ireland, Bose's visit to England frustrated him. In a cover story on him, *Time* magazine quoted him as saying that "Ethiopia, Spain and China have successively forced themselves on the attention of the Civilized World.... India has receded into the background and the British public appear to heave a sigh of relief that, whatever else happens, the knotty Indian Question has finally been solved...." He later claimed to have met Englishmen who actually wanted him to succeed, but none of them worked in government.[19]

Bose's experiences abroad gave him an international outlook unmatched by any other Indian nationalist, including Gandhi. By 1939, he intended to conduct India's revolution according to Western guidelines, and he needed the active support of Europeans to accomplish his goal. Two distinct movements caught his attention, and he considered them both. Bose carefully noted that the followers of either philosophy could never be friends of the British.

The Value of an Iron Fist

Bose began to follow a new path — a Western path — toward Indian independence. Before traveling, he had, of course, thoroughly studied the history of revolutions in Italy, Ireland, Turkey and Russia. The Young Turk Movement and Atatürk's regime utterly fascinated him. For Bose, Turkey illustrated a prime example of upheaval and subsequent reorganization of an Asian country. He realized that India, like Turkey, would need a powerful centralized government during those trying first years after liberation. He examined the rise of Communism in Russia and fascism in Western Europe, and he tried to determine the possible relevance of these two movements to India.[20]

While Bose had not yet visited the Soviet Union in the 1930s, he could not ignore Moscow's strong condemnation of imperialism, nor could he afford to overlook certain historical facts. A special relationship existed between Russia and India, which served as a precedent for a serious contact. India always glittered as the crown jewel of the British Empire, and Russia loomed as the only potential threat to it. However, Czarist Russia was weak compared to Great Britain, but that did not allay England's concern about India's giant neighbor. Russia's extension into Uzbekistan, Turkestan and other parts of Central Asia encroached on India. Viceroy Curzon warned that while "...neither Russian statesmen nor Russian generals are foolish enough to dream of the conquest of India, they do most seriously contemplate the invasion of India; and that with a very definite purpose which many of them are candid enough to avow."[21]

In contrast to Imperial Russian attitudes toward India, the Soviet Union took a patronizing interest in the Indian struggle by providing guidance and asylum to many of India's failed revolutionaries. The Bolshevik takeover gave many Indian nationalists revived hopes as World War I dragged on to its conclusion. Soviet officials encouraged Indian radicals with their frequent remarks about the British hold over Asia, and the possibilities of a Communist-inspired mass revolt against the Raj. In 1921, the Comintern recognized the Communist Party of India, which was headquartered both in Tashkent, Uzbekistan, and the USSR. Indian Communists joined forces with the Ghadr Party in California and the Berlin Committee, and so were included in the massive Indo-German Conspiracy of 1914–18. When the Allied victory in World War I canceled Indian plots in Western Asia, some revolutionaries escaped from Afghanistan and Iran into Soviet Central Asia, where they found new lives.[22]

The Soviet Union abetted the anticolonial cause by offering aid and education to the Indian nationalists. The new nation itself provided the perfect model for a leftist government in Free India. Jawaharlal Nehru toured the Soviet Union in 1926, and the wealthy young Anglophile returned home convinced that a revolution and land reforms would save his people. The future prime minister expressed his concern that Gandhi's Hindu views on nationalism anchored the movement to a stationary past. Satyagraha's soft stand kept the Indian masses from forcefully arising. The Russians scoffed at nonviolence, since they had climaxed their revolution with one of the bloodiest civil wars in history.[23]

The Soviets quickly discovered that Indian Communists were a new breed of extremist, and not easy to work with. M.N. Roy, the first outstanding Indian communist leader, not only clashed with Lenin, but also tried to persuade the Soviets to sponsor an Indian uprising. Between 1920 and 1921, Roy organized the first foreign unit in the Soviet Red Army, using Arabs, Iranians and renegade Pathans, formerly of the Royal Indian Army. Sequestered at the Tashkent Military School, Roy's Indian Brigade attracted the attention of Lord Curzon, then Britain's Foreign Minister. The Soviet government, insecure in the world community, feared additional economic isolation from Western Europe, so to avoid a confrontation with the British, the Russians closed the academy in Tashkent. They relocated the cadets to the newly opened Communist University of the Toilers of the East in Moscow, but Lenin did not go further with his Indian program.[24]

Bose's specific opinions about the Soviet role in an Indian revolution remain unclear, suggesting that he accepted fascism rather than *rejected* Communism. Undoubtedly his poor relations with Indian Communists influenced his decision. Certainly Roy's estrangement from Moscow in 1921 made an alliance with Josef Stalin seem uninviting, since Lenin's successor showed far less tolerance for independent-minded revolutionaries seeking Soviet aid.

In the early 1920s, numerous Comintern agents assisted Chinese nationalist Dr. Sun Yixian (Sun Yat-sen) in his attempts to wrest the Republic of China from warlord control. Although the Soviets promised to respect China's autonomy, they coauthored the charter of Sun's *Guomindang* (KMT), or National People's Party. After Sun's death in 1925, Jiang Jieshe (Chiang Kaishek) rose to power, and subsequently purged the Russians and Chinese Communists from the KMT. By 1936, Mao Zedong led Chinese Communists on the arduous Long March and established his headquarters in the barren foothills of Yenan, Shansi Province. Mao's rejection of the urban outlook in traditional Marxism and his success with rural peasants cost him Moscow's support.[25]

The Soviets' efforts to dominate China and their abandonment of an Indian program gave Subhas Chandra Bose no alternative; he willingly turned to fascism.

Realistically, the concept of fascism seemed as alien to India as yoga was to Adolf Hitler. The situation in India differed greatly from that in Germany and Italy, but Bose drew some connections. The void left by the end of World War I became a hothouse for political extremism throughout Europe. Economies had been shattered worldwide. Lives spun aimlessly as an entire generation was lost. As Subhas Bose turned 25, he discovered millions of Europeans wracked by the same problem faced by India: lack of identity.

Germany's defeat in the First World War stunned its population. Never aware that the Kaiser's armies were losing until weeks before the war ended, the Germans suffered a second psychological trauma adapting to the terms of the Treaty of Versailles. Postwar Germans tried to cope with a tremendous debt in a country suddenly deprived of its major industrial regions. While Germany sacrificed its gold reserves to pay the Allies, the people faced economic ruin in the wake of unprecedented inflation.

After Germany's last divine-right monarch, Kaiser Wilhelm II, fled to Holland, outside forces exerted pressure on the domestic affairs of the nation. The *Diktat*, or forced peace, established Germany's first democratic government, the Weimar Republic. The Allies encouraged this alien institution in hopes that the world would never see the rise of another sword-rattling, imperialist Germany. The Treaty of Versailles insured this by outlawing all but a token national defense force, and by the use of foreign troops to occupy the demilitarized Rhineland. In one last effort to completely demoralize the Germans, the international community unanimously condemned their nation in the War Guilt Clause. The financial woes and social transformation resulting from the *Diktat* left Germany in a whirlwind. The middle and working classes, naturally hurt the worst during the Weimar period, retreated into the protective bosom of history. They harked back to the days of Frederick the Great, when Europe stood in awe of Prussian strength and determination. Postwar Germans needed a hero, or at least someone to rebuild order. They chose Adolf Hitler.

Hitler, himself personally tortured by self-doubts and impossible goals, played upon the ideals of the conservatives by reviving Teutonic lore and Wagner's operas at the expense of his scapegoats — the Jews, Communists and other alleged traitors who had sabotaged the German victory and crawled under the diplomatic tables of Paris in 1919. After his Nazi Party won by a slender majority in the November 1932 elections, Hitler took power as Chancellor of Germany the following January. Within three years he flouted the Treaty of Versailles by launching full-scale industrial and defense programs, which immediately improved the economy.

The Führer required the unquestioning support of the German people, and in return, he gave them back their pride and identity. If one came from pure German stock, remembered the days when people felt patriotic, and still made a profit, one had a place in the Nazi Party. Hitler became the Kaiser of the Disgruntled, giving them a new sense of belonging. The swastika armbands, ornamental daggers and the good old songs gave postwar Germany *unity*. Nazism built a past, a present and a future. In Italy, Benito Mussolini had already developed a similar program some ten years earlier. The one-time left-wing journalist rose from patched-elbow poverty to take control of his country as the burly don of the Blackshirts. Strutting up to the podium, Mussolini offered a viable Italy in return for sacrificed civil rights. To revive the glory of the Roman Empire, claim Carthage and turn the Mediterranean into an Italian lake, he needed to liquidate the leftists and other undesirables.

As Subhas Bose learned about the meteoric rise of fascist governments, he began to admire the men who controlled them. He knew that powerful figures took over countries and steered them out of difficult times with strong hands. Hitler and Mussolini would have come from the lower castes had they been born Indians, yet they held absolute power. If such men thrived, could an upper-caste, Cambridge-educated philosopher unify India? Could an iron fist mold an Indian national character and expel the Raj forever? Would Bose's personalized melding of "Fascism and Communism" create an autocratic state more oppressive than the one imposed by the British colonial structure? Bose found comfort in the belief that India's multiple parties and factions would always keep India democratic, despite her centralized beginnings.[26]

One may question if Subhas Bose and his followers truly favored fascism. Bose himself certainly never adhered to fascism. He was a devout socialist in economic philosophy — a philosophy which contradicted pure fascism. Some historians doubt if he really understood the European right wing. Bose lauded fascism as anti-imperialism, yet he never publicly criticized Mussolini for his 1934–36 Abyssinian campaign. He denigrated Britain's condemnation of Italy by saying that the British acted solely in their own political interests. In fact, Bose resented England's use of Indian soldiers to "protect Indians and other British subjects" in Ethiopia.[27]

Bose claimed that India needed a highly paternalistic government with socialistic policies. Assuming that the young politician completely understood the ramifications of such a regime, and was not just dreaming of glory, how could he balance his hopes with his Hindu upbringing?

◆ 5 ◆

NOT A QUESTION OF SPIRIT, BUT OF COLOR

Although Subhas Bose personally enjoyed a warm reception in Europe during his tours of the mid–1930s, India's reputation abroad needed substantial improvement if he expected the Axis to support his struggle. Indians occupied a tiny niche in European affairs, so most Europeans never had a chance to become familiar with them. Far too many believed that India represented nothing more than a British hellpit producing millions of black, naked people, their heads swathed in filthy turbans. The more sophisticated Europeans overcame such prejudices, but what little they knew about India was equally wrong. For instance, many believed that the caste system created a divided nation. They did not realize that the traditional hierarchy protected traditional Indian society, and that having social layers insured everyone's place in life from the moment of birth. When the individual has his or her guaranteed niche, stability results. With the exception of those untouchables who converted to Islam, Indians looked to the afterlife for social mobility. Such alien ideals struck most Westerners ice cold.[1]

Not unexpectedly, India had its worst reputation in Germany and Austria. Though Bose found some sympathy in pre–Anschluss days through his participation in the founding of Vienna's Austrian-Indian Society, bigotry survived. Indian topic books and movies, such as the ever-popular film *Bengali*, were always made by Westerners who presented stereotyped material. Bose personally lodged his protest with the Archbishop of Vienna over the showing of *Bengali* in Austria.[2]

What could Bose expect from the Nazis? In the heart of every fascist throbbed a vicious racial prejudice. While the Italians never elevated the

43

Roman ideal to deity status, the twisted German mindset produced the saintly Aryan. The Aryans, a supposedly forgotten race of blond, cobalt-eyed Vikings, represented the pure, original, earthiest people of Father Deutschland — they were the *Volk*. By distorting Teutonic legends, Adolf Hitler urged Germans to sift society, remove the "dregs," and move on to glory once again. He roused the hopes of his people while convincing himself of the absolute truth of the madness. He never accepted the reality that the Aryans were an ancient, golden-skinned race from the northern half of the Indian subcontinent.[3]

The Führer's hatred of dark people made the thought of an Indo-Nazi relationship seem ludicrous. Had any militant survivors of the Kaiser's old Berlin Committee remained in Germany to see the rise of Hitler, they certainly never surfaced. It seemed that no Asian revolutionary stood a chance in Nazi Germany. Despite his racism, Hitler was a cunning political animal, skilled at bending men and countries to his desires. He and Mussolini viewed the Middle East as a powder keg aching for a fascist match.

After World War I, self-determination turned into a pipe dream for the Arabs, and they remained under the domination of France and Britain. Like Bose, a number of Arab nationalists looked to fascism, often with a foundation of ultraconservative Islam. For example, the Greenshirts of Egypt, the Syrian National Party, and the *Futuwwa* of Iraq all mimicked the Nazis and Italian Blackshirts. The Arabs had also seen how a local strongman such as Atatürk resisted European encroachment in the Middle East, and they hoped to create a cadre of such leadership.[4]

In a peculiar way, fascism linked Axis disgruntlement with Arab nationalism. Germany and Italy took strong interests in the region, which they believed the Allies denied them after World War I. Mussolini cast greedy eyes over the Mediterranean, while he smashed Libya and harried the Ethiopians. Although Italian avarice repelled most Arabs, Iraq and Saudi Arabia moved into Mussolini's sphere. Those two nations, unhappy clients of the British, asked Italy to aid them in their military affairs. Il Duce pushed the British and French out of Syria and North Africa by building schools and dominating the Arab media.[5]

Historically speaking, German-Arab contact had never been strong. Small pockets of German immigrants sprang up in a few Arab regions, and many German businesses dealt with the defunct Ottoman Empire. During the Weimar period, Germany and Egypt developed a thriving economic relationship, however closely a suspicious Britain monitored their activities. The Nazi government attempted to expand its market in Cairo to include military equipment, and tried to buy mineral rights, which the British naturally blocked. Politically speaking, German influence never competed with that of the Italians. The Germans frequently invited Arab notables to Nazi torchlight assemblies, and Berlin cooperated with Arab students attending German universities. Hitler Youth commandant Baldur von Schirach visited Iran, Iraq and Syria in 1937. In February 1939, Josef Goebbels journeyed to Egypt, and the reception he received from Arab right-wing groups delighted the Nazi Propaganda Minister.[6]

Berlin soon discovered that its greatest asset did not concern himself with economic affairs, but with anti–Semitism. To the joy of fascist Europe, Haj Amin el-Husseini, the Grand Mufti of Jerusalem, exhibited every character-istic of a Nazi — with a vengeance.

As with the Germans, the violent hatred of Jews was a longstanding theme of the Arab psyche, often encouraged by the authorities in British-occupied Palestine. The Palestinian Arabs had desired their own country since the League of Nations mandated the lost Ottoman colony to Great Britain in April 1920. The Palestinians blamed the British and the Jews for sealing off their road to independence. Two factors could have removed the hindrances: strong leadership and outside assistance. Palestine chose the Mufti as its leader, and he planned to work with the Axis in a joint effort to solve his own Jewish Question.

By the mid–1920s, Haj Amin el-Husseini, who came from one of Pales-tine's most successful families, inherited the title of Grand Mufti, or Chief Islamic Justice. He quickly murdered most of a rival clan and ordained two pogroms against the Jews. While a frustrated Adolf Hitler spent 1923–24 in jail for his futile Munich Putsch, Husseini honed his skills as a master manip-ulator of the British administration. After literally forcing the colonial high commissioner to appoint him governor of the Muslim population, the admin-istration changed hands, and the next high commissioner put the Mufti under house arrest. He escaped to Lebanon, and London incorrectly assumed that he had retired in exile. By 1936, the Mufti was speaking out in favor of both Mussolini and Hitler, and Arab residents of Europe began to lobby on his behalf.[7]

The Axis responded favorably to the Arab overtures. Germany immedi-ately alerted her agents in Baghdad to stir up an anti–British rebellion. With Italian funds, the Mufti secretly traveled to Iraq, then, as now, inhabited by some of the most militant Islamic fanatics in the Middle East. By 1941, British forces silenced the Iraqi revolt, and the Mufti fled to pro–Nazi Iran. Shah Reza Pahlevi, a brutal Cossack tribesman and the King of Iran, welcomed the Führer's emissaries heartily. The Iranians needed a religious figure to rally behind, so the Mufti worked in Tehran until Mussolini decided that Iran was endangering the Arab leader. So in the fall of 1941, a clandestine flight brought Husseini to Rome. Under the patronage of Count Galeazzo Ciano, Italy's able Foreign Minister, the Mufti enjoyed Roman hospitality and a pleasant work-ing environment. The Count arranged the Mufti's trip to Berlin, where For-eign Minister Joachim von Ribbentrop established the *Büro des Grossmufti*.[8]

Within a few weeks of his arrival, the Mufti endured his first meeting with Hitler. The emotional Führer behaved rudely toward his turbaned guest, and violated Arab custom by refusing to serve coffee. Even for one as unpredictable as Adolf Hitler, it seems strange that he alienated Husseini. According to his architect, war production director and confidant, Albert Speer, the Führer so admired the Islamic faith, that he *nearly* regarded the Arabs as his equals. Speer recalled Hitler's excitement after visiting Middle Eastern diplomats reminded him of Arab conquests throughout Europe. He responded that Germans and Muslims shared the same degree of natural aggression, but that innate racial inferiority kept the Arabs from taking over colder nations. Hitler assured his guests that had Islamic warriors reached Germany, Teutonic converts would have gladly fulfilled their legacy. The Führer rejected one Islamic faction outright. The Nazi government prohibited the teaching of Sufism, a Muslim love-and-peace sect not unlike the Baha'is, on the grounds that it was "alien to German culture."[9]

Hitler and Husseini never warmed to each other, but they readily agreed on one major item. The Nazi leader admitted that Germans and Arabs were engaged on the same side in a war against international Jewry. In reply, the Mufti said, "the Jews have changed the life of Palestine in such a way that it must inevitably lead to the destruction of our [Arab] race."[10]

If Hitler remained personally cold toward Husseini, SS Lieutenant Colonel Adolf Eichmann did not. The chief of the Gestapo's extermination program provided one of his officers as the Mufti's personal guide in Germany, and he escorted his guest on tours of concentration camps. The death camps elated the Arab visitor. For his efforts at eradicating Jews, Husseini called Eichmann a "diamond," and remarked that such facilities in the Middle East could have been "the solution to the Palestinian problem." In turn, Husseini offered to use his influence to assist Eichmann in the Final Solution. Indeed, the Mufti would be remembered as Germany's prized collaborator.[11]

From Berlin, Husseini forced the colonial government in Palestine to prohibit further Jewish immigration. In Europe, he constantly reminded Axis officials about the risk of releasing Jewish "spies." However, most of Husseini's activities pertained to broadcasting propaganda to European, Arab and Far Eastern Muslims. His two greatest successes in this area related to the formation of the Balkan Islamic panzer divisions and Project Mohammed. The Mufti urged Yugoslavian and Albanian Muslims to accept the Nazis and butcher as many Jewish and Christian enemies as possible. "Kill the Jews wherever you find them," he exhorted, "this pleases God, history and religion." The blond, blue-eyed Croatian Muslims, bloodthirsty knife-and-torch killers, eagerly accepted German automatic weapons.[12]

In Turkestan, Uzbekistan and Tajikistan, Muslims lived as miserably as

Russians did under Soviet rule. Significant numbers of Caucasians practiced Islam in Soviet Georgia and Armenia, and in Azerbaijan it was the national religion. These ethnic groups — approximately 17 percent of Russia's population — never considered themselves a genuine part of the Soviet Union. As in Iraq, the Nazis gambled that with Project Mohammed, the Grand Mufti could motivate Soviet Muslims to rebel against their colonizers. The *Büro des Grossmufti* met with success in persuading Caucasian and Central Asian Muslims to side with the Axis. Ironically, the Abwehr (the Nazi War Department's intelligence division) independently launched a similar plot, Operation Shamyl, but it failed miserably.[13]

Clearly, Nazi Germany's sympathy with the Palestinian Arab cause stemmed from a mutual hatred of Jews.

Subhas Bose offered no encouragement to anti–Semitic policies, as he usually kept his feelings about the Jewish question private. One notable exception took place in 1939, when he criticized Nehru's efforts to aid Jews fleeing Europe. Through his Jewish Committee, Nehru hoped to offer Jewish professionals a chance to live and work in India. Although not designed to sponsor large numbers of refugees, Bose referred to this plan as an attempt to make India an "asylum for the Jews." In response, Nehru described his achievement in relocating a famous Italian doctor, and felt that his colleague was overreacting to the situation.[14]

By 1939, Bose adopted a militant stand toward Indian politics, and strongly favored the European fascists. This factor could account for the incident, since among friends, Bose expressed a contrasting view. In private, Bose confided his belief in the Jews being an "old and fine race" of "oriental origin," and, like the Indians, they suffered from a historical tradition of being attacked by outsiders. Bose drew an analogy between Jewish-Christian conflicts and the tensions between parents and children.[15]

Curiously, the saintly Gandhi harbored ill will toward the Jewish refugee movement into Palestine. He remembered the days when Jewish business and community leaders of South Africa made life difficult for Indian residents. Still, Gandhi wanted no involvement with Hitler and Bose did.[16]

Hitler expressed his personal views on India in *Mein Kampf,* and they differed considerably from his opinions about the Islamic world. Not only did he have an unfavorable attitude toward the Indian people, but also firmly believed in the impossibility of Indians ruling their own country. At that time, the Führer preferred that the British keep India rather than have another colonial power, such as Russia, take it over. He believed that the British would be able to maintain their colony as long as they kept a firm and exclusive hold on the management level of India's civil administration. The Führer did acknowledge, however, that there were a few Asian patriots, without mentioning any Indians, who possessed the capabilities of leading their countries on to freedom.[17]

During the first half of World War II, Hitler apparently had no designs on India. In his private conversations, he seemed to admire the Raj as a model for an alien minority governing a majority. He frequently verbalized his hopes of dominating the Soviet Union in a similar manner. "The Russian space is our India," Hitler declared in 1941. "Like the English, we shall rule this empire with a handful of men."[18]

In Hitler's mind, the Indians, like the Russians, presented the image of needing masters. The Führer seemed both misinformed, and at times, even contradictory in his attitudes toward India. He once remarked to Party Secretary Martin Bormann that Britain's long reign over India could be attributed to her refusal to change Indian culture. Although India never experienced missionaries to the extent of, for example, China, British schools, the English language, and especially the foreign concept of bureaucracy all profoundly altered Indian life. Hitler also believed that the British brought industry to India, with the consequence of hurting labor at home. He apparently did not realize that the United Kingdom used India strictly as a source of raw materials and a market for expensive British products.[19]

At the onset of World War II, Subhas Chandra Bose was desperate for an alliance with the far right. Alienated from Communism and blind to the realities of Nazism, Bose tried to forge ties with Berlin. His own experiences should have warned him of the futility of his path.

In 1933, the British released Bose from prison on a health furlough, enabling him to seek treatment at a Viennese hospital. After a short stay, Bose struck up friendships with Indian exiles and attempted to contact the Nazi government. In the 1930s, only mild Indian exiles living in the area, such as the ailing statesman V.J. Patel, European academics, and caseworkers in the Indian Information Office seemed interested in him. This Berlin agency assisted Indian students in Germany and issued press releases on major Asian figures visiting Berlin. With the aid of Dr. Franz Thierfelder, the director of Stuttgart's German Academy for Foreign Relations, Bose made contacts in the Foreign Office, with the intention of applying for an interview with a high official to present the rough draft of an Indo-German alliance. The Foreign Office's public relations department turned him down, claiming that Germany wanted to remain neutral on the Indian independence issue.[20]

In a letter to Thierfelder, dated March 24, 1936, Subhas Bose wrote, "Today I regret that I have to return to India with the conviction that the new nationalism of Germany is not only narrow and selfish but arrogant.... When we are fighting the greatest Empire in the world for our freedom and for our rights, and when we are confident of our ultimate success, we cannot brook any insult from any other nation or any attack on our race or culture.... I hope that the present atmosphere will change and we shall ultimately arrive at an understanding."[21]

Bose encouraged Thierfelder to show this letter to German government officials. The Bengali patriot sensed more in the rejection than neutrality; the overt prejudice on the part of many Germans stung him. Nazi officials acknowledged that the Japanese and Indians were the only cultured Oriental peoples, but they still referred to the Indians as "colored." They remained suspicious of Indian motives. At one point, when the Nazis seemed to be over-powering Bose, his temper snapped and he said, "For the sake of my country, I have risked my neck to come to Germany. For the same reason I am prepared to risk my neck to return to India if I cannot achieve my purpose. The British CID is very efficient and just as I escaped in spite of it I shall escape your Gestapo also."[22]

During his 1933–36 excursions into Germany, rejection forced Bose to content himself by writing editorials to Nazi newspapers, such as the *Völkische Beobachter*, and by trying to contact the dissident wing of the Nazi Party. Were it not for the small clique of pro–Indian sympathizers, Bose's early trips would have been totally futile. Encouraged by Propaganda Minister Goebbels, some even promised arms and communications equipment to the Indians, but their offers proved to be barren.[23]

As long as Bose appeared like a beggar on the Nazis' doorstep, he stood little chance of getting any assistance from them. Bose needed to create a program of mutual benefit to India and Germany. Domestic circumstances made such a plan vital to the future of India, and for Bose personally.

Escape

Being pro–fascist had not only political consequences, but criminal ones as well. As Bose became even more outspoken, his exaggerated reputation as a terrorist surfaced again. He and his comrades were under the concerned and watchful eyes of the CID. British intelligence knew the sinister side to Bose's goodwill tours of Europe, including his appeals to Berlin. On his subsequent return visits to India, in 1934, because of his father's death, and again in 1936, he found a less-than-warm reception from the British. The police insisted that he remain in his own home or his brother's. The Raj banned Subhas Chandra Bose from walking the streets of his hometown; however, he was never a man to remain quietly indoors.[24]

As World War II began, Bose stayed in Calcutta to arouse the masses, despite a war ordinance that prohibited public meetings. On June 31, 1940, he gave an address in crowded Shraddhananda Park, but the police did not arrest him. In his speech, he demanded the destruction of various British monuments in India, such as the Holwell Statue. On July 2nd, the day before the target date for the Holwell Statue demolition, the police arrested Bose. He was sent to prison (it was his 11th time) without a trial, as was customary during India's rebellious years, especially during wartime. While in prison, Bose came to three major conclusions:(1.) the Axis would defeat the Allies; (2.) though a loser, England would tenaciously hold on to India; and (3.) India must aid the Axis, and in return, the Axis would set her free. But how? How to aid the Axis? [25]

Bose knew that he had to get out of jail for India's sake, then escape to either Germany or Italy to make firm plans. He decided to go on a hunger strike. He truly readied himself to be a martyr for his country, but for him, a hunger strike did not have the mystical Hindu connotations that it had for the Mahatma. No doubt, Bose expected the officials to react. The wardens threatened to use force-feeding, and he replied by threatening suicide. Bose's domestic and profascist activities certainly disturbed the British, but they knew if he died in their custody, a massive riot would erupt. On December 5th, after a grueling five-month stay, the British authorities released him.[26]

Due to both the war and his well-publicized views concerning the international role in an Indian revolution, the CID barred Bose from leaving the country. Obviously, the task had to be accomplished surreptitiously. On the night of January 16, 1941, Bose, bearded and dressed as a Pathan tribesman, was driven out of Calcutta by his young nephew, Sisir. They got to Bararee by next morning. In Bararee, Bose stayed with another nephew, and from there he was driven to Gomoh. At the station in Gomoh, he boarded a train for northern India. On January 25th, Bose's family announced his disappearance. Subhas Chandra Bose remained somewhat of a mystery for over a year. Various rumors about him surfaced: he was staying at a retreat in the Himalayas; he was making secret deals with the Japanese; then, finally, on March 28, 1942, Reuters announced that he had been killed in a plane crash off Japan. Reuter's news release prophesied an event to come three years later.[27]

Sisir K. Bose's biography of his uncle, *A Beacon Across Asia*, gives a detailed account of the "mystery period." On January 19, 1941, Subhas Bose arrived in Peshawar. He was still traveling incognito, under the alias of Mohammed Ziauddin, an occasional deaf-mute, shabby insurance salesman and part-time teacher. After a week in Peshawar, he and a political ally, Bhagat Ram Talwar, moved on toward Afghanistan. They walked and hitchhiked through mountainous territory, while dodging a sadistic Afghan policeman, who ended his harassment only after being bribed with a gold watch. Feeling lost and lonely, the pair reached the capital, Kabul, on January 31st.[28]

Oddly enough, they tried to make contact with the Soviet embassy, but Russian officials ignored their efforts. By early February, Bose had made some weak connections with the German Embassy in Kabul. The officer in charge, a Minister Pilger, did not trust Bose, but he showed a willingness to contact

Berlin for him. In his communiqué to the German Foreign Office, he warned that Bose probably belonged to the British secret service. After filing his negative report, Pilger put Bose and the Indian issue to the back of his mind, and did nothing for about three weeks. During this time, circumstances forced Bose to spend his days in a friend's house, since the Afghan government refused to guarantee his safety if he ventured outside. An impatient Bose became disillusioned with the Axis, and his thoughts once again turned to approaching the Soviet Union.[29]

How strange that the man who lauded the fascists in Calcutta attempted to meet the Soviets without trying to make a new approach to the German or Italian Embassy. The Soviets proclaimed themselves the avowed enemies of the fascists. Bose's consideration of an alliance with Stalin lends credence to the belief that Bose practiced "soap-box Nazism," while remaining a nationalist at heart.

When Bose fled Calcutta, he still had a few Indian Communist friends. They assisted him during his journey, and provided him with numerous safe houses. They encouraged him to work with the Soviets, since they loathed imperialism in thought and action. Despite their promises that the Soviet ambassador in Afghanistan would treat him as a fellow diplomat, Bose was unceremoniously ignored. The Kremlin had already given M.N. Roy a chance in the 1920s, and it had no interest in a second potential fiasco with another Indian radical. He did not grieve long; German Ambassador Pilger never really forgot him. In late February 1941, Bose received a message that Alberto Quaroni, the Italian minister in Kabul, had granted him an appointment. In March, Quaroni met with an anxious Netaji-to-be.[30]

This interview, published under the title of "Plan of Indian Revolution," outlined Bose's proposed Free India programs. Bose asserted that the Axis "should promise, recognize and guarantee the independence and the integrity of India." He explained that since the Axis would defeat Britain, Britain had no future, and therefore India had no future supporting her. Bose's plans called for the formation of a special army of rehabilitated Indian prisoners of war. Once the fascists released any Indian captives and Bose reeducated them to approve of the liberation, they would fight against the Raj. He also demanded the establishment of a government of Free India — the Azad Hind government. He emphasized the need for a massive propaganda barrage to mobilize the Indian populace and counter British "lies." Bose assured Quaroni that effective propagandizing presented no problem for him, since he believed that he was the most influential man in Indian foreign relations.[31]

Subhas Bose offered a potential Indian revolution, but he made only one request of Quaroni: he wanted the Axis to precipitate the revolution. Germany and Italy merely needed to send 50,000 soldiers into India as a catalyst.

Once the invasion took place, Bose believed that the Raj's troops would throw down their arms and flee. When the Indian masses saw their protectors scatter, they would know that India's only hope rested with the fascists. The Axis had to give technical advice and financial aid during the revolution, since old-fashioned Swadeshi-style terrorism never proved fruitful enough. The Italian ambassador agreed with Bose's assessment of the Anglo-Indian situation. Though he had some reservations about the plan, he realized that within India beat the heart of the British Commonwealth, so backing Bose's venture could be a worthy investment, despite the tremendous cost of an invasion. Quaroni genuinely liked Bose, and described him as possibly "the only realist among the Indian nationalist leaders."[32]

The Quaroni-Bose discussion led to a formal agreement by Italy, Germany, the Soviet Union and Afghanistan to cooperate with Bose, but the agreement was scanty at best. The Soviets only gave Bose permission to travel through their country, and that was the extent of their involvement. Apparently the Afghans refused to extend themselves much further than the Russians. While the Afghans remained indifferent to the British during World War I, the 1940s drove them toward a friendship with the United Kingdom. As the negotiations proceeded, the Afghan government considered extraditing Bose, and his associates in the capital encouraged him to leave. He took the identity and passport of one Orlando Mazzotta, a minor clerk with the Italian Embassy in Kabul. On March 18, 1941, Bose, sporting a trim goatee, and a party of three left Afghanistan for Russia. They spent the rest of March traveling through the Steppes until they reached the legendary city of Samarkand. They took a colorful train ride from scenic Samarkand to Moscow, where Bose caught a plane for Berlin. This escape was tight and exciting, as the wartime road from Kabul to Berlin was paved with spies, assassins and assorted secret police.[33]

Subhas Chandra Bose arrived in Berlin on April 3, 1941, still under the alias of Orlando Mazzotta. To maintain his secrecy, the Germans deliberately called him "*Signor*" or "His Excellency" Mazzotta. Few people knew who he actually was. Responsibility for Subhas Bose fell on the shoulders of several diplomats with the Information Section of the German Foreign Office. The director, Dr. Adam von Trott, and his assistant, Dr. Alexander Werth, specialized in British and Southeast Asian affairs. Von Trott and Werth steered Bose away from the more volatile Nazi Party officials to avoid any open conflicts over colonial or racial issues. In a chapter for Sisir K. Bose's *A Beacon Across Asia*, Werth reflected that Bose presented numerous difficulties because he never comprehended Germany's overall lack of sympathy toward India and its hardened racism. Bose embarrassed his hosts by making repeated requests to meet with either Hitler or Goebbels. Also, the Foreign Office faced the problem of finding or creating a position for him, worthy of his prestige and background.[34]

Bose remained seriously problematic, especially since he continued giving mixed messages regarding the nature of fascism. In a letter to Nehru, dated March 28, 1939, he wrote, "...Foreign policy is a realistic affair to be determined largely from the point of view of a nation's self-interest.... It is no use championing the lost causes all the time and it is no use condemning countries like Germany and Italy on the one hand and on the other giving a certificate of good conduct to British and French imperialism...." Then, ten months before he landed in Berlin again, at the June 1940 Forward Bloc Anti-Imperialist Conference, Bose himself referred to Nazism as colonialism. "In the war between rival Imperialisms," he commented, "the old ones have been faring very badly indeed."[35]

The Nazis failed to understand the Indian. Bose, in turn, grew angry at their coolness toward him, but, slowly, he broke down a few barriers. Even if Hitler and Goebbels refused to grant him an audience, he still had important friends in the diplomatic centers of Rome and Berlin. Also, in the five years that had elapsed since his prior overtures after being released from prison, the Netaji-to-be had developed concrete ideas about the nature of the Axis involvement in India he desired.

6

THE NETAJI

The outcome of Bose's 1941 German mission might have been similar to his 1933–36 efforts, but for his special, top-secret "Memorandum to the German Government." This document, marked "Berlin" and dated April 9, 1941, proposed an official alliance between India and the Axis. In it, he described the clandestine operations to occur in Europe and Asia, much of it to be accomplished with Indian sweat and skills, but with Axis support. He bolstered the credibility of his offer with historical and contemporary political evidence, while firing the emotions through the brash use of strongly worded opinion. He analyzed the karma of the Raj, while predicting their future of Mother Hind. He summed up world politics and showed the Germans how to move into the niche Britain seemed destined to leave. The German Foreign Office listened carefully to what Bose had to say.[1]

Drawing on British activities during and after World War I, Bose attempted to prove that Indians and Germans were locked in a struggle with the same domineering enemy. According to Bose, the British subjugated their millions of colonials by first breaking their spines, and then mercilessly exploiting the limp victims. The Raj had behaved that way in India since 1757, he said, and more recently, Britain had joined France in an effort to maim their neighbors, Austria and Germany. As Bose put it, "The iniquities of the Treaty of Versailles were manifold, but Great Britain and France did not nevertheless succeed in disturbing the fundamental integrity and homogeneity of the German Reich. On the other hand, the two Empires, Austro-Hungarian and Ottoman, were completely broken up and today we see clearly what the result of that break-up has been. But for the German Reich, there would have been no power in Europe at the present time to challenge the Anglo-French combination."[2]

54

Britain seemed bent on conquering the world, and a "New Order" was required to halt her campaign. Bose asserted that although the abuse of colonies may keep a mother country financially afloat, she ultimately collapses without moral fiber. Bose focused his wrath on the modern Englishmen in India. They had money, tradition and the other cultural accouterments that riled any socialist, yet they possessed no talents for "diplomacy and statesmenship [sic]" that even the old-fashioned Raj officials had. The rising tide of Indian nationalism weakened England, which potentially worked to the Axis' advantage. According to the Netaji, Great Britain's miserable military performance at the outset of World War II proved that it only existed as a shell waiting to be crushed by the fascists.[3]

Bose assured the Nazis that Indians felt none of the loyalty they mustered during the First World War. Indians knew that any impositions made by London on India only served the English. World War II was Britain's war, and the Crown obviously could not defend her colonies. He mentioned that British war propaganda, so effective in neutralizing the relatively scant German media efforts of 1914–18, failed to convince the people in 1941. Bose offered personal proof to back his contention. As part of his "one thousand lectures" throughout India, he polled his audiences about their attitudes. According to Bose, they all applauded the downfall of Great Britain.[4]

In his memorandum, Bose then described the value of India to the Axis. He discussed India's vast manpower, and cited the huge iron ore and steel companies in Jamshedpur and Mysore to support his claims of Indian industrial and resource potential. He emphasized the strategic importance of India and the related Middle East, primarily as the supply and communication link-up for the European and Japanese branches of the Axis. Here Bose began to consider the Japanese role. In recognizing Japan's resentment of the Western presence in Asia, he hinted that India could be a valued client. He maintained that Tokyo undoubtedly hoped to include India in the scheme that eventually emerged as the Greater East Asia Co-Prosperity Sphere. Bose warned that he did not intend to have his nation swallowed by the Japanese Empire, but to join and be protected by the Axis as a whole. He later clarified that point by mentioning the importance of creating a band of pro–Axis states in North Africa, the Middle East and Asia. He seemingly harbored no fears of the Germans conquering India; judging by the *Drang nach Osten*, or Drive to the East, Bose believed that the Nazis rooted themselves as a continental power instead of a colonial or sea force. He elaborated on British military strength in India in 1941, but reminded the Germans that current sentiment might easily lead to the sabotage of the Raj's forces.[5]

The specifics of this Indo-Axis alliance developed from the plans Bose discussed with Ambassador Quaroni in Kabul only one month before. Bose required a formal treaty between the Axis and independent India, hinging on an Axis guarantee of Indian statehood after a fascist victory in World War II. After Bose became President of India, he planned to grant unspecified "special facilities" to his benefactors. The fascists could show their faith by establishing a "Free Indian Government" in Berlin, with embassies in any nations favorable to the cause. As in his talks with Quaroni, Bose strongly advised that a propaganda campaign, especially by radio, commence immediately.[6]

Bose targeted Afghanistan and the bordering Independent Tribal Territories as an important field of operations, especially since the Axis opposed the pro–London Afghan government. The region potentially served as both liaison between Europe and the Far East, and as an espionage center to be used against Allied forces in India. Before penetrating Afghanistan, renegade tribesmen such as Mirza Ali Khan, the Fakir of Ipi, would be encouraged to raid British military installations in the area. While Bose talked about a few German and Italian personnel being sent to Afghanistan for assistance, he suggested that the communications base be manned by "existing legations" or "our agents already working in" the area. He could not legitimately regard the Fakir's warriors as his men, since maverick Afghans drew swords against British imperialists in their homeland, and had no concern for India. He made contacts with the leading Indian revolutionaries in the Middle East and the Orient only after he joined the Japanese in 1943. One cannot help but assume that Bose exaggerated the extent of his movement to arouse the Germans, as yet uncommitted to India.[7]

The future Netaji expected his countrymen to revolt against the Raj. Radio broadcasts from Berlin and seditious pamphlets from Kabul would urge Indians to strike in the civil, military and industrial spheres. Bose himself wrote propaganda speeches and articles advising Indians not to pay taxes. With imported explosives and a moonless night, no structure in British India remained safe.[8]

Despite the lofty goals and complicated methodology, less than one page of the memorandum covered the Axis' role in the agreement. Again, Bose requested an Axis invasion of India by 50,000 troops, to crush the Royal Indian Army with one blow. As with the Indo-German conspirators of World War I, Bose depended on outside funding for his Free India. He asked the fascists to pay for the revolution, but he insisted that they treat the money as a loan, to be repaid in full after independence.[9]

Berlin was impressed. Bose's memorandum awakened Nazi leadership to India, its problems and potential. The German Foreign Office realized that Hitler's conservative views about India and his admiration for the colonial structure had no place in a war against Great Britain. As Bose cleverly pointed out, the British granted protective custody over anticollaborationist leaders from overrun countries such as Holland, Norway and France. They headquartered free governments-in-exile in England, often with full ambassadorial status. These anti–Axis statesmen flooded the world with literature condemning Hitler, so Bose offered the Nazis a chance to reply with an oppressed patriot of their own.[10]

Of Interest to the Nazis

The Axis could not afford to underestimate the truth in Bose's statements about the latent military value of the Indian subcontinent, including Afghanistan. In September 1938, Victor A.J. Hope, the Viceroy Lord Linlithgow, told C. Giuriati, the Italian consul general in Calcutta, that "in the event of war he would be quite unable to maintain British rule in India." When coupled with India's weakness, the fact that Afghanistan remained vulnerable heightened the interests of the Axis nations. Taking Afghanistan would give Hitler the base he needed to cut Britain's east-west supply and communication lines.[11]

Before the war, London still worried about the chances of a Soviet attack on the subcontinent, and the Nazi-Soviet Nonaggression Pact of August 1939 only reinforced this concern. The Russian-German combination, however temporary, endangered the pro–British government of Afghanistan and opened the possibility of returning the throne to deposed King Amanullah, a favorite client of Mussolini. The Afghans found a silver lining in the cloud that suddenly overshadowed their government. If the British did not fight in Europe, Kabul hoped to influence England or the USSR by offering to side with one over the other. After the war broke out, the Afghans feared that the Russians would turn their country into a Communist sphere of influence. The Nazis capitalized on these fears by the spread of disinformation.[12]

More than one British official took Nazi propaganda seriously. Before joining the Foreign Office, the late Fitzroy Maclean served in the British embassy in Moscow. Having extensively explored Soviet Central Asia and Afghanistan, he knew the Soviet military situation in the region firsthand. In his travelogue, *Eastern Approaches*, Maclean described the growth of the Soviet rail system as it edged ominously toward the Afghan border, and he estimated that Stalin could spare up to 1,700 planes for an Afghan invasion without risking his country's defenses.[13]

After receiving reports from Maclean, the British Secretary of State for India became alarmed, fearing British India to be the next target if Afghanistan fell to Nazi-Soviet aggression. The secretary notified military intelligence, expressing his concern that the Red Air Force might easily destroy Indian defense forces, using bases in Afghanistan. In response, British military authorities maintained that even if the Soviets did take Afghanistan, India's border territory would prove quite difficult to break through, especially by land. While the military's reply to the secretary's warnings failed to address the issue of Soviet air strength, British generals felt confident that Stalin could not conquer India overnight, should that be his intention.[14]

In light of the potential for a Soviet invasion, the Afghan government began to pressure London for a commitment to protect the region. To both guarantee Indian defenses and avoid losing face with their Muslim allies, in April 1940, the British officially promised to defend Afghanistan. MI2, the section of the War Office's Military Intelligence Department that specialized in India, realized that manpower would be the major problem should Afghanistan be attacked. Interestingly enough, the Afghans owned more anti-aircraft guns than the Raj, but lacked skilled personnel to operate them. The British even considered importing Turkish army officers to train Afghans, but apparently dropped the idea later.[15]

The British wished for better relations with the often-rebellious tribes-men in the Afghan frontier, since Bose intended to use these groups for pro–Axis activities. Whoever won the allegiance of these mountain- and desert-born fighters automatically lured a superb guerrilla army to their side. Bose undoubtedly remembered that from 1936–1938, the Raj required over 30 percent of its army, with assistance from the Royal Air Corps, to defeat a lengthy insurrection led by the Fakir of Ipi.[16]

After the Germans saw the new value of Subhas Chandra Bose, his life began to change rapidly. Berlin began to take seriously the strangely eloquent gentleman from the East. His dedication, integrity and sharp evaluations of the Indian situation won him admiration and made him quite important to a select circle of Germans. Despite his increasing status, the Germans refused to consider him as an equal. That reality, combined with the prevalent colo-nial mentality regarding India itself, would continually hinder Bose's rela-tions with the Axis.

Germany's new attitude toward Bose was not without underlying motives. Pressing reasons directed the Nazis' attention to Bose's potential. By March 1941, Hitler considered the possibilities of India's role in an attack against Rus-sia or in the rescue of the Italians in Libya. Hitler still idealized the Anglo-Indian institution and certainly never wanted India as a German colony. He hoped, however, that by merely threatening the Raj, Germany could hold the British at bay in Europe. With or without an Axis assault on India, the Ger-man Chancellor saw Bose as an important propaganda tool for the war effort. Although his April 1941 Memorandum did not mention the POW militia that Bose had discussed with Italian Minister Quaroni in Kabul, such a program intrigued the Nazis. Each day, Rommel captured hundreds of Indians in North Africa and shipped them to POW camps in Germany. If Bose and other Indian exiles in Germany and Austria worked with the POWs, the fascists could use them against Britain. But how? Hitler left that question for Bose to figure out.[17]

Hitler decided that Bose offered useful skills, similar to the capabilities of the Grand Mufti of Jerusalem and ex–King Amanullah of Afghanistan, who were already furthering the Axis cause. In 1942, Propaganda Minister Goebbels noted that the Führer resented Japan's goal of pushing the white race out of Asia. Moreover, an association with Bose naturally kept German hands in Far Eastern affairs. To use Bose, Hitler only needed to dangle the pledge of Axis endorsement of Free India like a carrot. If the fascists insisted that any Indo-Axis agreement be kept secret, its political costs would be minimal. Still, Hitler felt uncomfortable about dealing with an Indian directly.[18]

Bose continued to work through the Information Department of the German Foreign Office. The Information Department set up two separate units for the study of Indian affairs: the "Working Group, India," and the "Special Department for India." Other government agencies, including the Press and Radio Departments and the High Command of the Wehrmacht (Armed Forces, literally "Defense Force"), ran their own studies of India. With Bose, a noted political scientist named Dr. Wilhelm Melchers directed the "Working Group, India." Melchers took the initiative in inviting Europe's Indian exiles to participate in the Nazi program of reeducating prisoners of war.[19]

Melchers found himself working alone during the summer of 1941— Bose left Germany in disgust. Bose had grown impatient at what he considered Nazi indifference. Within a week of arriving in Berlin, he generated a great deal of attention with his memorandum, and yet weeks later, only the preliminary steps of his program had been taken. Bose, by nature a temperamental optimist, did spark the Nazis' interest in his cause — no small accomplishment for an Indian amid diehard racists. After receiving what he considered to be a completely favorable initial response, the eager Bengali expected the immediate creation of a Free Indian government. Berlin held all the strings, and intended to keep its options open until the Foreign Office established a working format with Bose. Indeed, the Germans had not yet obligated themselves to India, and were not about to be rushed into any endeavor by an uninvited foreigner.[20]

Bose spent the summer of 1941 in Austria and Italy, but he did not remain idle. He tried to get more tangible support from the Italians, but had little success. The Foreign Ministry in Rome suggested that he be sequestered in a "neutral country" until the fascists prepared to act on the Indian issue. Bose ran into another brick wall when he approached Count Ciano in June 1941. The Italian Foreign Minister could not ignore Germany's hesitation, and wrote: "Nor must we be compromised, especially because the value of this youngster is not clear. Past experience has given rather modest results."[21]

Ciano's quote seems to be a flippant but barbed criticism of Subhas Bose. The facetious reference to him being a "youngster" downplayed nearly

20 years of political activism. Without further details, the meaning of "past experience" remains unclear. As of June 1941, the Nazis had merely established various Indian affairs committees. Bose had not been given the chance to yield "modest results." The other possible implication of Ciano's response was that Rome had become disillusioned with its own Indian program.

Throughout much of the war, Mussolini protected two nationalists from the subcontinent, ex–King Amanullah and Iqbal Shedai, yet they did relatively little with Italian facilities. Amanullah, a symbol of medieval Afghanistan, had some initial propaganda value, but spent most of his time hiding in his luxurious villa and never attempted to reclaim his throne. Shedai, an Indian Muslim, founded the "Friends of India" society, probably in the early 1940s. Despite a name suggesting a cultural exchange club, this Rome-based organization served as Italy's liaison with Indian radicals stationed in Berlin, Tokyo and Bangkok. In 1942, Mussolini placed Shedai in command of an unsuccessful Indian militia to reinforce the Italian Army. Bose maintained contact with Shedai, but they kept their movements separate.[22]

The German Foreign Office lured Bose back to Berlin with what appeared to be Hitler's approval of a government-in-exile. Before Bose returned to Germany in July 1941, his German colleagues developed the "Working Group, India," and put it under the personal direction of Dr. Wilhelm Kepler, the Secretary of State. Kepler arranged for official permission and the financial aid to build a Free India Center in Berlin. Sisir K. Bose, Subhas' nephew and the former director of Calcutta's Netaji Research Bureau, as well as his coauthors of *A Beacon Across Asia*, give the misleading impression that in Bose's mind, the Free India Center was synonymous with the provisional government of Free India. The diary of Josef Goebbels provides a more realistic picture of Bose's relationship with the Nazis. Goebbels did not believe that Bose had either the political force in India or the planning abilities to establish a pro–Axis government-in-exile. The German Propaganda Minister contended that an ersatz regime could never thrive in a "vacuum," so the Free India Center actually presented rather limited symbolic value to hopeful Indians, and, of course, to Germany.[23]

Despite the claims of his nephew, Subhas Bose quickly saw through his German sponsors, at least to the extent that he knew Berlin had no intention of declaring his government-in-exile. In a July 1941 meeting with Secretary Kepler and Under-Secretary Woermann of the Foreign Office, Bose warned that Indo-Axis relations needed serious attention. While the Indian intelligentsia conceived of both fascism and communism as likely partners in the fight against imperialism, the Indian masses hailed the Soviets as the liberators of the downtrodden. According to Bose, Nazi aggression against the USSR only lent credence to extremists' claims that Germany was the new imperialist superpower in Europe. Bose detracted from his Italian supporters by reminding the Germans of the Ethiopian victims of Mussolini's territorial expansion. Given the prevailing mood in India, Bose feared that the British could placate the masses with liberal legislation. If London's apparent generosity quelled Indian nationalism, the Raj remained secure. As his final argument, Bose predicted Britain's expansion beyond India toward the Iranian oilfields and the Soviet Caucasus.[24]

Bose insisted that Germany formally endorse the Government of Free India, or Azad Hind. Woermann, unimpressed with his diatribe, commented on Bose's unreasonable expectations of the Nazis. The Foreign Office politely dodged the recognition issue, and without giving details, also rejected the Italian plan to relocate Bose in a safer country. Woermann remarked that Bose seemed unconcerned with what the Nazis had already done for his cause, namely, the founding of the Free India Center. The under-secretary recommended that the Indian undergo fascist reeducation.[25]

At the onset of their relationship, Bose and the Germans tried to manipulate each other. Although neither party succeeded, neither wished to dissolve this unsteady alliance. The persistent Indian nationalist stood little chance of returning home without an extended prison sentence, and he had already harnessed his entire revolutionary program to the fascist movement. In turn, the Nazis realized that through Bose, India's value both strategically and as a propaganda tool increased tenfold. The uneasy partnership continued.

Having involved the German Secretary of State in the Indian program, Berlin gave Bose the erroneous impression that he had Hitler's personal backing. Through Kepler's endeavors, Bose was invited for an interview with Foreign Minister Joachim von Ribbentrop. The interview took place in November 1941. Bose made a point of thanking him for what the Nazis had already done for India, and clearly expressed his future goals, which was essentially a rehashing of the memorandum. He vainly asked Von Ribbentrop to persuade Hitler to alter the negative statements about India in *Mein Kampf.* Though the Foreign Minister freely allowed his staff to work with Bose, the Nazi maintained an icy reserve throughout the meeting. Bose left von Ribbentrop's office with the distinct feeling that any Nazi interests in his cause came from Germany's enmity toward England. Bose seemed to forget that his own concern focused on what the Nazis could do for India, rather than on what the Axis wanted from him.[26]

Difficult Days in Berlin

Although Subhas Bose hoped that his work in Germany and Italy would ultimately help India, his private life suffered in Europe. His exotic appearance and manner singled him out in any crowd. He was chatty, a quality exaggerated by a Victorian upbringing that made him use the maximum number of words. While talkative, Bose spoke neither German nor Italian, so isolating him from all but his immediate colleagues and educated acquaintances who knew English. Under the best of circumstances, one would feel quite lonely, but in lands in which racist ideology prevailed, the situation could hardly have been worse. While the crazed Mufti of Jerusalem enjoyed a certain amount of celebrity, the moody Bose had neither the personality nor the outspoken bigotry to win over many Nazis as friends. No Eichmanns wished to buddy around Berlin with him. The Indian frequently brooded over the lack of interest shown by many German high officials, not realizing that the Foreign Office, still unsure of how to use him, already protected him from those who might have shipped him off to a concentration camp.[27]

Bose had two important friends, both women, and in studying these relationships, one gains rare insight into the personal side of Subhas Chandra Bose. He first met Kitty Kurti on one of his early trips to Berlin in the 1930s. She and her husband, young newlyweds from Czechoslovakia, enjoyed the cultural scene in Berlin. Appalled by the cruel mob mentality of the Nazis, she found intellectual stimulation in attending lectures by India's roving ambassador of revolution. Impressed by his speeches, the Kurtis frequently invited the fellow expatriate to their home. More politically oriented than her spouse, Kitty Kurti found Bose's conversation enthralling, and his company enticing because of his notorious reputation in India. Obviously moved by his mere presence, Kurti, describing a lunch with him, wrote, "I look into the face of this unbelievable person. I see his Buddha-like smile[,] the great intelligence of the eyes, the keen[n]ess of the whole facial expression. And I feel, I intuit that this sweet and mysterious brother of mine is gifted with extraordinary understanding — that he senses more directly and quickly than other humans do. I also take delight in that smile that does not leave his face, for it signifies acceptance of my husband and me."[28]

Much of their conversation pertained to Kurti's efforts at understanding the nature of Bose's politics. At the podium and on the living-room sofa, Bose made it clear that India's independence motivated his every move. His socialistic leanings did not surprise Kurti, since many intellectuals drifted into the left wing before World War II. Bose denied being a communist, and according to Kurti, he "believed more in evolution than revolution, more in orderly ways of nature than in force and violence, even if at a given moment, for practical political reasons, he might use radical methods and go along with the Communists as he was now doing with the Fascists."[29]

Kurti found it difficult to accept that a man who grasped religions, political philosophy and psychology saw any value in Nazism, and yet, he justified his endeavors with thought-provoking evidence. Europeans tended to think that the British applied the Western tradition of liberalism throughout their colonial world. Bose informed his friends that English reforms extended only as far as the chalky cliffs of Dover, having no influence on India. Combating Raj brutality required the assistance of fascist strongmen like Hitler. To Bose, the Nazis represented a means to an end, and he fully realized their destructive capabilities. In private discussions, Bose unabashedly described his loathing of the fascists. Bose even knew about the concentration camps, and he condemned them. He urged the Kurtis to forget Czechoslovakia, flee Germany and move to the United States.[30]

Kitty Kurti remained Bose's friend and maintained a correspondence with him when he traveled. Like many Europeans, she learned about India, its history and contemporary struggle, through her association with Subhas Chandra Bose. He apparently touched her more than his average acquaintance; Kurti wrote a book about him. Although she never concealed her deep admiration for him, her reminiscences give support to the conclusion that Bose never truly adopted fascism.[31]

A friendship with a happily married woman held no romantic potential for Bose. His 45th birthday passed and he was still a bachelor. When his loneliness and frustration seemed overwhelming, he turned to Emilie Schenkl, an Austrian he met in Berlin and hired as his secretary. Her interest in his work drew them closer together, and in February 1942, the couple married in a Hindu ceremony. Their daughter, Anita, was born while they worked in Vienna. As in the case of most Indian leaders, very little of Bose's marital life is known or documented. Few outside the Bose family knew of his marriage, which saved Subhas from facing Indians who expected their Netaji to remain celibate in the tradition of Lenin or the Mahatma. Most Indians tended to regard marriage to Europeans as a sign of rejecting one's own people, while the Nazis considered Aryan–non–Aryan relationships miscegenation. Bose's choice of wife had little effect on his relationship with the Germans, since he kept all family matters private.[32]

The Voice of Indian Fascism

On February 19, 1942, the day Japan conquered Singapore, Bose made his first speech over Azad Hind Radio. Until he delivered that address, the world was not sure if Bose was alive or dead. He gave his audience the impression that he was broadcasting from a clandestine Indian locale, but he still remained in Berlin. The speech itself contained nothing unusual and it generated little effect in India. Once again, he predicted the demise of the British Empire and said that Indians and their Asian brothers deserved their freedom.[33]

In April 1942, Tokyo entered the picture. Astonishingly, the Japanese requested Italian and German support for a joint independence treaty for India and the Arab countries. Japan's sudden overture stemmed from difficulties within her own Indian program. Through the Black Dragon Society and other right-wing organizations, Japan unofficially sponsored Indian nationalistic activities from the 1920s until the beginning of World War II. After the rise of General Tojo Hideki, Japan openly endorsed any efforts to oust Europeans from Asia. Despite the close association between the Indian political gurus and Tokyo, Indian army units under Japanese command often resisted orders. When Imperial General Headquarters recalled a commanding officer sympathetic to the Indian cause and replaced him with a martinet, Indo-Japanese relations hit a critical low. Japan claimed to respect the idea of Free India, but wartime demands took precedence over long-term goals. Tokyo preferred to wait before issuing such a resolution, but further delays only strained their already shaky alliance. Even the unpopular new Japanese commandant urged his superiors to act quickly.[34]

The Japanese, faced with an Indian mutiny within their own forces, expected at least moral support from their Axis partners. Mussolini, rather excited about reports of Indian unrest in Southeast Asia and in India itself, wanted to back the Japanese proposal, as well as publicly establish Bose's government-in-exile. By early May, the Germans had convinced Rome to wait before making a commitment to the Indian-Arab issue. Germany reasoned that such a move should only be made after Axis forces occupied a position to control the situation in the Middle East.[35]

On May 4th, one day after Berlin vetoed the Japanese overture, Bose met with Ciano to express his disappointment. Bose avoided the issue of the rebellious nature of Indians working with the Japanese, and concentrated on a familiar theme: the Italian and German roles in the Indian revolution. He warned that with the Raj on its deathbed and Indians refusing to fight for the British, Japan naturally dropped into a position to work independently of its European allies. The headstrong Bengali insisted that Ciano arrange his second meeting with Mussolini on May 5th. Bose tried to pressure Il Duce to act alone. Mussolini thought it necessary to contact Berlin regarding Bose's appeal, and apparently Germany again rejected the idea.[36]

With this new failure of the Indo-Arab proposal, Bose saw the grim future of his entire German program. Even before he became the malignant voice of fascism and before he took command of a Berlin-sponsored Indian militia, Bose sensed the futility of his scheme. He interpreted Germany's stand as an official condemnation of Indian independence. Although the high point of his stay in Germany was literally months away, Bose sought other ties. Italy seemed unsure yet more encouraging than Berlin, and Japan seemed willing to back Free India, so the Bengali patriot turned to new partners.

It seems odd that Bose did not seek out Asia's leading power when he left India in January 1941, but in keeping with his Western outlook, he saw Nazi Germany and Fascist Italy as genuine revolutionary states. However, at the time, Tokyo had already organized a cell of Indian extremists, and did not need another militant guru. The Japanese, less sympathetic to the struggle itself but more determined to destroy the Raj, managed their Indian program quite differently than their European counterparts. By 1945, Bose discovered the cost which the Japanese Imperial General Headquarters demanded of its clients, and the severe penalties for those who challenged Tokyo's authority.[37]

Italy finally took the initiative. In the spring of 1942, Mussolini, at this point Bose's only European kindred spirit, officially committed Rome to the Indian cause. Il Duce's statement indicated both sympathy to Indian independence and his awareness of the need to weaken Britain. The Italian Premier believed that India could be freed by the use of revolutionary tactics, and that Bose was the man to apply them. Unfortunately, Italy did not compare to Germany in terms of military strength, but Mussolini's move prompted Hitler to agree to meet with Bose on May 29, 1942. Their conference did not favor the Indian cause. Hitler expressed his doubts as to India's readiness for revolution, as well as his fears of a Soviet takeover, and refused to change what he wrote in *Mein Kampf.* But Hitler did promise financial aid, and after Bose discussed relocating to the Far East, mentioned that some transportation might be arranged, in accordance with "the desires of the Japanese Government in the matter."[38]

Not many of the specifics of the Hitler-Bose interview have been documented, but in 1978, Washington declassified a number of MAGIC summaries — intelligence derived from decoded Japanese communiqués. The US War Department, it turns out, knew about Hitler's relationship with Bose, and learned that the Führer rejected Bose's request for military assistance. Through these MAGIC documents (available for more than 20 years yet still ignored by all scholars except those specifically researching Japan or the American war effort), it becomes obvious that Bose's association with the Nazis was tenuous all along. He had already made Japanese contacts. Shortly after talking with Hitler, Bose visited General Oshima Hiroshi, Japan's envoy to Berlin, to inquire about moving his program to the Far East. Oshima forwarded Bose's ideas to military authorities in Tokyo, but MAGIC failed to pick up the details.[39]

Although the specifics of the Hitler-Bose confrontation are not known, one can speculate about the scene in which two of history's most controversial characters shared the stage. For Hitler, who was known to be uncomfortable around Japanese diplomats and officers, and who certainly handled his Arab encounters badly, meeting with the Netaji must have been irritating indeed. Bose did not look like the epitome of a leader; he was a pudgy man of medium height, swarthy by European standards but normal for a Bengali, and dressed in rather plain European suits. Moon-faced and balding, he kept his hair close-cropped. His eyes were very large, soft, deep and brown. His expression was penetrating and gentle, perhaps the more so because of the small round dark-framed spectacles he wore. His mouth seemed full; his teeth were large. Bose looked like an Indian version of the actor Peter Lorre — a caricaturist's dream.

Bose sat looking at Hitler, a leader who was supposed to be a 20th century Napoleon, but saw only a small man staring back uncomfortably. Hitler was nearly eight years his senior, but already had a lined and flabby face, with crow's-feet around his legendary sea-blue eyes. His skin looked so pale and pink, his unkempt hair was lank and dark. The odd little toothbrush moustache, flecked with grey, twitched as he spoke that fast language only Frau Bose understood.

To Bose, an Indian long accustomed to the power of Oriental mysticism and Hindu charisma, the Führer probably seemed less than impressive. Furthermore, the linguistic and cultural barriers made Bose's encounter with Hitler more awkward than it would have been had Bose been a European. *A Beacon Across Asia* provides the following anecdote illustrating this point. Hitler summed up his feelings by saying that he failed to see Germany's advantage in supporting India. The Führer then asked Bose what his plans would be if the Axis refused to help him. Misunderstanding slightly, Bose told his interpreter to "please tell His Excellency that I have been in politics all my life and that I do not need advice from anyone."[40]

If his meeting with the German Chancellor dampened his spirits, Bose never let his depression hinder his work, as earlier setbacks had. He continued his activities at Berlin's Free India Center, or *Zentrale Freies Indien*, and worked to perfect his own propaganda style. Like the German and Italian fascists, Bose knew the importance of a complex propaganda machine, but the Indian aimed his toward counteracting British information and press releases, rather than imitating the aggressive Nazis.[41]

As a long-term project, Bose saw little value in racist ideologies, doomsday economic predictions and other standards of fascist propaganda. He realized that Britain's open society allowed a free flow of information that spread a positive image throughout the world. The British government kept up a good rapport with the press; after all, Prime Minister Churchill had been a journalist in his youth. In many countries, the British government also welcomed exchange students and encouraged international organizations to open offices in London. The British eagerly sponsored culture clubs, such as Vienna's Anglo-Austrian Friends. These methods inspired Subhas Bose.[42]

Bose hoped to eventually use British methods to win the world over to India's side, but for the time being, he settled for intelligent radio speeches and essays in various publications. One of his most controversial accomplishments was his use of the Azad Hind Radio. To make broadcasting a vital branch of the Free India campaign, he enlisted the help of Indian journalism majors studying in Germany. His fellow exiles gave speeches on the air and translated material into various Indian dialects. Bose even established a special Azad Muslim Radio station, clearly showing his concern for bringing all Indians into the movement.[43]

His broadcasts and articles all projected the same theme: this junction of history demanded India's freedom. In contrast to his old days as a Calcutta politician encumbered by alliances and compromises, the Nazis granted Bose the full use of propaganda, even allowing his movement to formally declare war on Britain on March 1, 1942. Considering that Bose represented neither a government nor an army, and that he broadcast from a tiny office in Berlin, London's lack of an apparent response is not surprising.[44]

Naturally, the Germans used Bose to their own end. Propaganda Minister Goebbels said in his diary that the Nazis pressured Bose into declaring war. Amazingly enough, Bose obeyed his sponsors without an official German commitment to Free India. Goebbels mistakenly assumed that the British still thought Bose remained hidden somewhere in or near India. He therefore believed that by using Bose, he damaged British morale without involving Germany. Bose launched a secret campaign against the British, and in return the Nazis merely funded a few useless programs, such as a new German-Indian Society in Hamburg, and an experimental "Indo-German Work Community" in Dahlem. These, too, served German political needs.[45]

Indeed, Bose was never able to compete with the British Broadcasting Corporation's Indian propaganda scheme. Knowing Bose's extremist politics and cloudy reputation in Bengal, the "Bluff and Bluster Corporation," as Bose nicknamed it, undertook a plan to neutralize any Axis disinformation, particularly the material broadcast on Azad Hind Radio. A clever socialistic admirer of the Axis like Bose had to be matched with a man of equal intelligence and political sensitivity and with a passionate resentment of totalitarianism. The BBC invited one Eric Arthur Blair, a 38-year-old drifter, writer, social critic and Loyalist veteran of the Spanish Civil War to manage its India Desk. Blair, better known to the world as George Orwell, gladly accepted the position in December 1941.[46]

Against Bose's barrage of enthusiastic promises of an impending fascist-sponsored liberation, Orwell wrote anonymous radio speeches directed to India, telling the people to patiently remain under British rule. To support his contention that, however restrictive, life under the Raj surpassed the fascists' idea of freedom, Orwell relied heavily on Germany's savage campaign in the USSR and, more relevant to Bengalis, Japanese atrocities in Southeast Asia. Orwell encouraged Indians to abandon any thoughts of an alliance with the Axis, while lauding the pro–Allied resistance movement in the Philippines. Strangely enough, during the 15 months of his employment at the BBC, Orwell never mentioned Bose or the Azad Hind movement by name; his method of attack was a simple weekly "news report" condemning all Axis activities and whatever Bose bragged about three days before.[47]

Orwell found his days at the BBC far from easy. He felt compassion for his radio audience and contempt for the Raj itself. He knew when his editorials bordered on lies, since he had briefly served in the Burmese colonial police force in the 1920s. His experiences in dealing with London's wartime censors, which came to an end in March 1943, actually did more to inspire his famed totalitarian warning, *1984*, than fighting Franco's Nationalists or living through World War II itself. Neither Bose nor Hitler nor even the Soviets — whom Orwell also despised — invented Doublespeak, the news medium featured in his 1949 novel. Doublespeak was the language in use at the British Broadcasting Corporation throughout the 1940s.[48]

While British documents tended to concentrate on the failure of Azad Hind Radio rather than on the effects of Orwell's appeals to India, London's propaganda would have reached the greater number of people. Bose's grand predictions touched only the most devout of his followers, if any at all. Orwell never promised domestic changes in India, but recounted news events that suggested a desperate Axis grinding down any nation caught in its path. The evidence showed that the Azad Hind Radio broadcasts were discredited in India.

While somewhat suspicious that Bose lacked a following at home, Goebbels never realized how little Bose influenced events in India. Without giving reasons for the sudden information release, the India Office in London sent a "secret" report to the BBC in April 1942. The report analyzed the impact of Bose's radio appeals. Many, including people from Bose's home state of Orissa, did not believe the voice was his, and felt that the Axis was behind this fraud. One of Bose's friends from the surviving Forward Bloc asserted that the party's guru would never join the fascists. The British communiqué concluded that "the message can be said to have aroused passing interest, not free from considerable scepticism, among certain sections of the public, but to have had a negligible effect, save in Forward Bloc circles, where the tendency to hail the message as the long awaited sign from Bose is not entirely whole-hearted."[49]

If Hitler had understood that Bose wielded so little clout at home, he might never have changed his mind about Bose's idea of Azad Hind, and sponsored the creation of an Indian National Army.

THE FAUJ

In August 1942, Bose theorized about the approaching conflict between India and Britain. His article, "Free India and her Problems," appeared in the German magazine *Wille und Macht*, and later in *Azad Hind*, the in-house publication of the Free India Center. Again he promoted the goal of an independent India, advocated the eventual linking of India's economy to a barter system with Germany, and suggested the immediate need for an Axis-supported Indian national militia. The key to Berlin's renewed interest, however, was in Bose's elaboration of the national military concept, which included an army, navy and air force.[1]

The general concept of an Indian National Army (INA), comprising Indians among British POWs and organized by the fascists, was not a particularly new idea. During World War I, the Berlin Committee, the German-supported unit of Indian extremists, had seriously considered recruiting POWs to fight for the Kaiser. In World War II, Japan, Germany and Italy independently experimented with their own Indian liberation armies. Their attempts began at virtually the same time — the early months of 1942. With 45,000 Indian captives, the Japanese claimed the largest number of soldiers to convert, especially after the conquest of Singapore in February. For nearly a year, Tokyo's INA tramped through Southeast Asia under the erratic leadership of Major Mohan Singh.[2]

Not to be outdone by either Tojo or Hitler, Mussolini quickly established an Italian-based Indian corps and immediately promoted Iqbal Shedai to the rank of generalissimo. The director of the Friends of India assumed command of the *Centro Militare India* (CMI) in April 1942. A smooth talker, Shedai canvassed POW facilities in Italy and Libya, suggesting that Indians take advantage of the golden chance to be patriots for their homeland. He managed to do this in violation of an agreement between Berlin and Rome that stipulated Germany's jurisdiction over Indian prisoners. Shedai even convinced a number of Indians at El Alamein to surrender to the Italians, and so avoid the humiliation and possible injuries that would be sustained during capture.[3]

In spite of Shedai's efforts, his men never believed that Italy wanted them strictly as a liberation force at home, and only 350 joined the CMI. Bose occasionally met with his Italian-based counterpart, but Shedai resisted Bose's attempts to dominate his brigade. By November 1942, Shedai knew that Italy only needed Indian soldiers as warm bodies to face the Allied push in North Africa; thus, any chance of the CMI being sent to Asia was eliminated. Furthermore, his own credibility among the POWs dwindled to nothing. Shedai watched helplessly as his men mutinied and refused to assemble. The CMI evaporated before reaching any battlefield.[4]

Bose's bulldog persistence and the prospect of his establishment of the German branch of the Indian National Army changed Hitler's attitude toward the Azad Hind movement. The Nazis loaned increasing amounts of money to the Free India Center, and the Wehrmacht helped Bose organize a POW army. The soldiers were usually frightened village youths who were still loyal to the Crown. German and Indian writers, especially those involved with Bose, later claimed that the POWs willingly allied with their German captors, and became an important part of the Wehrmacht's war effort. In his preface to Ganpuley's book, Adalbert Seifrig described the INA as a cooperative volunteer army of Hindu, Muslim and Sikh Indians.[5]

While accurate in that Bose appealed to all types of Indians, more objective works, most notably Roger Beaumont's *Sword of the Raj*, question the willingness of the captives to enlist in the INA. Apparently coercive measures, such as torture and even the killing of uncooperative prisoners, were used to encourage enlistment. Beaumont substantiates the charge that Bose even ordained the murders of many high-ranking prisoners to wipe out any possible POW resistance. Bose then subjected those "willing" to join — about 2,000 men — to an intensive preinduction brainwashing program under his personal direction.[6]

Subhas Chandra Bose's new role of army commander profoundly changed his legendary statesmanship. He moved from negotiating with government officials to a recruiting campaign among Indian prisoners of war. His steadfast diplomacy gave way to heavy persuasion and other techniques of modern advertising. The thoughtful angry intellectual left his cluttered desk and adopted the flamboyant style of his Western contemporaries. By August 1942, Bose acquired the typical fascist trappings: a uniform and a new title. He called himself the *Netaji*, or Revered Leader. His army, known as the Azad Hind *Fauj*, or the [Free] Indian Legion, had its special symbol: a springing tiger emblazoned on the tricolor shield of India. Bose enjoyed the personal honors of being an Axis leader. Hitler now granted him full diplomatic immunity, and gave him a home in the classy Charlottenburg section of Berlin. The Führer even agreed to change the offending passages in future editions of *Mein Kampf.*[7]

The German Chancellor became openly pro–Free India, and expressed his hope that Bose would lead the Axis assault on the Indo-Burmese front. In an artificially dramatic moment, Hitler said to Bose, "Your Excellency, I am prepared to tear [up] my tripartite agreement with Japan if she should refuse to honour your wishes in respect to India's independence."[8]

German officers trained the 2,000-man Indian Legion at Regenwurm, a major industrial facility in Frankfurt. About 100 prisoners qualified for entry into a special Indian commando course, which included training in sabotage, intelligence, communications, mountain combat and parachuting. These elites trained with the Lehrregiment Brandenburg, also known as the Brandenburg Fifth Column Training Unit, along with numerous Iranians and Soviet Asians who fell under the influence of the Grand Mufti of Jerusalem. After all POWs had received a general military education, the Wehrmacht stationed the Indian Legion at Koenigsbrueck, Saxony. Clearly, the Nazis ultimately hoped to use them for both European combat and insurrection activities in India.[9]

However, the Netaji insisted that his men be kept separate from the Germans. Although his own military background was limited to an archaic officers' training course in college, he served as advocate and liaison between his bewildered countrymen and their foreign hosts. Through the German Foreign Ministry, Bose demanded that the Wehrmacht grant the Indian Legionnaires the same rights and privileges as the Germans. His main concern was that the Azad Hind Fauj would not be exploited, or strictly used for fighting Germany's war.[10]

The Nazis regarded the Indian Legion the same way they did any of their other ethnic units — as a part of the German Army, and therefore under the jurisdiction of the German government. They forced Bose to swear his loyalty to the Third Reich, but the Bengali added a qualifying proviso, and said, "I swear by God this holy oath, that I will obey the leader of the German State and People, Adolf Hitler, as Commander of the German Armed Forces, in the fight for the Freedom of India, in which fight the leader is Subhas Chandra Bose, and that as a brave soldier, I am willing to lay down my life for this oath. I shall lead the army when we march to India together."[11]

Ganpuley, one of Bose's closest aides at the Free India Center, recalled the celebration when the Azad Hind Fauj commando students completed their basic training and joined the Brandenburg Regiment, under the command of cavalry officer Hauptmann Walter Harbich. On leave before their special disposition, the soldiers cheered and mingled with the Indian community of Berlin. The elite corps proudly displayed giant Springing Tiger banners signed in blood. The next day Bose reportedly wept as his men left their headquarters at Frankenberg. The Legionnaires responded to their Netaji's tears with enthusiastic cries of *"Azad Hind Zindabad"* and *"Netaji Zindabad"* ("Long Live Free India" and "Long Live the Revered Leader"). Yet, despite their German uniforms and professional reeducation, most were far from dedicated to Germany. They wanted a Free India, but found the idea of turning against the Crown disturbing. The Germans terrified them, and few adjusted to Prussian-style military training.[12]

After numerous consultations with Bose throughout 1942, the Germans agreed to use the Indian Legion in Western Asia. Bose and the Nazis planned to parachute some of the commandos into India's politically unstable northwestern Frontier Central to flood the region with propaganda. However, Bose required the bulk of his forces to be used in a pincer movement against India and Afghanistan, while the Germans swarmed into Soviet Central Asia. First, though, Berlin had other ideas. Against Bose's wishes, in July 1942, the Nazis demanded that the Indian Legion serve in the European and North African theaters before going on to Delhi. The Wehrmacht now ordered the Indians to pledge their fidelity to Germany over their Netaji.[13]

Another Kulturkampf?

The Indian Legionnaires quickly earned the reputation for being cowardly, rebellious and barbaric. Much of this image stemmed from German prejudice toward their foreign troops with strange Indian customs. One Indian unit in Holland staged a mutiny, and the German officers continually complained about them to Wehrmacht headquarters. Ironically, Bose felt insulted when Rommel refused to use his men. According to British historian Hugh Toye, Rommel "never ... considered the battlefield to be the place for the proving of Foreign Office ideas."[14]

The question of using the Indian Legion is one of the major controversies of Bose's German sojourn. Bose's close associate, N.G. Ganpuley, claimed that the Netaji never wanted his army to fight in Europe and North Africa. Throughout his negotiations with the Germans, Bose never showed any inclination to assist the fascists in their war effort, other than by sabotaging the British. In contrast to Ganpuley, Toye alleged that Bose wanted the Legion to give a show of force in North Africa. He claimed that Bose hoped to impress his fascist sponsors and alleviate the rampant boredom within his militia's ranks.[15]

Regardless of Bose's intentions, the Germans never used the Indian

Legion to any great extent. The skittish behavior of the regular troops discouraged the German field officers. Nonetheless, that fails to completely explain why Hitler's interest in India waned. Harbig respected his fifth column elites, and reported both excellent performances in training and high morale. Eventual German defeats at El Alamein and Stalingrad in November 1942 caused the Nazis to scrap their plans for a West Asian campaign. Without the West Asian attack, the Wehrmacht refused to keep even the 100-man special Indian unit. By the early months of 1943, Hitler and Mussolini concluded that the expenses of continued involvement in World War II meant abandoning their pet nationalists. The Italians withdrew their support from Amanullah of Afghanistan and Iqbal Shedai.[16]

As the Germans and Italians began to lose the war, and their Indian troops mutinied, Netaji Bose's status in Germany fell rapidly. He might have drifted into oblivion but for the appearance of a disturbing report. Despite Berlin's support for Bose's movement, he had been routinely investigated by the Gestapo and the *Reichssicherheithauptamt* (RSHA), the Supreme National Security Board. General Walter Schellenberg, chief of this secret service, relied on information provided by a mysterious agent known only as Jahnke. Jahnke, in turn, consulted with Sidi Khan, an Indian activist staying in Rome. Khan, one of Bose's political enemies, ingratiated himself with the Nazis by serving as an Indian analyst for the Asian branch of AMT VI, the Foreign Political Information Service.[17]

Jahnke's summary of Bose startled Schellenberg. "When I mentioned Bose's name to Jahnke," Schellenberg noted in his memoirs, "he at once gave me a warning. He said he knew that Bose had lived and studied in Moscow for a considerable time and that he had established close relations with the Cominform. In my own dealings with Bose I had time and time again come across indications of the influence of Moscow's teachings...."[18]

The RSHA's assessment of Bose was wrong. Between March and April 1942, Bose did travel through the Soviet Union after Ambassador Quaroni made special arrangements. However, spite of Bose's socialist beliefs, the Russians wanted no dealings with him. He certainly never attended a university there, and since the Soviets never recruited him as either a spy or a party protégé, he was never enrolled in any training center. While the possibility exists that even Schellenberg had no idea of Bose's activities during his January–April 1941 "disappearance" before appearing in Berlin, Sisir K. Bose and his collaborators all carefully documented this period, and Kitty Kurti kept track of him during his earlier travels in the 1930s.[19]

Could Hitler's security men have been so paranoid about Communism that even visiting Russia suggested the acceptance of Stalinism, and, worse yet, made one suspect of being a spy? In fact, neither Subhas Bose nor any of his family ever courted the Soviet Union; but Bose is a rather common surname in India, and a mix-up could have resulted. An extremely racist faction of the Nazi Party, or even Sidi Khan, jealous of the Netaji's power, may have deliberately tried to discredit Bose with the Germans. Lastly, one must consider the motives of the Nazi intelligence system, not particularly partial to even-handed analysis or accuracy.

End of a Dream?

The collapse of Germany's Free India program seemed inevitable, considering that Nazism promoted racism and showed no sympathy for subjugated peoples. If Indians harried the English like rebellious adolescents, then it served Hitler's purpose to encourage them. Although he respected the colonial system, Hitler needed to disable his enemy, and India was the heart of the British Empire. The Nazis tried to achieve their ends by using Subhas Chandra Bose as a mouthpiece.

Bose, determined to enlist the Axis as the sponsor of an Indian revolution, doggedly pursued the fascists until they saw the potential for India in an Axis-dominated world. By approaching Hitler and Mussolini, Bose accomplished something special. First, he introduced the Indian situation to Europeans with a modern, Occidental format. The West already understood England and accepted British ways, while remaining unfamiliar with the East. Bose downplayed Oriental values and challenged the issue of imperialism in the 20th century. He took the advice of his mentor, C.R. Das, and awakened the world to the Indian struggle. This period of Bose's career would soon be dwarfed by his spectacular rise to fame and shame in Southeast Asia, and yet, Bose's skills as a diplomat were never honed more sharply. That an Indian revolutionary earned the patronage of Axis officials seemed like a major coup; winning any concessions from them appeared to be impossible. The fascists, especially the Nazis, showed few reservations in making empty promises. In spite of German support that never came, Bose remained determined to use right-wing militarism to strangle the Raj. When he finally left India in January 1941, he felt optimistic that the Axis would treat him as a serious revolutionary nationalist. In contrast to his 1930s overtures, Bose proposed a detailed manifesto for the Indo-Axis alliance.

Within a few months of Bose's arrival in Berlin in April 1941, the German Foreign Office concluded that the Indian had propaganda value as a colonial militant and anti–British antagonist. Secretary of State Wilhelm Kepler arranged the creation of the Free India Center, which not only issued anti–Allied, pro–Nazi disinformation, but also coordinated the activities of numerous Indian exiles who shared Bose's sympathies. The dedicated Bose worked feverishly for his hosts, although his broadcasts never stirred up

Indians at home. Actually, his 1941–42 program generated little effect other than embarrassing London, but the Nazis never discovered this. Bose continually begged his sponsors to declare their intention of setting India free, and ordain his headquarters as a government-in-exile. While Mussolini approved of this request, Hitler felt uncomfortable about legitimizing a non–Aryan movement, and Propaganda Minister Goebbels assured his Führer that keeping Bose underground better served German interests.

Much to Bose's delight, the Wehrmacht adopted his idea of rehabilitating Indian POWs to fight against the British. Bose easily assumed the characteristics of a fascist demagogue and declared himself the Netaji, or Revered Leader. While fiercely loyal to his men, Bose was little more than a figurehead in the Azad Hind Fauj; Nazi officers led the 2,000-man army. While Bose lobbied for the rights of his men, Berlin decided to commit the Fauj to battle in Europe rather than India. By 1942, the Nazis had liquidated all but a handful of Indian units, after the troops mutinied in the European theater.

Subhas Chandra Bose's dream of creating an Indian Legion to liberate India disintegrated as the Nazis began to lose the war. He lost credibility with Berlin, but still had admirers elsewhere. While the Germans and Italians were still attempting to make the India issue part of their war effort, the Japanese had planted a revolutionary time bomb in the Far East. Since the beginning of the war, they had been sponsoring actively functioning, separate Azad Hind movements in all Asian countries except India. Those movements now needed a Netaji. In February 1943, Subhas Chandra Bose left Europe forever, to pursue anew his dreams of liberation.

◆ 8 ◆

DARLING OF THE AXIS

"Japan is firmly resolved to extend all means in order to help to expel and eliminate from India the Anglo-Saxon influences which are the enemy of the Indian people, and enable India to achieve full independence in the true sense of the term."

— Premier Tojo Hideki[1]

Japan: The Tiny Superpower

"So far and wide have the roots of Japanese victory spread that we cannot now visualize all the fruit it will put forth. The people of the East seem to be waking up from their lethargy." So said Mahatma Gandhi enthusiastically upon learning of Japan's 1905 victory over the Russians. Like many Indian leaders, he prayed that an Asian triumph would arouse all colonized Oriental peoples, and inspire them to oust their foreign rulers. Gandhi never dreamed of the eventual perversion in Japan's triumph, nor of Asians enslaved by other Asians. The evidence suggests that Japanese expansion into Western interests in the Far East was launched ten years before, with China's loss in the First Sino-Japanese War, yet planning began in earnest with Russia's defeat in the Russo-Japanese War. For centuries the Japanese fantasized about becoming the preeminent power in the Orient, and by the turn of the century, the Floating Kingdom proved the truth in the old historians' chestnut that a nation cannot undergo a rapid military buildup without intending to go to war.[2]

Aside from their new arsenal, the Japanese developed certain characteristics that gave them an edge over their neighbors. While most Asians, particularly the Chinese and Indians, lived on huge land masses divided by a variety of geographical boundaries and often hundreds of dialects, Japan

76

consisted of a small island chain with one language. In addition to these factors, Nippon's unity traditionally fused around the emperor and an iron-bound feudal heritage. Accepted as the Son of Heaven, his succession preempted any political tangles or occasional civil wars. The Mikado and his empire were defended by the samurai, who were guided by Bushido, the Cult of the Warrior, which taught those from this noble caste how to obey, fight and die with honor. Bellicose samurai guarded their homeland, which never endured colonization like most of the Orient. In fact, the first and only formal occupation of Japan took place after World War II. This unity, militancy and independence forged Japan's national character.

Japan's triumph over the Czar in the 1904–05 war proved the viability of Japanese nationalism and the strength of the Japanese military, especially the Imperial Navy. In an effort to uphold the 1911 treaty with Great Britain, Japan attacked the Kaiser's Asian and Pacific possessions during World War I. The Japanese attempted to expand their influence in the region with the infamous Twenty-One Demands of 1915, an unsuccessful bid to make China a vassal state. The West refused to tolerate the Terauchi Government's pressure on Beijing, nor would the Allies allow Japan to keep every area claimed by Tokyo in the Treaty of Versailles. While the Allies carved up Europe to suit their needs, they deliberately blocked Japan's road to preeminence. The Allies insisted that all nations deserved equal access to the Open Door of China, and that a hungry Japanese empire endangered trade. Disarmament treaties signed during the Washington and London Conferences of 1921–22 and 1930 further aggravated the situation by setting what Tokyo considered unfair limits on Japanese warships, while giving the great powers virtual control over the Western world. Tokyo responded to this betrayal by charting the course that led to the attack on the United States and World War II.[3]

Japanese policymakers advocated a program of controlling the Far East, called the Greater East Asia Co-Prosperity Sphere (GEA), as the only means of breaking the Western hold over the region while preventing further encroachment. At a 1941 policy conference, Japanese officials restated their intentions to "expel the influence of these three countries [the United States, Great Britain and the Netherlands] from East Asia, to establish a sphere for the self-defense and self-preservation of our Empire, and to build a New Order in Greater East Asia. In other words, we aim to establish a close and inseparable relationship in military, political, and economic affairs between our Empire and the countries of the Southern Region...."[4]

As Japan began to swallow countries in the late 1930s, many Westerners initially mistook this behavior for the sponsoring of national liberation movements. Instead of being a local "big brother" to the weaker countries — actually former protectorates — the Japanese military government merely improved on Western methods of oppressing these colonized people. Tokyo's version of the Gestapo, called the *Kempeitai*, replaced European security forces in Malaya, the Dutch East Indies and Indochina. Japan transformed the colonies into police states in order to serve Japanese interests.[5]

For the Japanese, the GEA had a three-fold purpose: to give the Rising Sun raw materials, particularly fuel and rubber, to press Southeast Asians into serving the Axis, and to satisfy their dreams of dominating the Far East and humiliating the white world. The speed with which the Kempeitai arrested, detained and deported Europeans dazzled the Asians; yet, they gradually realized that they remained third-class citizens in their own countries. Bedazzlement turned to despair when the Asians discovered that they now existed only for the benefit of the Rising Sun.[6]

Tokyo's activities melded conveniently with German wishes for the Orient, especially in terms of India. By 1942, Adolf Hitler regretfully accepted the fact that India, the bastion of white superiority over the Asian, would become part of the Nipponese Empire. Even while working with Bose, the Nazis always considered the Indian question under Tokyo's sphere. Berlin kept Bose as a client for his value as a propaganda mouthpiece and potential army organizer. While Bose's Indian Legion mutinied that year, and the Germans lost Stalingrad and El Alamein, Japan enjoyed virtual hegemony in the Far East. Bose and the Nazis agreed that to increase his effectiveness he needed to be relocated nearer to the Asian battlefields, and far from the scene of his European failure.[7]

The Nazis willingly relinquished their major interest in the Indian issue to those who never intended to actively promote India's independence. India's freedom was never the question. Liquidating the British Empire concerned the Axis, while the Japanese regarded India as the potential cornerstone of their GEA. In March 1942, Goebbels wrote that the Japanese told Hitler that their attempts on Australia were the stepping-stones before moving into India. They assured the Führer that an invasion of India would instantly kill England. The Axis believed that the Indians planned no resistance to the Japanese; Subhas Bose always maintained that his brethren sided against the unsympathetic Raj. Reiterating Bose's phraseology, the Germans accepted the idea that the Indians had finally achieved an international awareness, which created a vulnerable mood that enabled the fascists to take over as the British disintegrated.[8]

The Germans had an additional reason for rejoicing over Tokyo's intentions. In the paranoid delusions of Nazi leadership, a democratic harpy was lurking in the shadows, waiting to pounce on India. Goebbels noted that "Roosevelt makes no bones about his appetite for India."[9]

Indian Nationalists Look to Japan

In 1941, three years before the Japanese-controlled Indian National Army entered India, Tokyo began working with overseas Indians. After Japan entered the war, overseas Chinese vainly challenged its encroachment, which resulted in brutal extermination policies against them. On the other hand, Indian communities welcomed the troops of the Rising Sun as they conquered Southeast Asia. Despite the tendency for Indians to be more educated and politically sophisticated than their neighbors, they firmly believed that Japan justified its expansion by counteracting Western imperialism. After Bose's return to Asia in 1943, overseas Indians provided the financial base for Japan's Indian program.[10]

Japan also encouraged its own Indian exiles to guide India's entry into the GEA. After World War I, many Indian revolutionaries fled Germany and India for the Far East, particularly those involved in the Indo-German Conspiracy. Among them was A. M. Sahay, a physician and journalist who founded the Indian National Congress at Kobe, Giani Pritam Singh, a Sikh evangelist who created an Indian Independence League in Bangkok, and the infamous Raja Mahendra Pratap. By the 1940s, the former President of the 1915 "Provisional Government of India" had found new inspiration in fascism. Pratap preached a political philosophy called "World Federation," and he dreamed of a giant, pro–Axis state in West Asia named *"Aryanstan."*[11]

The dean of Indian expatriates in Japan was Rash Behari Basu, also known as Rash Behari Bose, although he was no relation to the Netaji. In India, he sparked various military rebellions, and in 1912, made an unsuccessful assassination attempt on Viceroy Lord Hardinge. During World War I, he collaborated with the Germans. In 1915, he went to East Asia, where he befriended Dr. Sun Yixian, who introduced him to Toyama Mitsuru of Japan. Toyama looked after Basu until Japan was ready for him. As godfather of the secret militant organization known as the *Kokuryukai*, or Black Dragon Society, Toyama hid the Indian fugitive in a pro–British country — in fact, London's closest Asian ally at the time.[12]

Toyama had established the Black Dragon Society at the turn of the century in reaction to Western dominance of Asia, or more specifically, Russo-Japanese competition for Korea and Manchuria. Membership flourished when ultraconservatives felt threatened by the "liberal" trends of the modern Japanese government in the 1920s and early 1930s. Viewing themselves as born-again samurai, Toyama and his superpatriots vowed to disfigure or kill any political, business or academic figure who succumbed to Occidental ways. Even military officers became targets for the Black Dragon and other secret fraternities. They loathed the round-eyed foreigners who polluted Asia, and so they felt kindred spirits with Chinese and Indian nationalists. As the international and domestic situations forced Japanese leaders to step to the right, the *yakuza* societies exerted political clout.[13]

The influential Toyama arranged meetings between Basu and important Japanese officials. After listening to Basu, Japanese interest in overseas Indians heightened. His words did not inspire a liberating sensibility within the Imperial General Headquarters, but quickened the military's opportunistic impulses. The Japanese desired an indigenous espionage network in Malaya and Thailand, and they realized the value of local Indians for this purpose. They concluded that Basu's colleague, Giani Pritam Singh, needed to be wooed to their side. As founder of the Bangkok-based Indian Independence League (IIL), Singh ranked among the most important Indians abroad; he was also a man in need of political and financial assistance.[14]

In September 1941, Tokyo ordered Major Fujiwara Iwaichi to establish a special liaison group to handle Indian revolutionary activities. Known as the Fujiwara *Kikan* or the F *Kikan* (Fujiwara Intelligence Agency), it functioned under Colonel Tamura, the military attaché in Bangkok. Major Fujiwara personally worked with Giani Pritam Singh, after offering Japanese aid in return for the IIL's active support. The F Kikan willingly gave Singh free use of radio stations in Japan and the occupied territories, since his speeches attacked Britain. Fujiwara arranged funding and publicity campaigns for the IIL, and put Singh in contact with Subhas Bose, then at the highpoint of his career in Berlin.[15]

Fujiwara asked the Sikh preacher to encourage his followers to compromise British defenses and convert Indian soldiers to the Axis camp. As Japanese units swarmed over the Malayan and Thai coasts in early December 1941, IIL members visited the Allies' Indian troops, and begged them not to shoot at the Japanese, who, they said, intended to liberate Mother India. Eventually the Fujiwara Kikan coordinated civilian and military intelligence operations throughout southern Thailand, Malaya, Singapore and Borneo.[16]

On December 8, 1941, the American war declaration against Japan prompted a vibrant speech from Rash Behari Basu, broadcast from Tokyo. He told his audience that Japan and the oppressed Asians emerged as a force to be reckoned with. Then Basu quietly approached his associates at the Imperial General Headquarters, to warn them of Allied strength in the Orient. He explained that British power in India seriously threatened the Greater East Asia Co-Prosperity Sphere, but a well-developed Indian Independence League undermined the Raj. Tokyo cooperated generously. On January 28, 1942, Basu convened the Tokyo chapter of the IIL at the Sanno Hotel. Two months later, he organized a Tokyo conference for all IIL branches throughout Asia, including fledgling clubs in Hong Kong and Shanghai. Delegates called for a massive IIL program, and many applauded as Rash Behari Basu became president of the coordinating body of the various branches of the League.[17]

Considering Basu's experience in founding local chapters of the IIL, and the fact that he wrote the League's manifesto, his appointment surprised none. His close ties with Tokyo while creating the IIL platform disturbed some Indian nationalists, who viewed him as more Japanese than Indian. Unlike Bose, who kept his personal life private, Basu's lifestyle was well known. Basu's enemies accused him of becoming foreign in habit and philosophy. The kimono-clad revolutionary had lived in Japan for nearly 30 years, married the daughter of a Black Dragon officer, and become a Japanese citizen. At least Giani Pritam Singh maintained his Sikh identity during his involvement with the F Kikan, while President Basu apparently had buried his heritage.[18]

The Story of Mohan Singh

The treatment of Indian soldiers captured by the Japanese concerned many Indian officials, but none as deeply as Giani Pritam Singh. Through Colonel Tamura, Imperial General Headquarters promised him that the Japanese routinely treated all Indian POWs with absolute respect, and not as Allied supporters. In fact, the Japanese showed a marked interest in using them as a resource. The Changi camp in Singapore overflowed with 45,000 trained Indian soldiers. Basu and his sponsors assumed that all Indians inherently despised the Allies, and with minor rehabilitation, could rejoin the war fighting for the Rising Sun. The Indian National Army (INA) began in 1941, several months before Bose founded the Indian Legion of Germany, so the Japanese never learned from the Wehrmacht's fiasco.[19]

Circumstances often drag individuals from their contented obscurity, and thrust them into positions of power. Mohan Singh fits this description perfectly. Singh, a Sikh captain in the 1/14th Punjab Regiment, led a small unit based in India's North-West Frontier. In early 1941, the entire regiment moved to Jitra, a town in the Malay State of Perak, near the Thai border. Noticing his battlefield performance, and his education at the respected military academy at Dehra Dun, Singh's superiors quickly promoted him, at age 29, to the rank of major. The British viewed him as a typically conformist Indian, a "good boy" who accepted Anglo-Saxon supremacy without question.[20]

In times of stress, however, Mohan Singh revealed a bitterness toward British authority and a rebellious side to his character. After an argument with a British officer, he reportedly mentioned to his fellow Indians that he might turn against the Crown. Like many Indians, he resented London for once again bringing India into a war without the prior consultation of Indian leaders. He took no pride in his promotion, since his active participation in the military had not been a matter of free choice. Historian K. K. Ghosh contended that Singh believed in the Axis cause, and went so far as to mention rumors that he collaborated with the Japanese before the war began.[21]

Regardless of his personal feelings, Major Singh fought in the British army in Southeast Asia for almost a year. On December 11, 1941, a Japanese tank unit mauled Singh's regiment, leaving him stranded in a swamp with two Indian noncommissioned officers and their British commander. As the Japanese closed in on the muddy quartet, Singh decided to defect. Ghosh speculated that Singh underwent a battlefield conversion from subdued soldier to enthusiastic revolutionary. He claimed that while still marooned, Singh plotted the foiling of Britain's Asian strategy and the liberation of India. The propaganda of the times and the rose-tinted memoirs of ardent INA veterans apparently seduced Ghosh and other writers of this genre. Singh's instincts probably told him to prepare for his defection. He knew that capture was imminent, and being a traitor seemed the safest approach when in the grasp of an enemy.[22]

The Japanese immediately decided that prisoner Singh made an ideal leader for their proposed Indian National Army. The Japanese had pressing reasons for choosing this discontented officer. For months, Major Fujiwara complained that his men found difficulty functioning in the wild Malayan city of Alorstar. Tojo's generals realized that the presence of a revolutionary Indian militia could persuade the Indian population of Alorstar to cooperate with the occupation.[23]

When Singapore fell to the Japanese on February 19, 1942, Imperial General Headquarters turned Changi camp into Singh's recruiting center. The Imperial Army granted Singh free access to 45,000 Indian captives. Singh acted according to four guidelines: (1) Tokyo completely endorsed the Indian National Army, and regarded it as a legitimate part of the Axis forces; (2) the INA remained separate from Basu's IIL; (3) Mohan Singh had control over the Indian POWs; and (4) Japan agreed to grant freedom to those POWs who cooperated with Singh. Those who refused to join the INA still had POW status, but nevertheless remained under Singh's jurisdiction.[24]

As with Bose's Indian Legion, this unit used coercion and stark brutality. Insecure POWs joined Singh's INA fearing for their lives, and were filled with disinformation about the war situation. Even so, crude training and brainwashing techniques failed to erase a longstanding devotion to the Crown. The majority of Indian soldiers had been raised in conservative homes not unlike Janakinath Bose's, where the parents regarded the Empire as a landed institution. Furthermore, the typical Indian officer treasured his commission as a vehicle for financial and social mobility. The INA did not encourage much support among ranking Indian officers with its policy of not recognizing previous Royal Indian Army titles.[25]

Some of the INA's best-remembered officers "enlisted" with deep reservations. Colonel P. K. Sahgal and General Shah Nawaz Khan joined only to keep a check on the Japanese and Singh, who, among Indians, was surprisingly not known for his leadership abilities. They believed that at best, Singh was a "very average" major who lacked the fortitude to handle the command of an Indian liberation force. Sahgal and Khan feared that once Imperial General Headquarters crushed Singh, the Japanese would destroy the Indian patriots in their war. Sahgal and Khan joined the INA with the noble intention of taking control after Mohan Singh's obliteration. In a delusion of grandeur, they believed that only through their presence, could their prisoner comrades and the other two million Indians in Southeast Asia be protected from Japanese sadism. General Khan and his men never forgot that chilling announcement made in the Changi camp soon after the fall of Singapore: Major Singh had been given "the power of life and death" over them. With that thought, they mobilized for action.[26]

Mohan Singh marched his army of 16,300 into Alorstar, and literally tamed the town. This initial achievement in the capital of the state of Kedah raised some eyebrows in Tokyo, and the INA gained prestige. Singh and his officers began a remarkable working relationship with Major Fujiwara and his agents. Fujiwara's seeming dedication to the Indian cause gave his orders an aura of sincerity, despite his imperialistic intentions. The director of F Kikan stressed the common Oriental background that made Indians and Japanese brothers. His adjutants lived in INA camps and learned to eat the curries and heavy stews that disgusted them. Fujiwara deliberately cultivated this singular rapport to prove the honesty of Nippon's quest for liberation, and to show the apparent difference in outlook between Japanese and British officers. The English, Irish, Welsh and Scots who gave him orders in the past never treated Mohan Singh so warmly.[27]

After witnessing Japan's cruel occupation of Malaya, Major Singh wisely chose to remain skeptical of Fujiwara's gilded promises. In March 1942, Singh convinced Rash Behari Basu to accompany him to Tokyo to demand a formal commitment to the Indian cause. Naturally taken aback, military officials refused their demands. In June, the Japanese implied support for Indian independence when they approved the platform developed by a Bangkok conference of the IIL. Consenting to this set of resolutions led to Japan's agreement to the establishment of a provisional government of Free India 16 months later. Mohan Singh still mistrusted Tokyo, even after he received increased funding for the INA and the Japanese built a special concentration camp exclusively for Indian resistors.[28]

Singh not only doubted Japan's program, but also the caliber of the Indians working on it. If, for one brief moment, Japan actually did pave the way for a Free India, who among them could lead the war against the Raj, and then take the country? A stunning thought dawned on Mohan Singh. He later recalled that "neither Pritam Singh nor I nor any other person in East Asia was fit for such a role. Besides why were they [the Japanese] to manufacture overnight cheap and third rate leaders when Subhas Chandra Bose was in Germany and the Japanese could, if they only tried, bring him over to East Asia."[29]

For the moment, the Japanese did not care about Singh's opinion of their Indian program. They desperately needed laborers to build airfields in Thailand and Borneo, so they chose INA troops for the job. Despite their talk of a unified Asia and of respecting Indian Army rank, the Japanese began to demonstrate the deep-seated racism of the Rising Sun. They ordered those Indians not working on constructions sites to guard Changi. The Imperial Army assigned only a small number of experienced Indians to artillery units. The Japanese dashed Singh's hopes for a cadre of sophisticated Indian officers in November 1942, when the Kempeitai detained Indian intelligence students from the Swaraj Institute in Penang. Despite his Japanese colleagues' cynical expectations, Singh refused to tolerate exploitation by the Axis. He responded to his loss of authority and dignity by ignoring orders.[30]

Complaints from Imperial General Headquarters rained down on Rash Behari Basu. He now had to deal with a new man, since Tokyo transferred Major Fujiwara in April 1942. Fujiwara's successor, Colonel Iwakuro Hideo, had no patience for diplomacy. Iwakuro refused to compromise his orders, and he never tolerated disobedience from the INA. Basu, enraged at Mohan Singh, accused him of alienating the INA from the Indian movement, and using it as his "private and personal army." Singh's acts of protest sabotaged the Indian Independence League, according to its hot-headed president. Basu fired the Commander in Chief of the Indian National Army on December 29, 1942, and ordered his immediate arrest by the Kempeitai. Singh prepared for the worst; he had already passed his last sealed order to his lieutenants. Singh ordered the INA dissolved.[31]

Bose Looks East

By late spring of 1942, Subhas Chandra Bose realized that his German alliance was tottering on the verge of collapse, and he began to look eastward. In the first of his "Call From East Asia" letters to the Nazi government, Bose reasoned that Japan's campaign in Asia undoubtedly heralded India's freedom. With the end of the Raj in sight, Bose hoped to increase his effectiveness by returning to the Far East. Since Italy, Germany and Japan shared a common enemy — Great Britain — wherever Bose worked served their mutual interests. He thanked the Nazis for their support, assured them that he intended to continue their common struggle, and maintained both his departments in the German Foreign Office and the Free India Center as his liaisons to the Führer. He then asked the German and Italian governments to arrange his trip.[32]

In December, Bose sent a second letter, which detailed the arguments he made in his previous statements. He mentioned that, from the Indian point of view, Japanese victories in the Far East overshadowed Axis defeats elsewhere. He did say that the North African campaign held relevance to Indians. This point probably referred to the idea of using the Indian Legion in that theater, a plan that never materialized. He then elaborated on the deteriorating hold of the Raj, which he wanted to accelerate by his presence in Asia. According to the Netaji, the British stood on the brink of oblivion, and he was prepared to give the final push. Again he asked for assistance in relocating.[33]

On June 23, 1942, the Bangkok conference of the Indian Independence League adjourned, having received some vague endorsement from Tokyo regarding Indian nationhood. In a resolution entitled the "Future of India," Kesar Singh Giani, Bose's future civil administrator, stated that "this Conference requests Sjt. Subhas Chandra Bose to be kind enough to come to East Asia and appeals to the Imperial Government of Japan to use its good offices to obtain the necessary permission and conveniences from the Government of Germany to enable Sjt. Subhas Chandra Bose to reach East Asia safe [ly]."[34]

Japan's indecision about permitting the Netaji to return sparked controversy even before Germany's Indian Legion failed and the 1942 military defeats forced Berlin to cut back on all international schemes. As mentioned in the previous chapter, after his meeting with Hitler, Bose secretly appealed to Ambassador Oshima Hiroshi to relocate his government-in-exile. In January 1943, German Foreign Minister von Ribbentrop discussed the possibility of sending Bose home in a German submarine. Once in the Indian Ocean, the Germans expected the Japanese to pick him up in one of their navy vessels. When Oshima forwarded Ribbentrop's idea to Japanese Foreign Minister Tani, he replied that there had been "no change in Japan's desire to have Bose come to East Asia," and that an oceanic transfer presented problems. Nonetheless, Bose left Kiel by German U-boat on February 9, 1943.[35]

In May, an unnamed India specialist from Ribbentrop's office informed Oshima that Bose's whereabouts remained a secret from the Allies, and that, if managed correctly, the release of information regarding Bose's return could have a tremendous propaganda impact. Acknowledging that Japan took the brunt of the responsibility for Bose, the German said that his government planned to assist in Azad Hind endeavors. Oshima reported to Tokyo that the Nazis were pleased by Bose's move, and described it as "a big thing" in Berlin's moral war against the British.[36]

On May 8th, the German submarine carrying Bose arrived at a "South Pacific base," where he boarded a Japanese submarine which he took to the Malay Peninsula. Tokyo's reaction to Bose's return seemed peculiar, considering the Japanese government's alleged sanction of it. Shortly after Bose left Berlin, Foreign Minister Tani reprimanded Oshima for approving the move without his backing. Mentioning delays in communications, Tani chided Oshima for allowing Bose to go before Japan's role in his transportation had been ironed out. MAGIC analysts noted that while Tokyo always claimed that the government wanted to work with Bose, the Japanese found travel difficulties or diplomatic formalities perfect excuses for not accepting him. The US War Department suspected that Japan did not want to impinge on its client of long standing, Rash Behari Basu.[37]

Tokyo gave instructions to Italy and Germany regarding Bose's Asian mission. The Japanese requested that the media in Axis nations announce the Netaji's move on June 18th, and not imply any assistance from Japan. "No articles, no matter how interesting they might be, will indicate that the Boses are tied up with the Axis." Tokyo also warned against suggesting that Subhas Bose had left either Gandhi or Nehru's political folds.[38]

This statement clearly showed the naivete in fascist intelligence gathering. By 1943, the sentiments of both the Netaji and Rash Behari Bose (alias Basu) were well known in India and Europe. Indians discredited Basu for taking a greater interest in Japanese right-wing politics than affairs at home. British intelligence indicated that Subhas Bose's exile in Germany aroused the emotions of only his staunchest followers, and again, the whereabouts of both men were common knowledge to Allied espionage networks. Given Bose's marginal track record in Europe and Basu's alienation from the Indian population, it appears surprising that the Axis continued to include either nationalist in its plans. Moving Bose apparently presented difficulties for Berlin and Tokyo, and the Japanese Foreign Ministry went to great lengths to brief all concerned parties on the Netaji's arrival.

If Oshima or Tani decided to gamble on the headstrong Bengali, then luck seemingly blessed all of them. From the moment Bose shook Premier Tojo's hand, Indians began to watch his every move with the utmost anticipation, and British officials finally took alarm. Historians remember Bose's turn to the East as the most significant part of his life. Within weeks of his arrival, he received three major titles and stepped into the media spotlight. How unfortunate that the last two years of his life gained him so much notoriety, and yet be so far out of character.

In the late 1930s, articles such as "European Chess-board" and "Europe — To-Day and To-Morrow" showed Bose's marked affinity for the fascist movement, and an apparent rejection of his earlier socialism. He asserted that the dynamic militancy and resentment of the Allies generated by the Germans and Italians resulted from 20 years of being short changed by the international community. Aside from Mussolini's adventure in Ethiopia, which Bose privately condemned, the fascists hoped to shatter the old imperialist order. The anticolonialist stand, more than any fascist goal of world liberation, brought Bose, Hitler and Mussolini together.[39]

When Bose returned to Asia, he forfeited his role of political philosopher and retired his skills as a statesman, to become the darling of the Axis. Personally, he disapproved of his Japanese patrons. In his 1937 essay, "Japan's Role in the Far East," he criticized the foreign policy of the Rising Sun. Like their European counterparts, Japanese right-wing leaders shook their fists at the Western establishment, yet unleashed their fury against weak China — one of Bose's pet causes. Japan illustrated its destructive capabilities by mutilating China and its false progressivism by creating the "autonomous" state of Manchukuo. Bose realized that Japan's undertaking stemmed from an imperialistic desire no less aggressive than Britain's. He apparently saw no similarity between Tokyo's activities and Hitler's assault of Poland and Czechoslovakia. Bose always accepted Central Europe as Germany's sphere of influence. He concluded his article with the plaintive hope that India would never attempt to reach her potential by destroying another nation.[40]

Then why did Bose work with General Tojo? His alternative was to remain in Berlin until he heard a knock on his door in the middle of some night.

Bose Becomes Established in Asia

Upon his arrival in Penang, Malaya in May 1943, Bose flew to Tokyo, where he met Tojo and Field-Marshal Sugiyama Gen, his Chief of Staff, on June 14th. In the days that immediately followed, Bose made several broadcasts and held a press conference. Now disavowing what he said in his 1942 "Call From East Asia" letters, he discounted the Axis armies in the North African and European theaters of war. He stressed the importance of Japan's impending glory in the Far East — the glory that meant freedom for all Asians. Apparently swallowing his loathing of imperialists, Bose extolled the virtues of the Japanese, and described them as the liberators of India.[41]

Behind his media fluff he touched two important points: overseas Indians must cooperate with the Japanese if they expected a Free India after the war; and that regardless of the outcome of the conflict, Britain would not willingly give up India. During a prison term in the 1930s, Bose reached a similar conclusion, but softened it with the belief that Britain had no chance against the fascists. America's entry into the war in 1941 certainly bolstered England, thus reinforcing her hold on India. Bose warned his radio audience that under these circumstances, no Indian needed to accept Allied promises of post war self-government.[42]

In a broadcast made on June 24, 1943, Bose reemphasized the value of Japanese assistance in the Indian revolution. He stressed that the Axis planned to devastate the colonizing nations, including the United States. Compromising his 1937 study, Bose spoke of Japan's commitment to a Free India. He reminded his listeners that India and the Axis warred against a common enemy, and so he trusted the fascists. To dispel any skepticism, he assured the Indians that Tojo aspired to keep his promise of granting freedom to conquered Burma and the Philippines within the year.[43]

Of course, doubt among India's population flourished. Under the direction of George Orwell, the BBC's India Desk gave the British government the advantage of predicting these very promises over one year before. In March 1942, Orwell described the situation in the Philippines as not one of liberation, but of a people's struggle against the Japanese. He delivered a savage condemnation of Japanese activities in Burma in an April 1942 radio program. He analyzed the actual plunder of the colony and its tragic economic outlook under the Greater East Asia Co-Prosperity Sphere. Instead of prosperity or freedom, the Burmese faced starvation, with burial urns crammed full of worthless paper money.[44]

By May 1942, Orwell anticipated a Japanese invasion of India. He expected a bloody campaign, quite similar to the Nazi attack on the Soviet Union and the Japanese massacre in China. He suggested that the Indians were unprepared for war, compared to the battle-scarred Chinese and Russians. Without specifically condemning Bose the man, Orwell criticized the efforts of the Azad Hind movement. In the event that fifth columnists succeeded, the Raj would disappear and Indians would suffer the same fate as the Burmese, Chinese and other vanquished peoples of Asia. As Orwell put it, "[Japanese] efforts will be to paralyse Indian resistance, by terrorism, by lies and by sowing dissension among the Indians themselves. They know that if India has the will to resist, India cannot be conquered, whereas if that will fails, the conquest might be comparatively easy."[45]

Bose countered Orwell's propaganda by describing his cooperation with the Axis as the augmentation and extension of Gandhi's civil disobedience. Japanese occupation served as a uniting factor for the scattered Indian communities in the conquered territories. With Tojo's backing, Bose and his followers proposed to work outside of India to bring down the Raj. The Netaji generated confidence among his fans as he said, "No power on earth was able to hamper my movements since January 1941; and no power on earth will be able to prevent my crossing the frontier once again in order to participate in the last phase of our national struggle."[46]

Ironically, Bose made the following plea in that same June 1943 speech: "I would ask those countrymen [Indians] to put their trust in me. For the powerful British Government that has persecuted me all my life and has imprisoned me eleven times, has not been able to demoralise me. No power on earth can hope to do so. And if the wily, cunning and resourceful

British Politicians have failed to cajole and corrupt me, nobody else can do so."[47]

On July 4, 1943, Rash Behari Basu relinquished power to Bose as head of the Indian Independence League in Singapore, and Bose took command of the Indian National Army 24 hours later. The Indians of Singapore experienced the Netaji's charisma, and suddenly felt more hope and patriotism than Basu and Mohan Singh ever drew out of them. Young girls threw leis of flowers. The INA, which remained in limbo after Singh's order to dissolve, rallied with renewed vigor. The masses cheered Bose and Basu, and perhaps out of habit, they called out for Gandhi and Nehru. Although Bose had been estranged from these two towering figures for years, his followers believed in the unity of Indian nationalist leadership.[48]

A speaker opened the ceremony by reading a letter from Tojo. He lauded the overseas Indian patriots for their activities thus far, and guaranteed that Japanese successes in China and Thailand insured a viable Greater East Asia Co-Prosperity Sphere, which indirectly helped India. Then Basu reminded the crowd that Nippon and Mother Hind shared their victories. He then turned over the podium to the Netaji.[49]

Bose, too, complimented India's sons and allies, and called for unity. He claimed that Japan's vitality and the Crown's deterioration were moving history in India's favor. Bose noted that the violence which occurred whenever the CID arrested Gandhi proved India's readiness for an armed struggle. The Netaji also told his supporters that he now coordinated the Indian revolutionary movements both at home and abroad. Bose dared to make such a flamboyant and misleading statement only because he was no longer subject to British authority.[50]

Amid the cries of *"Azad Hind Zindabad"* ("Long Live Free India") and *"Inquilab Zindabad"* ("Long Live the Revolution"), Bose walked toward the Singapore Municipal Office complex to inspect his troops. Pleased by the sea of khaki, he compared the ex–POWs to the legions of Washington and Garibaldi. The Netaji instructed them in their dual purpose — to win and then protect the new nation of India. He did not forget that a fascist army willingly ran into fire when given a symbol to uphold, and for this militia, it would be the Red Fortress of Delhi, the chief military headquarters of the Raj. When the INA marched into the Red Fortress, the immoral British occupation of Mother India would soon be over. The Nazis, Bose told them, marched to the slogan "To Paris" and the Japanese to "To Singapore"; the INA charged to the victory cry of "To Delhi."[51]

The next morning, July 6th, the Rising Sun shone on Singapore's Indian population. Premier General Tojo flew to the island. He came to salute the Netaji and the INA. Overcome with joy, Bose told his benefactor, "This day will ever remain a red-letter day in the history of the newly organised Army of Free India."[52]

Subhas Bose's work began after the speeches ended. Although the soldiers presented themselves in full uniform, the Indian National Army remained in shambles. In contrast to the opinions held by Mohan Singh's top officers, most of Singh's men came to like him at the end. They admired him for his resistance to Japanese domination, and morale fell upon his dismissal. Rash Behari Basu ignored Singh's orders and attempted to keep the INA intact, but only the knowledge of Bose's imminent return to the East kept the soldiers together. Unlike the Indian Legion of Germany, this unit swore allegiance to Free India, not the Axis. Under the Netaji's "Unity, Faith and Sacrifice" ideal, equal opportunity became the guideline for both the Indian Independence League and the Indian National Army. Caste and religion, the cornerstones of appointment and promotion in the Indian Civil Service and Royal Indian Army, never mattered to Bose. Lastly, the Netaji banned English in favor of the "Indian language" as the official tongue of the INA.[53]

On July 13th, Bose revamped the Indian Independence League. He hoped to change the IIL from a revolutionary organization into the civilian side of the future Free Indian government. His design had the potential of becoming the long-range plans for managing India. In this area, he excelled far beyond his contemporaries. Bose's experience as a Cambridge-trained bureaucrat and an observer of German centralization proved useful. While many, including Basu, rejected all things Occidental, Bose even adopted the British practice of summer vocational schools. While in Berlin, he studied the German public health system and the Nazi Labor Service Corps. He intended to use such measures to develop his country.[54]

The Netaji divided the defense area into four major departments: the Military Bureau, and the Departments of Recruitment, Training and Supply. The training branch included the Naujawan, a group inspired by the Hitler Youth. Other notable wings of the new League were the Overseas Department, to promote the international Azad Hind movement, a Reconstruction Department to develop a program for running independent India, and a General Secretariat, the IIL's main governing body and link with Imperial General Headquarters in Tokyo. Bose clearly showed Western progressivism with his establishment of a Women's Department, which eventually mobilized the Rani of Jhansi Regiment, a unit primarily consisting of frontline medics.[55]

Three weeks after taking control of the IIL, Netaji Bose expressed his desire to lead his army into battle. Always the internationalist, he initiated his campaign for support at the diplomatic tables, the setting most comfortable to him. He left Singapore for a brief visit to Burma and Thailand, where Tokyo exerted a great deal of influence. On August 1, 1943, Bose celebrated Burmese Independence Day with Dr. Ba Maw, himself an outspoken client of General Tojo. Less than a week later, Thai Premier Field Marshal Plaek

Pibul Songgram assured Bose that he encouraged Indians in Thailand to support the IIL. Bangkok highlighted Bose's junket. The Indian community greeted him at the airport and invited him to speak at Chulalongkorn University.[56]

Bose met with Italian and German consular officers in both Bangkok and Rangoon, and he approached them as equals. He no longer entered embassy back doors, using assumed names and feeling humiliated by polite rejections. He stopped analyzing revolutionary politics and ceased practicing diplomacy in any real sense of the word, but parroted the anti–British propaganda as ordered by Tokyo. The Axis ministers listened skeptically to Bose's rhetoric, remembering his checkered reputation in India and his disaster in Germany. This Indian who left Berlin after a Gestapo investigation now had the endorsement of Imperial General Headquarters, and so they tolerated him.[57]

Bose's whirlwind summer progressed to autumn, and his war had not begun yet. The Netaji harangued the public throughout Japan and Southeast Asia concerning the upcoming battle for Free India. Tojo's generals recognized that morale in the INA had reached an all-time high, and Bose's dire predictions about the fall of the Raj could only help the Japanese propaganda machine. In Europe, Bose made a limited impact on Indian politics, but in Asia, he seemed to wield greater power as he adopted a malevolent fascist persona. Both Downing Street and the colonial authorities in Delhi saw the danger as Bose moved closer to India, and in his charismatic hold over an apparently loyal following among overseas Indians.

Tokyo found a way of rewarding Azad Hind supporters for their early success, while simultaneously enhancing the Netaji's propaganda capabilities. The one thing Bose wanted — and the best way of undermining British confidence — would be the establishment of Free India. So Japan created Free India.

◆ *9* ◆

NOBODY'S DARLING

"Free India" At Last

Tokyo officially recognized the Indian Independence League as the Provisional Government of Free India, or Azad Hind, on October 21, 1943. Subhas Chandra Bose automatically became the President of Free India. Though it was headquartered in Singapore's Cathay Cinema Building, Bose's supporters looked upon his government-in-exile as a symbolic regime, in much the same way that the French Resistance regarded the London office of *La France Libre* as an exiled government. While the concept of organization-as-government had appealed to Bose since his Berlin days, Japan's timing may have surprised him. Fueled by pots of coffee and chain-smoked cigarettes, Bose had written the "Proclamation of the Provisional Government of Azad Hind" in one draft, composed during an all-night push 48 hours before.[1]

It seems rather odd that Tokyo never prepared Bose for such a major move, but neither the primary nor secondary sources offer further insight. Perhaps Imperial General Headquarters wanted to reserve the right to cancel this plan suddenly. Had the publicity-loving Netaji announced Tokyo's intentions, and then Tojo decided against Azad Hind, Japan would have been seriously discredited in the minds of Indians.

Nevertheless, officials of the Azad Hind Association and other Indian civic groups hastily attended to all ceremonial details. These gave the false impression of legitimacy. The converted movie house was festooned with colorful flags, banners and posters. Uniformed INA officers, Japanese diplomats and Asian statesmen surrounded the dais, waiting to hear the Netaji's long-awaited announcement: Free India was born healthy and active. Bose compared his government to Atatürk's regime, and made two firm offers to prove the vitality of Azad Hind. He pledged aid to starving colonial India, and presented a monetary gift to his Japanese benefactors.[2]

If any one document captured the essence, the historical context and contemporary significance, of Bose's movement, it was the "Proclamation of the Provisional Government of Azad Hind," read by the Netaji on October 2lst. Bose gave his audience a nutshell history of the fabulous noblemen, warriors and thinkers who had vainly tried to usurp the Raj. Indians fought the English at the political level after convening the Indian National Congress in 1885. After Swadeshi and the Gandhian movement, Indian nationalism jelled, but India needed militant strength to actually break the chokehold of imperialism. Bose credited the Axis with weakening Great Britain. World War II, as no other time in history, gave Indians the chance to liberate themselves.[3]

Although Bose essentially renounced most of his values when he landed in Penang five months before, he still found comfort in history. He understood that any appeal to arms brought India that much closer to freedom. If the Swadeshi strikes of 1905 and the civil disobedience of the 1920s and 1930s raised the national consciousness, then war was needed to emancipate India. Blood had to rain over Southeast Asia before the INA rescued Mother India from her oppressors. The Netaji knew that two centuries of living under British rule justified any costs for his crusade. Bose's speech tempted many Indian extremists in India, as well as those overseas. No level-headed warnings from Orwell of the BBC could neutralize the value of Japan's latest propaganda coup. Even the Netaji's own earlier broadcasts never matched the one delivered on October 21st, live from the Cathay Cinema. Perfect timing gave Bose his atypical impact at home. Earlier that month, Gandhi, Nehru and other Indian leaders happened to be imprisoned during a CID crackdown on revolutionary activities.[4]

The Netaji chanced his own brave move. Since Tokyo granted the Azad Hind governmental status, Bose told his people that they had to accept him as Indian Head of State, Prime Minister and Minister of both War and Foreign Affairs. Bose admitted that heavy security prevented him from establishing a government on Indian soil. Setting aside the caste system, he promised equal rights for all Indians. He called for an armed struggle, which he described as "Total Mobilisation," blessed his military and civilian followers, and concluded by swearing to build a nation.[5]

In addition to Bose's signature, the proclamation was endorsed by numerous members of the INA, including Lieutenant-Colonel (later General) Shah Nawaz (Khan), as well as civilians S.A. Ayer, Bose's active Propaganda Minister and main author of *Unto Him a Witness*, and old Rash Behari Basu, whom the Netaji invited to become Azad Hind's Supreme Advisor. Bose and his cabinet swore to uphold Free India, with the Netaji invoking God's blessing, a surprising move for a Hindu. Azad Hind's ministers soon discovered that since Bose claimed all positions of power, devotion to the Netaji took precedence over any other considerations.[6]

On October 23, 1943, Bose spoke at a rally of 50,000 people. He proposed an Azad Hind declaration of war against the Allies, but he asked for the symbolic approval of his followers. "I want you to demonstrate to the world that you are resolved as one man to follow up this declaration with action that will show to the world that you mean bloody war when you declare war," bellowed the Netaji. "The British know very well that I say what I mean and that I mean what I say. So when I say 'War' I mean WAR — War to the finish — a war that can only end in the Freedom of India." Such populist talk seemed grossly out of character for Bose, but it sparked the desired effect. The crowd went wild.[7]

Bose's international activities skyrocketed after the IIL became a legitimate government-in-exile. Japan, Germany, Italy, Croatia, Burma, Thailand, Occupied China, Manchukuo and the Philippines quickly recognized the Azad Hind's status. Oddly enough, Vichy France refused to acknowledge the Netaji. Undaunted by the Allies, who questioned his legitimacy, Bose opened consulates in Bangkok, Saigon, Java, Sumatra, Borneo, Manila, Tokyo, Nanking and Hsinking, Manchukuo.[8]

On October 28th, Bose flew to Japan to speak at the Greater East Asia Conference and make his first state visit to Emperor Hirohito. In Japan, Bose made two masterful political strokes that stunned any who doubted his loyalty to India. At the conference, Bose refused to join the Greater East Asia Co-Prosperity Sphere. Tojo tolerated this move, smugly confident that war would force Bose to depend on Japan regardless. Then, on November 6th, Tojo presented the Japanese-held Andaman and Nicobar Islands to the Azad Hind, which the grateful Bose renamed Shaheed (Martyrs) and Swaraj (Independence). Although these strange island chains had little commercial or military value, the transfer made symbolic impact, since the Springing Tiger flag now flew over Indian territory.[9]

Subhas Chandra Bose justifiably regarded these coups as great moral victories. To his supporters, having control over the islands constituted the first step toward securing the mainland, and showed that Tokyo obviously respected the IIL and Azad Hind. The fact that Bose resisted the invitation to join the GEA and still kept both the alliance with Tokyo and his neck intact was by far the greater credit to his movement. While Bose will always be considered one of Japan's puppets, he desperately intended to maintain his country's identity. That was the last act of defiance in Subhas Bose's life.

Bose's action at the conference surely disappointed the Japanese Premier, yet he rewarded Bose with the Andaman and Nicobar Islands. Unlike Basu, the Netaji had no connections with the inner circle of Japanese powerbrokers.

Bose received needed political leeway, which certainly built up the confidence of the new President-in-exile of India. Maybe Tojo realized that even if India never officially subscribed to the GEA, supporting the Bengali maverick still served Japanese interests in the psychological war against England.

Bose made a trip to China following his attendance at the GEA Conference. Writers, including Bose's closest associates, often treat this official visit lightly. While on the surface it appeared to be little more than another goodwill tour, US War Department documents released in 1978 suggested that Bose made his appearance in response to a man who betrayed him. In February 1942, the British and Americans asked Generalissimo and Madame Jiang Jieshi to go to India, in hope that they might mend some of the differences between the Indians and the British colonial government. This controversial trip, which even disconcerted Viceroy Archibald Percival Wavell, proved ineffective, but it showed that the Chinese felt no sympathy for their fellow Asian nationalists. Any remaining credibility Jiang had with regional anti-imperialists crumbled after he fought for Britain against the Japanese on the Indo-Burma frontier.[10]

On November 17, 1943, Bose arrived in Nanking, where a fellow puppet, Wang Jingwei, the President of Occupied China, showed Bose the honors due India's chief executive. In a November 23rd radio speech, he admonished the Nationalist Chinese about their horribly misguided sense of optimism, which only extended their draining war, particularly in Chungking. Bose promised the Chinese that the Axis could never be defeated. The Netaji blamed Jiang — whom he described as a "man without the character" to make peace with Tokyo — for inflaming the situation by campaigning in Burma. Bose took Jiang's policies as a personal slight, since he had long felt akin to the Chinese people. Jawaharlal Nehru himself remembered that as Congress President in 1937–38, Bose turned against the fascists he so admired by openly favoring the Chinese in their war against Japan. His support included allocating Congress funds for medical aid to China.[11]

Money for the Movement

After establishing himself as the political and military leader of the overseas Indian freedom movement, Bose needed to fatten Azad Hind's pocketbook before going to war. Lieutenant-Colonel A.C. Chatterjee, his first Minister of Finance, chaired the Board of Management for Raising Funds. According to Indian sources, the Azad Hind charity drives worked. Western studies, such as Hugh Toye's *The Springing Tiger*, often accuse Indian writers of inflating both contribution and population figures, but apparently the Indian residents of Southeast Asia numbered less than two million. Bose expected 30 million Straits (Malayan) dollars from them. The economic form of "total mobilization" particularly applied to those who did not join the INA.[12]

In a strongly worded appeal to civilians to adopt a Spartan lifestyle for the cause, Bose complained:

> I cannot understand why those who do not want to give their lives are even grumbling to part with their possessions. What is money after all; compared with life, money is nothing. Supposing a foreign government tells you that either you have to give the [wealth] you possess or your life, surely you would rather choose to part with your [wealth] than your life.... The Indians as a nation believe in the ideal of self-sacrifice.[13]

Those words, taken from Bose's speech at a 1943 Indian businessmen's convention in Singapore, brought positive results. Donations began to arrive from Malaya, Singapore, Thailand and Burma. Gifts to Azad Hind came as money, gold or silver ingots, jewelry, cattle and even land. Some offered food and equipment for the INA's direct use. One unofficial patriotic group in Rangoon made a door-to-door campaign, vowing to collect one yard of cloth for every Indian resident. Members from all levels of society made Bose's charity drive their personal cause. A publicity photograph showed a decrepit street hawker who allegedly gave every penny he made to Bose. An obscure gentleman named S. Iqbal Singh Narula promised to donate his portly Netaji's weight in silver. He happily turned over 200 pounds of ingot. A Rangoon philanthropist — like a number of prominent Muslims — donated a fortune, and Bose awarded him the Sevak-I-Hind Medal in 1944. Bose's colleague Kesar Singh Giani summed up the fund-raising crusade with, "the rich gave [money] but the poor gave all they had."[14]

Giani estimated that Bose received about Str.$15,000,000 from Malaya in 1944 alone. The hard-sought funds of Azad Hind had far-reaching effects. In April 1944, Bose appointed his Propaganda Minister, S.A. Ayer, to direct the new Azad Hind Bank of Rangoon. Bose used both the bank and the Azad Hind treasury to fund various projects designed to further erode the power of the British in Asia. As Viceroy Lord Wavell faced a severe Bengali famine in 1943, the Netaji pledged 100,000 tons of rice. The Raj never acknowledged this wild promise, which apparently went unfulfilled. While the war ravaged the Far East, Indian Independence League hospitals and charity centers sprouted up throughout Southeast Asia, the Andamans, China and Japan, primarily to give relief to overseas Indians. Kuala Lumpur's Indian Welfare Center, for example, spent Str.$840,000 annually. By 1944, Bose began to repay his German loans, although his movement was still indebted to Tokyo for its financial base and weapons supply. Perhaps Giani merely oversimplified the case when he claimed that Bose kept Azad Hind economically independent from Japanese patronage.[15]

One must give credit to Subhas Bose's personal charisma for Azad Hind's financial success. The Bengali politician who once divided his colleagues in Congress now stirred diverse groups of Indians who never unified before, let alone exerted political clout. Bose's civilian followers differed radically from the people Rash Behari Basu criticized in 1942:

> ...of the two million Indian residents in the Far East, ... the majority of them have no interest whatsoever in India. They are only concerned with their own daily bread, and of their leaders, with the exception of very few, none is worth the name. These so-called leaders, just to save their skins, are prepared to sell the 400 millions [*sic*] in India. They love to go about in big cars, attending tea parties and such like things. Can you expect anything noble or honourable from them?[16]

Bose certainly did.

On to Delhi

Feeling politically and financially secure, Bose left Rangoon on February 4, 1944, to mobilize his army and send them into their long-awaited battle. Out of a pool of 230,000 Indian POWs and civilian volunteers, 40,000 prisoners formally pledged, though only 25,000 actually joined the INA. Despite his charity drives and Tokyo's support, Bose had the facilities and equipment to accommodate only 12,000 troops. The previous September, he was forced to unite the cream of his Gandhi, Azad and Nehru Brigades to form a Subhas Brigade, under the command of General Shah Nawaz Khan. Those unable to participate in active service were immediately shifted into nonmilitary endeavors. Bose actually expected this force — the only viable unit in the INA — to invade and liberate India, naturally with heavy Japanese assistance. The Netaji and his scant troops embarked for battle, crying "*Chalo Delhi*" ("On to Delhi"). [17]

Determining the precise number of INA troops can prove tricky. Besides giving the number of POW collaborators, Majumdar mentions some 20,000 Indian residents of Singapore and Malaya who supported Bose. That figure does not necessarily reflect actual enlistment. In *Asia: The Winning of Independence*, editor Robin Jeffrey discussed the INA in terms of 25,000 POWs, but did not suggest the number of troops in actual combat.[18]

On Christmas Day, 1941, Japan occupied Hong Kong. Exactly one month and one day later, the new Hong Kong branch of the Indian Independence League held its inaugural meeting for an uninspired cadre of would-be nationalists. Unlike the branches in other parts of Asia, this chapter catered to newly acquired Indian POWs, rather than civilian residents of the territory. As a result, its main goal was to establish a new unit for the INA.[19]

Generally speaking, the group failed. Despite a membership fee of only HK$2, and a choice of venues on either Hong Kong Island or the Kowloon side, only a handful of Indians joined. Most probably signed up since meetings guaranteed a short-term pass from the POW camps. According to the late Professor George B. Endacott of the University of Hong Kong, only 400 joined. As in neighboring countries, the Hong Kong branch of the IIL supplied food relief to local Indians.[20]

If the League there seemed uncertain, Hong Kong's battalion in the INA offered even dimmer prospects. Once settled in the territory, the Japanese moved most Indian prisoners to the Mau Tau Chung Camp, near Kai Tak Airport in Kowloon. There they allowed the IIL to begin a recruitment drive for the INA. They chose "Major" Hakim Khan, a minor soldier from a Punjabi regiment, to organize the program. The Japanese rewarded Khan by granting him the rank of major and the privilege of being Hong Kong's official delegate to IIL functions overseas. Khan's supporters — meaning those Indians who enlisted — numbered only 400. This figure was given by British defense official and military historian Oliver Lindsay, and it is certainly not coincidental that this was the exact number Endacott gave as total IIL membership in Hong Kong.[21]

By December 1943, those willing to enlist in the INA were moved to Murray Barracks on Hong Kong Island. The Japanese apparently intended to send them to their brothers in Singapore. The majority of Indian POWs flatly refused to join the traitorous INA, but many collaborated by serving as police in British POW camps, or as security guards for the wharves, train stations, radio stations and other sensitive locations. The Japanese sent some to work in a similar capacity in South China and nearby Hainan Island. The Indians who agreed to this were not traitors in the deepest sense of the word, since they did virtually nothing but stand guard, while Japanese soldiers watched *them*. The Japanese did arm them, so fewer of their own troops needed to be deployed for security work.[22]

While the Japanese vainly tried to get local Indians to support the INA, pro–British Chinese infiltrated Indian POW holding areas. While the Indian and Chinese populations traditionally mistrusted each other in Hong Kong, those resistance agents who worked for the British Army Aid Group (BAAG) had few difficulties convincing them that the 400 were in the wrong. In camp circles, the BAAG found an important ally in M.A. Ansari, an Indian officer who loathed the Japanese and the Azad Hind movement. When Captain Ansari's outspoken criticisms and attempts to hinder the INA's success reached the attention of Japanese military authorities, the BAAG feared for his life. The Chinese contacts offered to smuggle him out of prison, but the loyalist Ansari refused to abandon his men. After one of his fellow inmates reported his activities, Ansari was executed.[23]

As in other Axis-held territories, the Japanese military command in Hong Kong seemed to have little faith in the INA program. They kept their contacts with Indian nationalists to a minimum, perhaps paying more attention to local Chinese, Portuguese and even British collaborators. They did send the Hong Kong battalion to Burma, where, Lindsay notes, 40,000 of their comrades eagerly awaited orders from the Netaji.[24]

By March 1944, the INA had successfully fought a skirmish against a British unit of fierce West African soldiers. Moving with Japanese forces, the INA took the Burmese Arakan Front with relative ease. The extent of Bose's personal involvement in these victories remains somewhat murky. While Giani noted that the "Netaji himself visited the front," Bose spent most of this period shuttling between his headquarters in Singapore and Rangoon. Bose assured his enthusiastic troops that "our long-awaited March to Delhi has begun, and ... we shall continue that march until the tri-colour National Flag that is now flying over the Arakan mountains is hoisted over the Viceregal Lodge and until we hold our victory parade at the ancient Red Fortress of Delhi."[25]

Two years later, Raj officials conducted a highly disputed yet inconclusive investigation at the Red Fortress.

None of Bose's troops dared to think of defeat on the night of March 17-18, 1944. The INA crossed India's eastern border to launch a raid on Mowdok. The soldiers kissed the ground and planted the Springing Tiger flag. Bose issued a statement, calling for the support of all Indians in India to join the INA in ousting the Raj. Forgetting his former patrons in Rome and Berlin, he emphasized Indo-Japanese cooperation in this venture, reminding his followers of Japan's "unparalleled" achievements in its Asian campaign and Tojo's gift of the Andaman and Nicobar Islands. He concluded by saying that "Nippon is therefore determined to redeem her pledge to help the Indian people to create an India for Indians."[26]

The Netaji's detractors in Delhi and London could say what they wanted, but his movement became a reality in the border states of Mizoram and Manipur. Less than one year after his arrival in the Far East, Bose attained his secondary goal (the primary goal was, of course, India). His Indian National Army marched out of Singapore and came home to Mother Hind, and the Azad Hind movement enjoyed the peak of its success for a few short weeks.

Mother India in Turmoil

It seems rather surprising that some secondary sources on modern Indian history choose to forget Subhas Chandra Bose, considering the world's reaction to his Azad Hind crusade. While both American intelligence and the India

Office regarded Bose's European efforts to be of minimal influence in India, by 1943, he had angered London. Unlike the Germans, the Japanese made no attempt to keep the nationalist hidden. Despite Tokyo's original directives to keep public attention from linking Bose to the Japanese, Bose flaunted Tokyo's cooperation in the Indian struggle. The West fully understood the subversive nature of Bose's Indian struggle, and this soon disturbed England. By 1942, Sir Stafford Cripps, the Leader of the House of Commons and dean of British Liberals, began pressuring Conservatives to reconsider the Indian question.[27]

The Raj weathered the violence that occurred in India during Bose's 1940–44 absence. Aside from general strikes, much of the anti–British activity was either poorly organized or engineered by thugs and gangsters who immersed themselves as much in wartime black marketeering as they did in politics. Some chose action of a paramilitary character. In the spring of 1942, an ambitious Muslim mystic named Pir Pagaro led a small band of Farqi Hurs on a wild rampage against the British, which included a paralyzing attack on the Lahore-Karachi rail system. In August 1942, Jayaprakash Narayan, Bose's successor in the Indian left wing, organized 36 Nepalese tribesmen into a futile terrorist army.[28]

The Raj handled these problems as it always had — with increased police brutality. Interrogators used whippings, airtight smoke-filled cells, and the rape and torture of women to curtail the revolution. Historian Ram Gopal reported that police allegedly threatened to insert bamboo sticks into the rectum of Bose's nephew during his detention in the early 1940s.[29]

Bose's presence in the Axis camp understandably frustrated London. Unlike the rebels in India, British security forces could not silence Bose as he was outside their jurisdiction. In light of the Japanese conquest of Singapore in February 1942, the British had to treat Bose's 1943 return to Asia as more than an embarrassment to their colonial regime. Bose had grown into a serious threat. British concerns centered on two fears: that Bose planned to turn the essentially neutral Indian majority toward Japan; and if he reconciled with Gandhi and Nehru, Tokyo might well make significant inroads into India, with or without a Japanese invasion.[30]

On March 23, 1942, Churchill's cabinet sent Sir Stafford Cripps and an impressive delegation of government officials and academics to placate India. Bose's prophecy of Britain's hopeless attempts to hold India proved correct. Cripps, the Liberal leader, promised India's leadership eventual self-government as a dominion. The British insisted on the establishment of a national constitutional congress, and guaranteed the individual Indian states a choice of whether or not to join the united country. The Crown swore to uphold minority rights as well as states' rights in India's future course. Cripps's offer gave Indians little freedom in their national affairs, but his mission failed completely when he pledged Britain's continued role in defending India. To

London, the defense of India meant using the military to suppress all nationalistic activities. The Indians rejected the Cripps mission proposals, and continued to call for India's freedom. The Raj responded by arresting Gandhi and his colleagues.[31]

After Cripps left, Gandhi and Nehru — still both anti-fascist — authored a resolution which showed some sympathy with the Forward Bloc, Bose's old party. They revealed that they spurned England out of a belief that she would soon lose the war, and while abhorring Tokyo's politics, admitted their admiration for the Japanese military machine. Nehru feared the annihilation of pitiful bands of conscripted village recruits fighting England's war. Both urged the creation of a nonmilitary Indo-Japanese alliance, since India's unhappy membership in the British Empire had been the only reason for her participation in the war.[32]

While Bose gives this resolution much attention in *The Indian Struggle 1920-1942*, he concedes that Nehru and Gandhi acted pragmatically and that there was no indication of a change in their philosophy. Whatever the rhetoric, the British worried needlessly about a coalition between Nehru, the Mahatma and the Netaji. Bose regarded Gandhi as too pedantic, and he felt a personal animosity toward Nehru. Gandhi reacted to the Azad Hind movement by exclaiming, "we do not seek our independence out of Britain's ruin." Nehru stunned his followers by saying "launching a civil disobedience campaign at a time when Britain is engaged in a life and death struggle would be an act derogatory to India's honour."[33]

Gandhi and Nehru issued such strong statements against Bose's movement only because of his involvement with the Japanese. While neither leader wished to postpone independence or fight in World War II, they felt uncomfortable joining the Japanese army. An ingrained sense of Victorian loyalty to the United Kingdom prevented them from assisting Britain's enemies in a military effort.

In July 1942, the Working Committee of Gandhi's Indian National Congress issued the Quit India Resolution in protest at the Mahatma's incarceration. The Congress, banned by the Raj and meeting in secret, demanded the immediate termination of British rule and influence. It seems rather interesting to compare this act — quite extreme for a body as conservative as a Gandhian Congress — to Bose's similar manifesto of 1931.[34]

The Quit India Resolution brought further repression by the Raj. As Indians saw most of their politicians carted off to jail, their attention turned toward the Azad Hind. The failures of both the Cripps mission and the Quit India Resolution occurred at a time when Japan reached the highpoint of its Asian offensive, further enhancing India's choice of either Japanese-sponsored liberation or Tokyo's brand of slavery. After the fall of Singapore, Britain feared for India's questionable security. Naturally, Bose and Basu capitalized on this in their propaganda.[35]

Some British officials downgraded the threat of pro–Axis elements in India. Dr. R. Coupland, an esteemed professor invited to join Cripps's diplomatic mission, reported that Bose's broadcasts only appealed to his followers in Bengal. Coupland described Bose's orders as "given from Berlin," and insisted that the Indian masses felt more in touch with Russian or Chinese nationalist programs — never fascism. In hindsight, Prime Minister Winston Churchill concurred with this opinion, dismissing Bose as a demagogue for the extremists who was ignored by a Gandhian majority. However, one must defer to the conclusion of an official who actually lived in India. Viceroy Lord Wavell wrote that the widespread unrest as a consequence of the Quit India demands certainly helped Bose and the Japanese propaganda cause.[36]

Over a year before Bose arrived in Penang, Britain's anxieties over an impending Japanese attack became a reality. In April 1942, bombs suddenly rained on the east coast of India. Unbelievably, the Raj had no established civil defense program, and could only barely evacuate the local civilian population.[37]

The India Office in London noted that the Japanese supported Indians in Burma and Malaya, and encouraged them to fight under the banner of the Rising Sun. The Japanese General Staff Headquarters had allegedly created an Indian High Commission in occupied Malaya, so the Raj naturally suspected spies among the waves of Indian refugees returning from occupied Southeast Asia. British authorities paled at rumors that prominent Bengalis had already begun learning Japanese, and that a secret league of Indian businessmen and Japanese industrial magnates conspired to control the Indian economy. Historian Arun Chandra Bhuyan described a "Free India" newsletter circulating in rural villages, urging Indians to show their patriotism by sabotaging the rails, fuel stations and dreaded police vehicles.[38]

Gandhi still maintained his nonviolent stance, professing that militancy only inflamed Nipponese aggression against Mother Hind. Peaceful protest, on the other hand, would force Japan to either retreat from India or face the unthinkable option of destroying every Indian. Oddly enough, Gandhi's position led to accusations from the *Eastern Times* of Cuttack, Bose's hometown newspaper, that he and the Axis had made a deal. Some British officials believed that the Congress used Japanese contacts, especially for its illegal use of the radio airwaves. The fact that Congress broadcasts only contained pro–India propaganda, while ignoring the British and Japanese war efforts, did little to support such allegations.[39]

The INA Readies Itself

When Bose took to the battlefield, the Western press began its comprehensive coverage of his movements. Most articles reflected a marked fear of the outspoken Bengali. Strangely enough, few discussed his relationship with the Nazis, and those writers who did tended to dismiss it as a training period for his later role with the Japanese. Unlike most of Tokyo's other clients, Bose represented more than just a propaganda mouthpiece.[40]

As the INA marched out of Burma toward India, journalists warned that Bose's forces endangered the balance of power in Asia. The early victories of the INA lent credence to Bose's frequent radio announcements that with Japan's help, he would soon claim India. Regardless of the Netaji's chances of liberating India, *Nation* correspondent John W. Gerber suggested that Japan depended on the INA to block the Burma-India supply line to China. The Allies hoped to use this route to weaken Japan's stronghold in China.[41]

The size of Bose's army became a matter of controversy. The wire services estimated the number of Indian POWs throughout Southeast Asia as 30,000 to 60,000. Bose certainly wanted the world to believe that every POW joined the INA. At the other extreme, the Raj informed the media that the INA had only 3,000 troops. Given such conflicting information, the Western press settled on 25,000–30,000 as a reasonable figure. This, in reality, was more than twice the number of men truly outfitted for battle.[42]

Nation, Collier's, the *Saturday Evening Post* and other magazines warned America of the potential for disaster if Bose entered Delhi. John Gerber, Alfred Tyrnauer, Alfred Wagg and other reporters admitted that the Netaji did have a following in India. Not surprisingly, Bengal was the center of the domestic Azad Hind movement. For those starving under an unfeeling Raj, Bose sent rice to feed them. His philosophy and politics uplifted the impotent masses. He encouraged every citizen — women included — to join the oncoming legions of front-line soldiers. For those disgusted with passive resistance, the Netaji told them to burn down the Raj.[43]

It seemed as if Bose was planning a holocaust.

THE FALLING TIGER

The INA Unravels

In March 1944, just within the eastern border of India, Bose and the INA cheered with unfounded confidence. While the Raj was failing and Gandhi bouncing in and out of jail, Japan still triumphed in Southeast Asia. In the Netaji's mind, all of India prayed for the return of the Springing Tiger of Bengal. Japanese Foreign Minister Shigemitsu Mamoru intended to establish the Government of Free India on Indian soil, once he received Bose's assurance that he had secured his position. Shigemitsu asked the Italian and German embassies to recognize Bose's conquest. The Nazis swore that Germany "welcomes the establishment of a Bose Government [in India]," but needed to inform Hitler first.[1]

Military considerations soon overshadowed any political ramifications of the Netaji's return to India. The "Road to Delhi," a proverbial path of victories that Bose had dreamed of since the war began, virtually closed before the end of the month. When the INA entered India, three Japanese units attacked the outskirts of Imphal, a British stronghold and the capital of the Indian State of Manipur. Allied air rangers cut Japanese communication lines in Burma, and British troops began fighting Japanese and INA forces. Azad Hind Propaganda Minister Ayer promised that an INA victory at Imphal would be the swan song of the Raj. However, neither the Japanese nor the INA could compete with Allied air power, and on July 20, 1944, the Japanese withdrew from Imphal. The British snared the abandoned INA with ease.[2]

Only two weeks before, Subhas Bose completely recanted his previous pro–China stand. In a broadcast message to Gandhi, Bose restated his position. Apologizing for his earlier ignorance of the situation, Bose told his old rival that through his close relationship with Tokyo, he realized the error in his thinking. "...since the outbreak of the War in East Asia, Japan's attitude towards the world in general, and towards Asiatic nations in particular, has been completely revolutionised.... A new consciousness — what I may best describe as an Asiatic consciousness — has seized the souls of the people of Japan. That change explains Japan's present attitude towards the Philippines, Burma and India. That is what explains Japan's new policy in China."[3]

Bose's reference acknowledged Dr. Ba Maw's regime in Burma and Dr. José Laurel's puppet government in Manila. Bose reminded Gandhi that Tojo's personal endorsement of the Azad Hind movement and the return of the Nicobar and Andaman Islands proved Japan's earnestness. Bose again criticized Jiang's resistance activities in Chungking, yet neglected to give reasons why the Chinese should accept Tokyo's indirect rule. He did offer a ludicrous theory to explain Jiang's failure to surrender. "It is India's slavery that is at the bottom responsible for the chaos in China. It is because of the British hold over India that the Anglo-Americans could bluff Chungking into hoping that sufficient help could be brought to Chungking to enable Chungking to continue the war against Japan.... I go so far as to say that the freedom of India will automatically bring about an honourable understanding between Chu[n]gking and Japan...."[4]

Despite his impressive titles, flashy uniforms and elaborate Azad Hind bureaucracy, this statement illustrated the extent to which Bose had fallen. The man who once dared to be insolent to high Nazi officials and even Hitler himself finally kowtowed to Tojo. His purity and legendary dedication faded, only to be replaced by utter hypocrisy. The Japanese manipulated his apparent triumphs, and these staged achievements seduced the Netaji. The failure of the Japanese in Burma and India left their onetime darling fighting with words and empty guns.

After the Japanese retreated on July 20th, Subhas Bose tried to remain calm and boost the morale of his confused men. He kept up a philosophical outlook, insisting that Imphal was theirs, and that he expected the Japanese to send materials and provide air coverage. Sadly, the combined pressures of losing the war and the rapidly deteriorating relations with his Japanese sponsors proved too much for Bose. Far from dead, the Raj launched a counteroffensive in the summer of 1944. As this army of two million — the largest volunteer force in history — went into battle, an INA unit in Singapore mutinied. Bose panicked and resorted to fascist methods in order to crush the impending rebellion in his camp. The Netaji used violent psychological torture on Captain Mahmood Khan Durrani, a security officer who apparently betrayed him. For other traitors, Bose ordered hasty courts-martial and immediate executions.[5]

By autumn 1944, Bose doubted the future of his movement. He sent urgent messages to German and Japanese attachés in Kabul, complaining about the lack of information regarding the complete military situation in India. He seemed deeply worried that Indians had lost faith in Azad Hind and that so few had actually turned against the Allies. He vainly hoped that some senior Allied pilots might defect with planes, but that was as likely as the Axis agents in Kabul making his requests a priority.[6]

Lastly, Bose implored Tokyo, Berlin and Rome to counteract the widespread anti–Japanese propaganda that destroyed his credibility at home. He needed to project an image of being aligned with India's liberators, rather than with the new colonizers. Indians needed to understand that the Azad Hind represented a purely Indian effort, with Japanese assistance being in the form of weapons only. After Bose's defeat at Imphal, India rejected his movement and dubbed him a Japanese puppet. Bose told his contacts in India to meet with Gandhi to tender his support. Gandhi's acceptance might have saved Azad Hind, but no conference was ever arranged.[7]

In September 1944, Bose sent a memorandum to his disappointed apostles in Southeast Asia. He begged all Indians to keep up the war effort, and prepare to "pay with blood" for Free India. A Japanese official in Bangkok wrote that the Netaji's once-powerful words now failed to convince the overseas Indians. Japan's withdrawal from India and the Allied recapture of the Andamans made anti–Axis propaganda seem more relevant. The core of Bose's support eroded beyond repair.[8]

By 1945, the Japanese could no longer afford the costs of sponsoring nationalist movements, particularly that of the unsuccessful Subhas Chandra Bose. When Tokyo attempted to resolve the situation by sending Hachiya Teruo as a special emissary, Bose refused to see him without ambassadorial papers. Hachiya complained to the Azad Hind Acting Foreign Minister, A.C. Chatterjee, that Japan need not register with provisional governments. Chatterjee insisted, fearing both the Netaji's loss of face with other Asian leaders, and the potential for bad publicity with the Indian masses. Chatterjee hinted that Tokyo's lack of respect tempted Bose to turn over his authority over to an ultranationalistic junta. Ayer further elaborated on Bose's anxieties over the obvious puppet-master relationship with Japan.[9]

As the helpless INA soldiers began to desert back to the British, or even commit suicide, the Japanese Imperial General Headquarters completely scorned Bose. The Japanese warlord of Burma, Field Marshal Count Terauchi Hisaichi, personally disliked Bose and his men. His resentment may have been somewhat inherited; Terauchi's father had been Dictator-General over the Sovereign Colony of Korea, and he had taught his son contempt for independence movements. Terauchi reluctantly agreed to include 3,000 INA troopers in his invasion plans. Unfortunately, the INA reinforced the Count's prejudices when 25 percent of the unit in the Arakan ran off into the rainforests, many defecting back to the Allies.[10]

On April 23, 1945, Azad Hind's military headquarters in Rangoon received word that the British had captured Pyinmana, in central Burma, and would be marching to the capital shortly. The Japanese evacuated, once again leaving their Indian comrades to their karma. Bose's cabinet and officers discussed suicide to avoid certain capture; the Netaji himself was only concerned with who would govern the Azad Hind regime — after he escaped. On the pretense that his women's medical corps, the Rani of Jhansi Regiment, had not been provided for, Bose volunteered to escort them to safety in a truck caravan, along with Propaganda Minister Ayer.[11]

Bose, like Burmese President Ba Maw, believed that Bangkok offered temporary asylum. However, Thai government officials, including the new Premier, Pridi Phanomyong, had always remained lukewarm toward the Azad Hind government. Despite Bose's friendship with his predecessor, Pibul Songgram, Pridi had avoided an offer to establish formal diplomatic relations two months before. Then the premier excused himself on the grounds that Rangoon lacked a suitable building for an embassy, and that there was a shortage of officers in the Thai foreign service. Japan's ambassador in Bangkok implied possible negative effects on Japanese-Thai relations should two failing nationalist leaders be sequestered there.[12]

Against the recommendations of its Bangkok embassy, Japan permitted Bose and Dr. Ba Maw to relocate to Thailand. Bose stayed in the home of an IIL financial officer, who informed him of Azad Hind's empty treasury. The poor may have given all they had to the movement, but the Netaji gave all he had for the expenses of maintaining a lost cause. With mustered pride, Bose decided against asking the latest Thai Premier, Khwang Apaiwong, for funding. A destitute S.A. Ayer, however, took the pitiful course of begging Thailand's chief of state for a job. Such an act of humiliation embarrassed the Thai leader, who tactfully ignored Ayer's request. In typical Thai fashion, Khwang tolerated Bose's presence in his country, but made no contact with the Azad Hind authorities.[13]

In his memoir, *Unto Him a Witness*, Ayer suggested that Bose began to reconsider the Soviet Union as a source of aid, especially after Germany surrendered on May 7th. Throughout the spring of 1945, Tokyo stepped up its attempts to convince Stalin of the great potential in a Russo-Japanese alliance. The Japanese foreign policy experts maintained that the United States and Britain would always side against the Soviets, while together, the USSR and Japan could happily rule Asia. Moscow, though, knew that the Rising Sun was, in fact, a setting sun.[14]

American intelligence revealed that Japan approved of Bose serving as the architect for such a plan. Tokyo hoped that if Moscow accepted Bose, Stalin might be persuaded to help force the British out of India. Through Hachiya Teruo, by then the official Japanese Minister to the Provisional

Government of Free India, Bose asked Tokyo if he could be headquartered in either Shanghai or northern China. Bose insisted that such a move became a "vital prerequisite to the improvement in Japan's own situation and the establishment of a new order in East Asia," that being "the formation of a Soviet-Japanese coalition." Hachiya noted that Bose believed that "the Indian and Chinese problems might well furnish a basis for a strong coalition between Japan and the Soviet Union, which might then be used in launching a diplomatic offensive aimed at the United States."[15]

In June, Bose offered to formalize relations between the USSR and Azad Hind. Later, Japanese Foreign Minister Shigenori Togo forwarded a communiqué to one Dr. Meghnam Saha, a physicist and Indian legislator who happened to be attending the International Scientific Congress in Moscow. Bose mentioned that the Soviets did not want to damage their alliance with Britain, but he still encouraged Saha to ask for Russian support in the floundering Indian independence movement.[16]

It seems rather unlikely that the Soviets would have wanted to deal with Subhas Bose, considering his fascist ties and the general attitude of Indian communists toward him. Ironically, the decline of the Azad Hind program paved the way for the communists to take hold of the extremist movement in India. Until 1945, the Communist Party of India (CPI) was never considered strong, and, in fact, Bose always regarded its factionalization as a major problem within the Indian Left. Like Gandhi's followers, the communists resented India being dragged into Britain's war, but they condemned Bose as a despicable traitor for openly courting India's greatest enemy, the Axis. Through its newspaper, the *People's War*, the CPI launched a mudslinging campaign against Bose. Comparing him to Quisling and Pétain, *People's War* called Bose the "running dog of Jap Fascism." The paper claimed that the Netaji lived luxuriously in a Rangoon villa, on money supplied by the corrupt, Axis-sponsored "South Regions Development Bank." Cartoons showed the Azad Hind leader as an obese cat held up to a microphone by Goebbels, and as a donkey carrying a Japanese officer. One particularly bitter cartoon portrayed Bose as a Dr. Strangelove type of character, riding a Japanese bomb as it fell on starving Indians.[17]

In February 1946, S.S. Batiwala of the CPI's Central Committee revealed a secret alliance that had existed between party official P.C. Joshi and Sir Reginald Maxwell, a Home Member of the Indian Legislative Assembly. The Raj agreed to maintain positive relations with the CPI, and, in turn, a communist theater ensemble would stage pro–British, anti–Bose plays for the Royal Indian Army. Maxwell seemed an unlikely figure to negotiate with communists, as he may have been a secret admirer of Hitler. Nehru's editor, S. Gopal, claimed that Maxwell was the subject of a letter written by Nehru to the American military representative Colonel Louis Arthur Johnson in May 1942. In the letter, Nehru described a "very prominent member of the Government of India" who promoted Nazism and advocated the detention of all Indian dissidents in concentration camps.[18]

While the CPI attempted to discredit the Netaji, another old extremist was cuddling up to the Raj. M.N. Roy, the father of Indian communism, identified himself as both a Social and a Radical Democrat by the 1940s, during his frequent meetings with Viceroy Lord Wavell. Wavell liked the aging revolutionary, who had been a terrorist before World War I. During Roy's lengthy exile, he befriended many important Germans during both wars, was deported from France, and gave Lenin and Stalin headaches while involved with the Comintern. The gutsy Roy pushed for a position on Wavell's Executive Council, but the Raj's chief of state did not wish to formally embrace a militant leftist. Wavell once joked, "I was Viceroy and did not propose to be vice–Roy."[19]

The End

At midnight, August 10, 1945, all hopes of an Indo-Soviet pact died when Stalin formally declared war on Japan. Ayer remembered that upon hearing the news, Bose remained outwardly calm, joked with his colleagues, and professed that Azad Hind would survive the Rising Sun. On August 17th, an exhausted and emotional Bose left Saigon in a Japanese bomber. The plane headed north, probably for either Manchuria, by then occupied by Stalin's Red Army, or to the Soviet Union. The plane landed to refuel in Taiwan. Shortly after takeoff, an engine exploded, and the aircraft dropped to the ground in flames. The Netaji staggered away from the fiery wreck, nearly in shock. About seven hours later, Subhas Chandra Bose died from burns in the Taipei Army Hospital.[20]

While the subject of Bose's possible overtures to the Soviet Union remains one of the more nebulous areas in the study of his diplomacy, the US War Department's MAGIC reports shed new light on the matter. Historians often believed that Bose suddenly approached the Soviets in an unplanned, last-ditch effort during the last 48 hours of his life, but these American documents suggest otherwise. He had been reconsidering the Soviets for support for at least two months before he left Southeast Asia on that fateful flight. Still, one can only speculate about the details, since the paper trail only reaches Tokyo. Ultimately, though, the Kremlin had rejected previous Japanese proposals, so the Soviets did not want any business with a nationalist contaminated by fascism — especially one who had failed to gain their confidence in 1941.[21]

* * *

For about a decade after the war ended, persistent and conflicting rumors concerning Bose's fate circulated through India and elsewhere. Much of the mystery, as expected, revolves around the uncertain destination of Bose's plane. Ten days after his death, US intelligence noted a dispatch from a Japanese mission in Saigon. Unfortunately, they had some difficulty decoding it. MAGIC officers could only report that "on the 17th, at his own request, Bose set off by air for the — [place name uncertain, probably 'Manchukuo'] area." According to the MAGIC report, the Japanese embassy in Bangkok suggested that Tokyo avoid "suspicions among the enemy" by not releasing any information regarding Bose's fatal accident.[22]

A number of peculiar stories surfaced immediately after Bose's death. In India, many of his followers believed that he survived the crash, but went into hiding. Some claimed that he adopted the quiet lifestyle of a monk. Others said that he actually joined a monastery in the Himalayas, intending to burst again on the Indian political scene when his nation was ready for him. Those convinced in the truth of this story may have remembered that in March 1941, the Bose family announced Subhas's death in a plane crash, when in reality, he had escaped to Germany.[23]

In 1948, Louis P. Lochner, a Pulitzer Prize–winning journalist and editor of the Goebbels diaries, suggested that the Americans captured Bose in Japan — and executed him! Lochner did not give his source of this false information. The *New York Times* did not publish Bose's obituary until 1956. During the 11-year interim following the Netaji's death, the Indian government created a committee to investigate the events of August 17–18, 1945. In an exclusive release to the *Times*, Delhi concluded that Bose was, in fact, traveling to the Soviet Union.[24]

* * *

The strange death of Subhas Chandra Bose brought an end to one of history's more enigmatic figures, a man who came from a land famous for producing enigmas. As no one can be certain about the precise circumstances of his demise, historians will always have doubts about his life. Like most of the collaborators who emerged during the war, Bose came forward as a failed opportunist, an "also-ran" politician whose extremism cost him his credibility in his native land. After his German-based movement collapsed in 1942, only sheer luck kept him from incarceration or execution. The more inflammable Nazis found the idea of Germany supporting Free India unthinkable, while the highest echelons of German intelligence remained certain that Bose really worked for Stalin. Being falsely labeled a Soviet agent put Bose at grave risk, and yet *he survived*.

He survived long enough to move into the second stage of his Axis program. Tokyo had an active recruitment drive for puppets dating back to the early 1930s, and, in fact, started their own Azad Hind campaign under Mohan Singh. Bose happened to be seeking a new sponsor at the exact moment of Singh's fall from grace. Premier Tojo willingly adopted the slightly soiled Netaji.

On the surface, it seemed as if Japan treated him far better than the German government did. The honors and awards bestowed on Bose served Tokyo's propaganda interests, or Tojo would never have granted them. The spanking-new uniform, command over a POW army, the staged rallies, the "return" of the Andaman and Nicobar Islands, and most important of all, official recognition of a provisional government made Netaji Bose the short-lived darling of the Axis, and journalists' favorite nemesis to British security in Asia. In sharp contrast to the holy Mahatma and the erudite Nehru, Bose gave the international media its "Would-be Führer" and "Indian Quisling." A fat man in tight officer's fatigues, with thick little glasses and an overbite, he presented an unlikely figure as the commander in chief of the army that would end two centuries of British rule and liberate Mother India. Calling for blood, sacrifice and financial contributions, Bose promised to lead his people to victory and prosperity — but not "Co-Prosperity."

The man who gave the Asian press corps its flamboyant Netaji gave the Axis diplomatic corps its severest headache. Bose insisted on maintaining all rules of protocol, especially at critical times when Japanese military officers and government personnel would have preferred expediency to formality. The darling of the Axis arrived in Tokyo for the 1943 Greater East Asia Conference amid fanfare usually reserved for a head of state. The atmosphere radiated the spirit of brotherhood created by Japan and her client states. This mood was as phony as the gold braiding on Bose's dress uniform, but at any Axis function, image took precedence over reality. The convention was stage-managed to be a propagandist's dream, with nearly all puppet leaders present, and gestures of support carefully awarded by Tojo.

The Japanese premier restored the Andaman and Nicobar Islands to Indian rule by presenting them to Azad Hind. The Netaji showed his gratitude by refusing membership in the GEA. Laurel, Ba Maw and representatives from numerous other collaborationist governments throughout occupied Asia all fully cooperated with Tokyo and joined the GEA. Bose's act of independence earned him the respect of his followers, but could have proven to be a serious embarrassment to his benefactors. Fresh from his Berlin disaster, the Netaji took a tremendous chance by not accepting Tokyo's offer. Japanese leadership saved face by later saying that they never considered India as part of the GEA; their interest in the British colony was strictly as a potential trade partner. The Japanese Foreign Ministry and Imperial General Headquarters certainly went to extraordinary efforts for mere business, considering the fact that Japan had a proper empire.

Why did the Japanese tolerate Bose? His propaganda activities always alarmed the British. His time in Germany proved that, but the Nazis always remained uncomfortable cultivating an Indian ally. Despite British intelligence reports that claimed he would always be a questionable personage in India, London still hired Orwell to direct the BBC's counterpropaganda campaign against him. They knew that Bose's effectiveness would likely increase if he was closer to home, so they allowed him to replace Mohan Singh. The Japanese made a wise decision, considering the times and their ambitions. Once given his commission and a ragged band of POWs, Bose generated more journalistic attention than Tokyo's other traitors, even overshadowing Puyi, the last monarch of China's Qing Dynasty and the puppet Emperor of Manchukuo.

Bose had no military training to speak of, but he knew how to pose for a camera and more importantly, he had a gift for public speaking. Asian-based news correspondents watched his media antics, read his aggressively worded press releases, and reported that he would invade India if at all possible. Bose served as a weapon against British morale, and nothing else.

The Netaji's military exploits, which have received a great deal of study in secondary sources, resulted in utter failures. The tragedy of the INA eclipsed any successes Bose had as either a propagandist or a diplomat. The Japanese never relied on their Indian forces, and with good reason. Historically, rehabilitated POWs and disgruntled minority units proved ineffective. The German Kaiser attempted such a scheme during World War I, using various kinds of prisoners. In the early 1920s, M. N. Roy clashed with the Soviet government over an Indian brigade in the Red Army. In more recent history, Bose's Indian Legion of Germany and Iqbal Shedai's Rome-based *Centro Militare India* all mutinied on the battlefield. The Mohan Singh Affair showed Tokyo that Indian revolutionaries could not be trusted. Establishing a new INA with Bose at its head served propaganda interests. In practical terms, the Japanese did not mind using Indians for coolies and rifle-bearers, but as a combat force, they were reserved for cannon fodder in battles on the Indian subcontinent.

* * *

Subhas Chandra Bose sacrificed a great deal when he shook hands with Tojo Hideki, the cost being his integrity. At this point, calling Bose a controversial figure is, of course, an understatement. In India, contemporaries and voters either lauded or hated him; few ever took a moderate stand toward the Netaji. Despite his extremism, his early qualities of determination and ethical behavior were admired by many, including his most vehement political enemies. Even Gandhi respected Bose's dedication to values that greatly differed from his own.

In his dealings with the Germans, these values never changed. Bose had very definite plans for the future of India. They included liberation with Axis support, and a few initial years of totalitarian rule just to stabilize the new nation. India would then be ready for a liberal government with a socialist economy. Naturally, the Axis powers would be India's closest allies, militarily, politically and tradewise. This was a bold proposition from a colonial revolutionary, but at least midlevel German diplomats took it under review, and funded and sheltered him. The Nazis intended to *use* him, and, in turn, Bose obviously tried to take advantage of them as well. When Berlin hesitated to endorse an Indian government-in-exile, Bose openly showed his irritation and considered parting with the Germans.

When he joined forces with the Japanese, Bose's moral strength apparently dissolved. Since Tokyo had its own program, Bose moved into an existing slot, rather than having to negotiate for a new position. As the Japanese heaped on all the usual fascist trappings, Bose gradually came to believe the words Tokyo told him to say. His squabbles with Ba Maw and some Japanese field officers showed impatience rather than commitment to principle. Rejecting GEA membership seemed to be his only act of defiance in the East, and yet his movement functioned completely under Japanese control, suggesting the refusal was more symbolic than intentional.

Unlike collaborators such as Laval, Quisling and Puyi, the Netaji died before he could be investigated, so he never explained the last year of his life. British military authorities detained INA survivors at the Red Fort in Delhi, and made plans for their courts-martial. With the mood in postwar India anything but settled, the Raj decided to release the soldiers, who enjoyed brief popular appeal. As for Bose, the people of Bengal regard him as a hero — even going so far as to name Calcutta's newest stadium after him.

> "...in the last days perilous times shall come."
> 2 Timothy 3:1

> "Thorny indeed is the road to freedom, nevertheless, it is a road also to immortality."
> — Subhas Chandra Bose[25]

CONCLUSION

Born out of violence, India today is the world's largest democracy, yet this troubled nation has rarely known peace. Her national anthem begins with "Hindu, Muslim, Christian, Jain...," yet intercommunal violence there has been a recurrent theme. While the Muslim nations of Pakistan and Bangladesh exist, India still has a huge Islamic population — larger than the entire population of Pakistan! The Kashmiris pressure the Delhi government either to grant them independence or to make them a part of Pakistan. Hindu-Muslim violence erupts there, as it does in other states.

Within recent years, however, much of the violence has been generated by the Sikhs in the north and the Tamils in the south. The Sikhs of Punjab are perhaps the best known of India's martial tribes; the others are the Rajputs of Rajasthan and the Nepali Gurkhas. Legends among of the warrior caste, the Sikhs combined elements of Hinduism and Islam, and they have a tradition of soldiering dating back to the days of the Mughals.

Throughout the early 1980s, the Sikhs conducted an armed struggle for an independent Sikh state in the Punjab, which would have been called Khalistan, after the warrior goddess of Hinduism. Her name was behind some of the most shocking events of 1984. By the spring of that year, it was no secret to Delhi's intelligence community that the Golden Temple of Amritsar, Sikhdom's holiest shrine, had been converted into an illegal arsenal. On June 28, 1984, Prime Minister Indira Gandhi ordered the army to raid the Golden Temple. Her troops killed over 10,000 Sikhs, whose survivors immediately plotted revenge.

Despite the increasing tensions, Mrs. Gandhi never thought of breaking with the custom of having Sikhs in her secret service. As the prime minister walked to an interview with actor Peter Ustinov on the morning of

October 31, 1984, her Sikh bodyguards gunned her down. While her son, Ranjiv, took the oath of office, intercommunal rioting erupted, leaving thousands dead in a widespread revenge massacre. After assuming his position, Ranjiv Gandhi enacted numerous antiterrorist measures throughout India, and, in return, Sikh nationalists put his name at the top of their assassination list.

While threatened by the sons of Khali, Ranjiv Gandhi had to deal with growing separatism from the southern state of Tamil Nadhu. Like the Sikhs, the Tamils felt that the Indian government had failed to address their needs. Inflamed by the distant government that ignored them and the civil war in Sri Lanka that captivated them, the Tamils launched their plot. On May 16, 1992, a young female suicide bomber took the lives of both herself and Ranjiv Gandhi.

Subhas Chandra Bose appealed to a darker, more common side of human nature. He saw value in rebellion and revenge. While Mahatma Gandhi attempted to uplift the conscience of the British people, the Netaji simply tried to force the imperialists out of India. He did not care if the British ever realized their moral error in being there; he never planned any concordat with London. From the days of his youth, Bose felt attracted to those patriots who had turned to hard-line Swadeshi economic warfare and terrorism following the 1905 Partition of Bengal. As the campaign for independence gained momentum, both the revolutionaries and the Raj had used increasing violence against each other. Bose embraced that savagery. As World War II commenced, he bitterly hoped not only to free his nation but shatter Great Britain as well.

Subhas Bose was certainly as idealistic as any of his colleagues. He earnestly believed that India shared a goal with the Axis powers. He clearly wanted a Free India, and the kind of initial international assistance that a developing country needs. For their part, the fascist nations let anger and utter madness guide their policies. Among their numerous resentments, Hitler, Mussolini and Japan's wartime premiers condemned imperialism. This, of course, had little to do with sympathy for colonial peoples, but highlighted the fascists' jealousy of the establishment powers, most of which enjoyed extensive colonial empires. Rome, Berlin and Tokyo merely felt cheated out of the world's prime territories. Obviously, the Axis' interest in Bose rested in his propaganda value, rather than his role in a future Free India.

Both the Germans and the Japanese, though equally prejudiced, disguised their sinister foreign policies by securing the cooperation of various eager nationalists, most of them politically active but unsuccessful before the onset of the war. Misguided Henry Aisin-Gioro Puyi was the deposed last Manchu emperor of China when Japan recruited him into their service in the early 1930s. While merely establishing the puppet state of Manchukuo in 1932, Japan took credit for recreating the Manchu Empire. In China, the ailing Wang Jingwei suffered a string of failures before his Axis sponsors put him at the helm of a regime in Nanking in 1940. Dr. Ba Maw collaborated with Japan in an effort to drive the British out of Burma, and spent most of his postwar years imprisoned by the new Burmese government. Dr. José Laurel shared a similar goal regarding the American presence in the Philippines. Interestingly enough, the Laurel family name was washed and repainted after the collaborator's son, Salvador, was Vice-President in the Aquino government.

Given this mixed cast of characters, Tokyo welcomed the chance to work with an experienced activist like Subhas Chandra Bose. Although discredited in Europe because of the Indian Legion fiasco, he had proven to be a major headache to London as the voice of Azad Hind Radio. The very fact that the BBC responded with Orwell's program for India showed that the British government worried about Bose's following at home, especially in Bengal. Even in confidential documents, various government departments tried to pacify each other by describing Bose as a has-been politician whose radio harangues meant little, and yet London went to fairly great lengths to counter him. If Germany saw little significance in this, Japan certainly saw much more. The Germans obviously had mixed feelings about dealing with a colonial rebel, especially one whose skin color represented everything that was wrong with the world. This forced Berlin to keep its Indian program relatively secret and limited. Of course the Nazis did not mind funding Bose and providing him with a radio station, but they did not want to be directly linked to an Indian revolutionary. In contrast, Tokyo openly supported such nationalists. Since the Japanese rarely attempted to hide these alliances, they easily came to terms with Subhas Chandra Bose.

In those radio broadcasts from Germany and Southeast Asia, Bose's message was always the same: an independent homeland. As one witnesses the political convulsions torturing India at the beginning of the 21st century, one cannot help but recall the radical masses who wholeheartedly supported the Azad Hind movement. When the Sikh soldier tore off his Crown insignia and saluted the Springing Tiger flag, or the Indian Muslim businessman of Kuala Lumpur donated ingots of hard-earned gold to an Azad Hind charity, tribe, caste and religion never clouded the issue. Indians of all levels of society — rich, poor, high-born or untouchable, Muslim or Hindu, overseas or local — cheered for the simple goal of *Jai Hind* — Free India. The idea of an India divided into ethnic or theocratic states would have offended Bose as much as having his country remain in colonial chains. Throughout his career, he advocated a free and united India — born out of violence, yes — but still united.

ENDNOTES

Chapter 1: Janakinath's Son

1. Sisir K. Bose, et al., eds., *A Beacon Across Asia* (New Delhi, 1973), p. 3. Until the 1905 partition, Orissa was a section of the Presidency of Bengal. From the Partition through today, Orissa has remained an individual province.

2. Subhas Chandra Bose, *An Indian Pilgrim: An Unfinished Autobiography and Collected Letters 1897–1921* (Calcutta, 1965), pp. 1–3. Quote on p. 2.

3. *Ibid.*, pp. 4, 19–26, 33–36, 44–50, 104–110.

4. Dhananjay Keer, *Mahatma Gandhi: Political Saint and Unarmed Prophet* (Bombay, 1973), pp. 7–9. Bose is often referred to as "Babu" in Indian literature. Here the title is meant as a sign of respect. In Leonard A. Gordon's *Bengal: The Nationalist Movement 1876–1940* (New York, 1974), p. 7, the author uses "bhadralok," a term similar to babu. This word has the somewhat negative connotation of the high-minded, politicized elite.

5. Bose, *Pilgrim*, pp. 3–4, 19–26, 33–36, 44–50, 104–110. Quote on p. 3.

6. *Ibid.*

7. Gordon, *Bengal*, p. 50; and J.N. Vajpeyi, *The Extremist Movement in India* (Allahabad, 1974), p. 1.

8. Percival Spear, *A History of India 2* (Baltimore, 1970), pp. 158–159; and William Yale, *The Near East: A Modern History* The University of Michigan History of the Modern World, rev. ed., (Ann Arbor, 1968), pp. 4–8.

9. Arun Chandra Guha, *First Spark of Revolution: The Early Phase of India's Struggle for Independence* (New Delhi, 1971), pp. 141–144.

10. Spear, *History*, pp. 158–162.

11. Geoffrey Moorhouse, *Calcutta* (New York, 1971), pp. 68–69.

12. Bose, *Beacon*, p. 8; Spear, *History*, pp. 158–162; and Vajpeyi, *Extremist*, pp. 11–12.

13. Vajpeyi, *Extremist*, p. 6; Allan and Wendy Scarfe, *JP — His Biography* (New Delhi, 1975), p. 6; and Shaileshwar Nath, *Terrorism in India* (New Delhi, 1980), p. 12. The Scarfes' study is a biography of leftist leader Jayaprakash Narayan.

14. Spear, *History*, pp. 158–162; and Roger Beaumont, *Sword of the Raj: The British Army in India 1747–1947* (New York, 1977).

15. Spear, *History*, p. 158.

16. *Ibid*, p. 159.

17. *Ibid.*
18. Bose, *Pilgrim*, pp. 39–41.
19. *Ibid.*
20. *Ibid.*
21. *Ibid*, p. 44.
22. Gordon, *Bengal*, pp. 1–11.
23. *Ibid.*
24. *Ibid.*, pp. 68–77.
25. Guha, *Spark*, pp. 35–36, 42–46, 144–145, 221–223.
26. *Ibid.*
27. *Ibid*, pp. 36, 42–45, 223; and Annie Besant, *How India Wrought for Freedom* (New Delhi, 1915, reprinted in 1974), pp. 418–429. Besant was an English educator who dedicated her life to the Indian cause. Even without the Swadeshi movement, Hindus burned their clothing as part of the seasonal *puja* (celebration), after which everyone would get new outfits. As of 1905, the new suits and saris came from Indian-owned factories, and were made from materials obtained in local mills.
28. Gordon, *Bengal*, pp. 85–86; Moorhouse, *Calcutta*, pp. 69–71; B.R. Nanda, *Gokhale: The Indian Moderates and the British Raj* (New Delhi, 1977), pp. 191–194; D.V. Tahmankar, *Lokamanya Tilak: Father of Indian Unrest and Maker of Modern India* (London, 1956), pp. 107–135; Stanley A. Wolpert, *Tilak and Gokhale: Revolution and Reform in the Making of Modern India* (Berkeley, 1962), pp. 166–185; John S. Hoyland, *Gopal Krishna Gokhale: His Life and Speeches* (Calcutta, 1933), pp. 131–134; R.C. Majumdar, et al., eds., *Struggle for Freedom* The History and Culture of the Indian People Series (Bombay, 1969), pp. 20–38, 43–67; Ram Gopal, *How India Struggled for Freedom* (Bombay, 1967), pp. 139–167; M.N. Das, *India Under Morley and Minto* (London, 1964), pp. 30–45; and Pardaman Singh, *Lord Minto and Indian Nationalism 1905–1910* (Allahabad, 1976), pp. 16–35. Other proposed changes, including alcohol prohibition and women's rights (equal education and outlawing the dowry), all meant profound reforms within the Hindu community. In Nanda, *Gokhale*, p. 342, the author notes that one of Gokhale's associates toured Bengal in 1907, and reported that Muslim participation in Swadeshi had been vastly overrated, with activity from only a few paid roughnecks, sponsored by the Nawab of Dacca. Sir Surendranath Banerjea, the distinguished editor of *The Bengalee*, pointed out that many English residents of Bengal disapproved of the Partition, and supported Swadeshi. See Surendranath Banerjea, *A Nation in Making*, 4th edn. (Calcutta, 1963), 177–180.
29. Keer, *Gandhi*, p. 91; and Mahatma Gandhi, *Swaraj in One Year*, 2nd edn. (New York, 1972), pp. 8–9, 35–42. Gandhi was an enthusiastic supporter of Swadeshi from the very beginning. See Mahatma Gandhi, "Will India Wake Up?," "The Boycott," and "Brave Bengal" in the *Collected Works of Mahatma Gandhi (1905–1906) 5* (Ahmedabad, 1961), pp. 44, 92, 114. These articles first appeared in the South African newspaper, *Indian Opinion* (Durban). In future references, Gandhi's *Collected Works* will be abbreviated *CWMG*.

Chapter 2: Money Always Helped

1. See Chapter 4.
2. Gandhi, pp. *Swaraj*, 8–9, 35–42; and *CWMG (1905–1906) 5*, pp. 44, 92, 114. Mahatma Gandhi always credited Swadeshi with encouraging all Indians to participate in the politics of self-rule. His younger colleague, Jawaharlal Nehru, expressed a different opinion. The Calcutta-based boycott never convinced Nehru that Swadeshi had the essential roots of the so-called "All India" archetype. The varying opinions of those two great Indian leaders illustrated the controversy in trying to determine the nature of dynamic patriotism in India.

3. Guha, *Spark*, pp. 120, 252.

4. S. Bhattacharya, "Cotton Mills and Spinning Wheels: Swadeshi and the Indian Capitalist Class, 1920–1922," in K.N. Panikkar, ed., *National and Left Movements in India* (New Delhi, 1980), pp. 27–44; and Gordon Johnson, *Provisional Politics and Indian Nationalism: Bombay and the Indian National Congress 1880–1915* (Cambridge, 1973), pp. 11–16, 128–130. The Tagore family, historically in the vanguard of Calcutta's cultural and political scenes, actively promoted all aspects of Swadeshi. The Tagores urged their relatives and associates to form *samitis* to promote and finance Swadeshi. A *samiti* consisted of distant members of a family, or even friendly clans of the same caste, all joined to assist a cause or perform some public service. Often they emerged as India's earliest political parties. See Gordon, *Bengal*, pp. 27–30, 79–83.

5. Subhas Chandra Bose, *Famous Speeches and Letters of Subhas Chandra Bose*, ed. by Ganpat Rai (Lahore, 1946), pp. 152–155.

6. Guha, *Spark*, pp. 87, 120, 141–144, 327–329; Banerjea, *Nation*, pp. 177–185, 193–203; and Majumdar, *Struggle*, pp. 45–46, 61–67. In 1908, the Morley-Minto Reform Acts increased the size of the Indian Legislative Council and added Indians to the Viceroy's Executive Council. These laws gave the Muslims distinct representation while bringing "moderate" nationalists closer to the colonialist side. The Raj even rescinded the Bengal Partition in 1911, in hopes of stifling Swadeshi by placating the Hindus. The British efforts were in vain. See Das, *India Under*, pp. 183–249; and Singh, *Minto*, pp. 180–250.

7. Gopal, *How India*, pp. 111–119, 182–192; and Vajpeyi, *Extremist*, pp. 101–102, 136–137, 197.

8. Guha, *Spark*, pp. 92–94, 116–117; Vajpeyi, *Extremist*, pp. 175; and Majumdar, *Struggle*, pp. 69–70, 200–201.

9. *Ibid.*

10. *Ibid.*

11. Sankar Ghose, *Political Ideas and Movements in India* (Bombay, 1975), pp. 29–30; Selig S. Harrison, "Troubled India and her Neighbours," in K.P. Misra, ed., *Studies in Indian Foreign Policy* (New Delhi, 1969), pp. 195–214; and Guha, *Spark*, pp. 32–33, 49–50, 85–86, 92–93, 120.

12. *Ibid.*

13. Quote from Guha, *Spark*, p. 86.

14. See Chapters 4 and 5.

15. Mahatma Gandhi, "Japan and Russia," in *CWMG (1903–1905) 4* (Ahmedabad, 1960), pp. 466–467; and Mahatma Gandhi, "The Rise of Japan" and "Australia and Japan," in *CWMG 5*, pp. 57–58, 115. These articles were first published in the *Indian Opinion*. Also see P.B. Sinha, *Indian National Liberation Movement and Russia 1905–1917* (New Delhi, 1975), pp. 86–91, 172–180.

16. Mahatma Gandhi, "Russia and India," in *CWMG 5*, pp. 131–132 (originally published in the *Indian Opinion*); Keer, *Gandhi*, p. 92; and Sinha, *Liberation*, pp. 258–259.

17. H.W. Hale, *Political Trouble in India 1917–1937* (Allahabad, 1974), pp. 1–8; Nath, *Terrorism*, pp. 34–42, 57; and Majumdar, *Struggle*, pp. 68–73.

18. *Ibid.*

19. Guha, *Spark*, pp. 130–133, 324–330; Sinha, *Liberation*, pp. 86–94, 226–227; and Gopal, *How India*, pp. 111–119, 181.

20. *Ibid.*

21. *Ibid.*

22. Singh, *Minto*, pp. 36–59; Ghose, *Ideas*, pp. 54–64, 334; and Vajpeyi, *Extremist*, pp. 192–195.

23. *Ibid.*

24. *Ibid.* Also see D.S. Sahota, *Lala Lajpat Rai: His Life and Thought* (Dhudike, 1974). Vajpeyi suggests that Rai and Singh were actually deported.

25. Keer, *Gandhi*, pp. 152–155; Majumdar, *Struggle*, pp. 169–170, 206, 230; and Guha, *Spark*, pp. 134–175.
26. *Ibid.*
27. *Ibid.*
28. *Ibid.*
29. Guha, *Spark*, p. 267.

Chapter 3: Thieves, Spies and Saboteurs — The Friends of Wilhelm II

1. Besant, *Wrought*, p. 582; and Vajpeyi, *Extremist*, pp. 135–136.
2. Guha, *Spark*, p. 414; Besant, *Wrought*, pp. 418–429; and Ghose, *Ideas*, pp. 34–44.
3. Guha, *Spark*, pp. 424–445.
4. *Ibid.* Also see Ghose, *Ideas*, pp. 65–67; and Gopal, *How India*, 221–228. Related to the Berlin Committee was the *Deutscher Verein der Fremde Indien* — the German Union of Friendly India — which had a shipping magnate and close friend of the Kaiser for its president. For more information, see Majumdar, *Struggle*, pp. 213–216.
5. Guha, *Spark*; Sinha, *Liberation*, pp. 99–102; and Sir Algernon Rumbold, *Watershed in India 1914–1922* (London, 1979), p. 32. Also see Arnold Krammer, "Soviet Propaganda Among German and Austro-Hungarian Prisoners of War in Russia 1917–1921" in Samuel R. Williamson, Jr. and Peter Pastor, eds., *Essays on World War I: Origins and Prisoners of War* (New York, 1983). Krammer's article provides unique insight into the Soviet and German efforts to brainwash their POWs. Baron Von Oppenheim appears to be a rather mysterious figure indeed. Guha is the only source to mention him, and despite his apparently important role, neither his full name nor his position in the Kaiser's government is given. He may have been an intelligence officer using an assumed name, or even a Krupp executive with an honorary title.
6. Guha, *Spark*; and Majumdar, *Struggle*, pp. 206–218. It is interesting to note the opinion of Hardayal's Punjabi colleague, Lala Lajpat Rai, on the subject of using Germany's armed forces in India. In *Lala Lajpat Rai: His Life and Thought*, Sahota offered this unattributed quote: "I am a Hindu Nationalist working for the attainment of self-government for India but I do not believe that it would be worth our while to achieve that end by foreign military intervention" (p. 16).
7. *Ibid.* The revolutionaries also wanted Germany to build a special mint to issue counterfeit Indian currency. Von Oppenheim did not approve of this operation, claiming that it presented complications that outweighed any potential value. The baron may have been aware that during the early Swadeshi period, the Bengalis engaged in a similar endeavor, with few effects on the colonial economy.
8. *Ibid.*; and Hugh Toye, *The Springing Tiger* (London, 1959), pp. 5–6. Working through future chancellor Franz Von Papen, then the military attaché to the United States, Germany planned to use the Krupp office in New York City as a weapons broker. See Majumdar, *Struggle*, pp. 216–218.
9. Guha, *Spark*; and Sinha, *Liberation*, pp. 100–118
10. Guha, *Spark*, p. 438. Unfortunately, neither Guha nor any other source provided an estimate of the number of operatives in the United States.
11. *Ibid.*, pp. 430–445.
12. *Ibid.*
13. Nath, *Terrorism*, p. 94; Vajpeyi, *Extremist*, pp. 204–207; and Rumbold, *Watershed*, p. 43.
14. Guha, *Spark*, pp. 430–445. On April 23, 1918, a spectacular murder took place

during the trial. While Ram Chandra, a hard-core revolutionary, appeared at the bench to testify, gunfire cut through the courtroom air. A Sikh, allegedly on orders from the Crown, assassinated Chandra, only to be gunned down by a court policeman. Guha quotes a message from O'Brien to Palmer: "[Chakravarty] has given valuable information to the Government and may again be useful to the Government. In our opinion there is little prospect of his being harmful to the country" (p. 445). Chakravarty later returned to India and died in obscurity.

15. *Ibid.*

16. Werner Otto Von Hentig, *Mein Leben — Eine Dienstreise* (*My Life — A Business Trip*) (Gottingen, 1963), pp. 91–191; Uma Kaura, *Muslims and Indian Nationalism: The Emergence of the Demand for India's Partition 1928–1940* (Columbia, Missouri, 1977), pp. 21–22; Sinha, *Liberation*, pp. 102–103, 161–164, 257; and Guha, *Spark*, pp. 446–460.

17. Guha, *Spark*; Tahmankar, *Tilak*, pp. 289–301; Rumbold, *Watershed*, pp. 23–27; and Majumdar, *Struggle*, pp. 220–221.

18. Guha, *Spark*; K.K. Ghosh, *The Indian National Army* (Meerut, 1969), p. 3; Gerard H. Corr, *The War of the Springing Tigers* (London, 1975), pp. 53–54; and Gopal, *How India*, pp. 229–232.

Chapter 4: His Path

1. Bose, *Pilgrim*, pp. 51–57, 64–70, 78–81, 93. Quote on p. 64.

2. *Ibid.*, pp. 85–103; Bose, *Beacon*, pp. 8–18; and N.G. Ganpuley, *Netaji in Germany: A Little-Known Chapter* (Bombay, 1959). Ganpuley worked with Bose at Berlin's Free India Center.

3. *Ibid.*

4. Rajat Ray, *Urban Roots of Indian Nationalism: Pressure Groups and Conflict of Interests in Calcutta City Politics 1875–1939* (New Delhi, 1979), pp. 78–95.

5. Bose, *Pilgrim*, p. 93; and Bose, *Beacon*, pp. 12–18. Bose later wrote that if "the Mahatma had spoken in the language of Dictator Stalin, or Il Duce Mussolini or Fuehrer Hitler — John Bull would have understood and would have bowed his head in respect." See Subhas Chandra Bose, *The Indian Struggle 1920–1942* (London, 1964), p. 229.

6. Bose, *Struggle*, pp. 42–51; and Romain Rolland, *Mahatma Gandhi: The Man Who Became One with the Universal Being* (New York, 1924), pp. 63–72.

7. Bose, *Struggle*, pp. 44–45, 370–371; and Jawaharlal Nehru, "Satyagraha," in D. Mackenzie Brown, ed., *The Nationalist Movement: Indian Political Thought from Ranade to Bhave* (Berkeley, 1961), pp. 134–151.

8. Bose, *Struggle*; and Subhas Chandra Bose, "The Anti-Imperialist Struggle and Samyavada," in Sisir K. Bose, ed., *Fundamental Questions of Indian Revolution* (Calcutta, 1970), pp. 1–32. "The Anti-Imperialist Struggle and Samyavada" was Bose's keynote speech for the Third Indian Political Conference, held in London in 1933. Bose used the "fortress under siege" analogy to argue for revolution. First, one must weaken the fortress through "economic blockade," then "capture the fortress by force of arms." (p. 15).

9. Krishnalal Shridharani, *My India, My America* (Garden City, New York, 1943), pp. 460–463; and Subhas Chandra Bose, "To the Youth," in *The Mission of Life* (Calcutta, 1965), pp. 144–179. See p. 178. Also see Ganpuley, *Germany*, p. 9; Bose, *Beacon*, pp. 43–44; and B.R. Nanda, *Gokhale, Gandhi and the Nehrus: Studies in Indian Nationalism* (London, 1974), pp. 58, 86–87, 113. "To the Youth" was Bose's presidential address to the Pabna Youth Conference of 1929. The Independence for India League should not be confused with organizations of similar names that functioned in Europe, Southeast Asia, Japan and the United States throughout the revolutionary period.

10. A. Appadorai, *Essays in Indian Politics and Foreign Policy* (New Delhi, 1971), pp. 27–29; and Bose, *Struggle*, pp. 341–347. Actually, Bose reached the Mayor's office by default. The elected man was in prison with an extended sentence.

11. Bose, *Struggle*; and B.R. Tomlinson, *The Indian National Congress and the Raj, 1929–1942: The Penultimate Phase* (London, 1976), p. 111. Quote from Toye, *Tiger*, p. 53. Jawaharlal Nehru's writings provide excellent coverage of Bose's 1939 reelection. See the *Selected Writings of Jawaharlal Nehru 9*, ed. by S. Gopal (New Delhi, 1976), pp. 477–490. In the future, this series will be referred to as *SWJN*.

12. Bose, *Struggle*, pp. 333–334. The entire text of "Forward Bloc — Its Justification" appears on pp. 395–414. Quote from p. 395. For general information concerning the rift between Bose and Gandhi's supporters, see Sankar Ghose, *Indian National Congress: Its History and Heritage* (New Delhi, 1975), pp. 160–161; Prem Nath Bazaz, *The Role of Bhagavad Gita in Indian History* (New Delhi, 1975), p. 531; Tomlinson, *Congress*, pp. 123–136; Louis Fischer, *Gandhi: His Life and Message for the World* (New York, 1982) (originally published in 1954), pp. 93–95, 107; Yogesh Chadha, *Gandhi: A Life* (New York, 1997) (originally published as *Rediscovering Gandhi*), pp. 351–361; and Nanda, *Studies*, 82–93. In 1938, Bose analyzed India's lack of unity and the resulting inhibition of social progress in his contribution to the series "India in Transition" in *The Living Age* magazine. Naturally, he blamed the colonial administration and the Congress for the confusion. See Subhas Chandra Bose, "As We See It," *The Living Age* 354 (April 1938): 150–152. Political affairs specialists in Britain's India Office took interest in Bose's fall from grace and subsequent formation of the Forward Bloc. According to British observers, Bose's resignation showed that Gandhi still controlled the Congress. They pointed out the uniqueness of the situation in which a Congress president left office after a dispute with a leading member. The India Office mentioned his unstable support base in Bengal, and concluded that he "made a sorry spectacle of provincial politics." See "Subhas Chandra Bose. Addendum to Previous Note on his Career." This is part of a report titled "Subhas Chandra Bose: Effect of his Broadcasts in India". From : India Office (communicated), April 27, 1942, Public Records Office, London, FO371/31799 XC/A/048065.

13. Bose, *Struggle*, pp. 333–334, 342–344, 392–394. Quote on p. 393. Also, Bose, *Beacon*, pp. 91–98; Toye, *Tiger*, pp. 50–53; Subhas Chandra Bose, "Gandhi-Irwin Pact and Lahore Executions" (part of Karachi speech, March 27, 1931), in *Famous Speeches and Letters of Subhas Chandra Bose*, ed. Ganpat Rai (Lahore, 1946), pp. 113–115; and Subhas Chandra Bose, *Impressions in Life* (Lahore, 1947), pp. 277–280. Congress' recognition of Bose's new party did not mean that every Indian legislator supported him. Not unexpectedly, Nehru became one of the most outspoken politicians to condemn the Forward Bloc. He had little faith in the radical new party, and in a May 1939 speech, expressed his fears that European fascists would manipulate it to gain a foothold in India. According to Nehru, the Forward Bloc platform, which included an antiwar stand, only created more dissent in Congress, rather than forcing it to unite and move. In a July 1939 speech in Colombo, Ceylon (now Sri Lanka), India's future prime minister discounted the Forward Bloc's membership for acting on "personal" beliefs, rather than a party ideology. One month later, he conveyed to an audience in Poona his dismay that Bose felt that Nehru regarded the Forward Bloc as both pro-fascist in its ideals and mercenary in its goals. In a 1939 letter to fellow statesman V.K. Krishna Menon, Nehru complained that Bose kept a regional outlook, and was unable to picture the political scene beyond Calcutta. In 1940, he suggested to Menon that only the youth of Bengal supported the Forward Bloc, while provincial elders resented the "Bose brothers' dictatorship." In November 1939, Nehru erroneously told a political ally, Rajendra Prasad, that "the Forward Bloc practically does not exist here now." See the following entries in *SWJN 9*: "[Letter] To V.K. Krishna Menon" (April 4, 1939), pp. 550–553; "On the Formation of the Forward Bloc" (Kanpur speech, May 23, 1939), p. 574; "The AICC [All-India Congress Committee]

and After" (editorial in the *National Herald*, May 27–28, 1939), pp. 575–580; and "The Congress is the Only Weapon" (Poona speech, July 27, 1939), pp. 594–595. See the following entries in *SWJN 10*, ed. S. Gopal (New Delhi, 1977): "The Need for Cooperation" (Colombo speech, July 19, 1939), pp. 17–19; "The Role of Youth in Revolutionary Times" (keynote address at the Students' Conference, Lucknow, September 22, 1939), pp. 159–160; "[Letter] To V.K. Krishna Menon" (October 11, 1939), pp. 182–184; "[Letter] To V.K. Krishna Menon" (March 2, 1940), pp. 343–346; and "[Letter] To Rajendra Prasad" (November 11, 1939), pp. 476–479. In a review of Marcus F. Franda's *Radical Politics in West Bengal* (Boston, 1972), Columbia University's Leonard A. Gordon criticized the author for calling the Forward Bloc a communist party. Gordon described Bose as "a devoted Hindu, … a socialist (with some fascist interpolations) and a secular nationalist." See Leonard A. Gordon, "Radical Bengalis: Alliances and Antagonisms — A Review," *South Asian Review*, 5 (1972): 341–344.

14. *Ibid.* Quote from Bose, *Beacon*, p. 98. Also see Subhas Chandra Bose, "The Nagpur Address" in *Crossroads* (New York, 1962), pp. 310–321. "The Nagpur Address" was also published as "Intensify the Struggle" in *Famous Speeches*, pp. 97–112.

15. Subhas Chandra Bose, "The Ramgarh Address" in *Crossroads*, pp. 269–274. This piece was published in an expanded form as "No Truck with Imperialism" in *Famous Speeches*, pp. 73–96.

16. Sita Ram Goel, *Netaji and the CPI* (Calcutta, 1955), pp. 1–4, 17–28. Quote from p. 4.

17. Bose, *Impressions*, pp. 13–27, 138–147; and Bose, *Beacon*, pp. 46–47.

18. Subhas Chandra Bose, "India Abroad" and "A Friend of India in Poland" in *Through Congress Eyes* (Allahabad, undated), pp. 76–93, 154–158; and Ganpuley, *Germany*, pp. 9–12.

19. "India: Chariot of Freedom," *Time*, 31 (March 7, 1938): pp. 19–20; Bose, *Impressions*, pp. 13–27, 138–147; and Bose, *Beacon*, pp. 46–47.

20. Bose, *Beacon*, pp. 64–74.

21. Taraknath Das, *India in World Politics* (New York, 1925), pp. 19–25; Sneh Mahajan, "The Defence of India and the End of Isolation: A Study in the Foreign Policy of the Conservative Government 1900–1905," *Journal of Imperial and Commonwealth History*, 10 (January 1982): 168–193; and George Nathaniel Curzon, *Russia in Central Asia* (New York, 1967), (originally published in 1889), pp. 321–361.

22. Guha, *Spark*, pp. 452–460; and Vajpeyi, *Extremist*, pp. 264–273.

23. S. Gopal, "The Formative Ideology of Jawaharlal Nehru," in Panikkar, *National and Left*, pp. 1–13; Jawaharlal Nehru, "The Fascination of Russia," "Lenin," and "Russia and India" in *SWJN 11*, ed. S. Gopal (New Delhi, 1972), pp. 381–383, 403–408, 447–451. These articles were first published in the *Hindu* in 1928.

24. Guha, *Spark*, pp. 452–460; and Vajpeyi, *Extremist*, pp. 264–273.

25. Sterling Seagrave, *The Soong Dynasty* (New York, 1986), pp. 166–197.

26. Subhas Chandra Bose, "Wake Up India" in *Famous Speeches*, pp. 213–216; Bose, "Ramgarh Address" in *Crossroads*, pp. 269–274; and Bose, *Beacon*, pp. 64–74. It is worth noting the Mahatma's attitude toward fascism. In 1931, he met Mussolini while visiting Rome. He never condoned fascism, yet a number of his colleagues criticized his trip. While a brief tour of Italy could not have exposed him to the excesses of totalitarianism, many of Gandhi's later statements show a clear lack of understanding. After the war began, he said that nonviolence and surrender on the part of the British would have not only disabled the German war machine, but taught the Axis a valuable lesson as well. The finest account of Gandhi's meeting with Il Duce can be found in Louis Fischer, *The Life of Mahatma Gandhi* (New York, 1983), pp. 330–339. Fischer was a journalist who interviewed Gandhi extensively. He wrote two books about him. For further information on Gandhi and fascism, see Chadha, *Gandhi*, pp. 362–363; and Lawrence James, *Raj: The Making and Unmaking of British India* (London, 1997), p. 541.

27. Subhas Chandra Bose, "European Chess-board," *The Living Age*, p. 353 (November 1937): pp. 201–207; Bose, *Beacon*, p. 77; and Toye, *Tiger*, pp. 48–49. Quote from Bose, *Impressions*, 124. In *Impressions in Life*, which he wrote from 1933 to 1937, Bose expressed a general admiration for Italy's adventures in Ethiopia and Spain. See pp. 64–67. In private talks, however, Bose had stronger opinions about the Abyssinian issue. He told the Italian Foreign Minister, Count Ciano, that Indians might not accept Italy's support, since they favored the Ethiopians. See Count Galeazzo Ciano, *Ciano's Hidden Diary 1937–1938*, with trans. and notes by Andreas Mayor (New York, 1953), (entry for January 20, 1938), pp. 65–66.

Chapter 5: Not a Question of Spirit, but of Color

1. Bose, "Forward Bloc — Its Justification," in *Fundamental*, p. 62.

2. *Ibid*. Also Bose, "Chess-board," *Living Age*, pp. 201–207; and Nanda, *Studies*, pp. 95, 149.

3. Nehru's writings make many references to his personal loathing of national socialism. In contrast to his colleagues in the Forward Bloc, he worried that in the eyes of the world community, the anti–British character of Indian nationalism already linked its participants with fascism. He made frequent references to the anti-fascist mood of the All-India National Congress. Ironically, Nehru condemned India's *National Herald*, which published many of his editorials and speeches, for an alleged pro–German slant. He accused the editors of making Hitler appear to be a peace-seeker. See the following entries in the *SWJN 9*: "Spain, China and India" (interview with *Rude Pravo*, Paris, July 31, 1938), pp. 91–92; "Germany and War" (interview with the *Hindustan Times*, New Delhi, September 4, 1938), pp. 129–130; and "[Letter] To Eduard Benes" (May 31, 1939), pp. 304–305. Benes led the Czech government-in-exile in London during the Nazi occupation. See *SWJN 10*: "Congress Resolution on India and the War" (September 1939 report), pp. 122–138; "Clearing the Decks" (editorial in the *National Herald*, October 31, 1939), pp. 212–215; "The Standpoint of the Congress" (Delhi speech, November 4, 1939), pp. 220–225; "Presidential Address to the U.P. Political Conference" (Mathura, November 28, 1939), pp. 254–258; "The Responsibility of the Congress" (Amritsar speech, December 31, 1939), pp. 270–271; "India's Demand and England's Answer" (article for the *Atlantic Monthly*, April 1940), pp. 273–282; "The Forward March" (Aligarh speech, January 9, 1940), pp. 285–287; and "Masses the Real Arbiters" (Ghaziabad speech, January 10, 1940), pp. 423–425. Also see the following items in the *SWJN 12*, ed. by S. Gopal, (New Delhi, 1979): "India's Attitude to the War" (Bardoli speech, December 26, 1941), pp. 43–44; and "Congress Unity" (Bombay speech, January 2, 1942), pp. 61–72. While Nehru remained tormented by the rise of Nazism and fascism, Bose, of course, thrived on it. He even encouraged Hitler's nonsense about race by linking Indians and Germans. He made ridiculous speeches, calling the Führer an ally to all Aryans. See James, *Raj*, p. 555.

4. Lukasz Hirzowicz, *The Third Reich and the Arab East* (London, 1966), pp. 12–19.

5. *Ibid*.

6. Joseph Goebbels, *The Goebbels Diaries 1942–1943*, ed, and trans, by Louis P. Lochner (Garden City, New York, 1948), (entry for March 20, 1943), p. 311; and Hirzowicz, *ibid*.

7. Joseph B. Schectman, *The Mufti and the Fuehrer* (New York, 1965), pp. 15–94.

8. *Ibid*., pp. 95–127. Also, "Joint Letter from Grand Mufti and Gailani to Ciano" (May 12, 1942). This message was intercepted by the United States War Department as

part of the MAGIC Operation. See [United States] War Department, Office of the Assistant Chief of Staff, G-2, MAGIC Summary SRS598, May 12, 1942, reel 1, frame 0258. This is part of *The MAGIC Documents: Summaries and Transcripts of the Top Secret Diplomatic Communications of Japan, 1938–1945* (University Publications of America, Inc., Washington, DC, 1980).

9. Schectman, *Mufti*, p. 95; and Albert Speer, *Inside the Third Reich*, trans. by Richard and Clara Winston (New York, 1970), p. 96. The quote regarding Sufism is from William Stevenson, *A Man Called INTREPID: The Secret War*, 2nd edn. (New York, 1982), p. 236.

10. Schectman, *Mufti*, p. 41.

11. *Ibid.*, pp. 138–142, 159–163.

12. *Ibid.* Quote on p. 296.

13. Heinz Hohne, *Canaris* (Garden City, New York, 1979), pp. 490–491; Goebbels, *Diaries*, pp. 56–57, 136; Fitzroy Maclean, *Eastern Approaches* (London, 1949), pp. 94–95; and "Memorandum of a Conversation between Hiroshi Oshima and Heinrich Himmler" (January 31, 1939), Appendix B of Carl Boyd, *The Extraordinary Envoy: General Hiroshi Oshima and Diplomacy in the Third Reich 1934–1939* (Washington, DC, 1980), pp. 157–158. In Sinha, *Liberation*, p. 242, the author noted that Raja Mahendra Pratap consulted with German officers involved in a similar plot in 1916.

14. "[Letter] To Subhas Chandra Bose" (April 3, 1939), in *SWJN 9*, pp. 534–549. The quote is taken from p. 537. Also see "[Letter] To V.K. Krishna Menon" (April 6, 1939), in *SWJN 9*, pp. 550–553.

15. Kitty Kurti, *Subhas Chandra Bose As I Knew Him* (Calcutta, 1966), pp. 38–40.

16. Keer, *Gandhi*. Gandhi had resented Jews for four decades. In his "Deputation to Lord Elgin" (November 8, 1906), he blamed South African anti–Indian legislation on less-successful Jewish immigrants from Europe and the Middle East, or, as he put it, "the very off-scourings of the international sewers of Europe." See *CWMG 22*, pp. 113–126. Quote on p. 115.

17. Adolf Hitler, *Mein Kampf*, ed. John Chamberlain, et al. (New York, 1939), pp. 954–956; Bose, *Impressions*, pp. 155–166; and Bose, *Beacon*, pp. 46–50. In an editorial for the *National Herald*, Nehru emphasized that both Hitler and Neville Chamberlain agreed on India's continued subservience. Nehru later said that "Herr Hitler has painted us, as every other man of Asia except the Japanese, in black colours." See "The Congress and War" (editorial, April 28, 1939), in *SWJN 9*, pp. 294–295. The quote is from "Britain Clouding the Real Issues" (Meerut speech, January 11, 1940), in *SWJN 10*, pp. 290–292. At the June 1942 Bangkok Conference of the Indian Independence League, Axis diplomatic officials gave speeches to a receptive crowd of overseas Indian activists. Both the German and Italian ministers to Thailand described the respect for Indian culture held by their people at home. See Kesar Singh Giani, *Indian Independence Movement in East Asia 1* (Lahore, 1947), pp. 76–77.

18. Adolf Hitler, *Hitler's Secret Conversations 1941–1944* (New York, 1976), pp. 13, 20–21, 28, 35. Quote on p. 28. At the 1942 IIL Bangkok Conference, Italian Minister Guido Crolla stated that "Italy, Germany and Japan have no territorial ambitions in India." See Giani, *Indian 1*, 77. In an unsigned editorial for the *National Herald*, Jawaharlal Nehru suggested that fascist aggression posed little threat to India. Italy and Germany focused their power on the European and North African theaters, while India was too far away from Japan to be a target of the Rising Sun. Bose had expressed similar sentiments at the time. See "The Defence of India" (editorial, April 22–23, 1939), in *SWJN 9*, p. 648.

19. *Ibid.*

20. Bose, *Beacon*, pp. 46–56; and Arun Coomer Bose, "Netaji and the Nazis: A Study in their Relations," *Journal of Indian History*, p. 50 (1972): 321–332.

21. Bose, "Netaji and Nazis," 324. Indian historian Arun Coomer Bose translated certain sections of the letter for a footnote to his article. He cited the original letter as appearing in

H.O. Guenther's *Indien und Deutschland: Ein Sammelband* (*India and Germany: An Anthology*) (Frankfurt am Main, 1956).

22. Bose, *Beacon*, pp. 46–56; Bose, "Netaji and Nazis," pp. 321–332; and Bose, "India Abroad" in *Eyes*, pp. 76–93. Quote from Ganpuley, *Germany*, p. 19. Albert Speer explored the dichotomy in Hitler's attitudes toward the Japanese. While he admired their suicidal patriotism, which he attributed to a religion superior to Christianity, he found working with nonwhites disconcerting. He took comfort in Britain's precedent with the London-Tokyo agreement which bound the two kingdoms in World War I. Hitler told Speer and others that Japan represented a military power comparable to Germany, while Italy did not. See Speer, *Inside*, pp. 96, 121.

23. *Ibid.* It is possible that the Nazis did finance Indian terrorists in the 1930s. In two letters to an acquaintance, Jawaharlal Nehru referred to the Khaksar Movement, led by Inayatullah Khan and his fanatical Muslim followers. Khan started this little-known nationalist group in the 1920s, and within a decade, he, like Bose, spoke in favor of Hitler. Nehru accused Hitler of sending money to build a Khaksar paramilitary unit. See "[Letter] To V.K. Krishna Menon" (April 4, 1939), in *SWJN 9*, pp. 550–553; and "[Letter] To V.K. Krishna Menon" (March 3, 1940), in *SWJN 10*, pp. 433–436.

24. Subhas Chandra Bose, "Letter to the *Manchester Guardian*" (March 17, 1936, postmarked Badgastein, Austria), in *Famous Speeches*, pp. 197–198; Bose, *Struggle*, pp. 344–345; and Bose, *Beacon*, pp. 45–46, 69, 99–100. In a letter to the Superintendent of Presidency Jail, dated October 30, 1940, Bose criticized the Raj for its use of what he called "super–Nazism". See "Second Letter" in *Famous Speeches*, pp. 176–178. There is some question about Bose's alleged meetings with the German consuls in Calcutta and Bombay in the fall of 1938. Nobody is sure if they actually took place, but if such talks occurred, the Nazis obviously failed to respond to Bose. See Bose, "Netaji and Nazis," pp. 321–332.

25. *Ibid.*

26. Bose, *Beacon*, pp. 100–103. In his "Second Letter" to the Superintendent of Presidency Jail, a suicidal Bose compared himself to the Irish patriot Terence Macswiney, the Mayor of Cork. "...I shall have the further satisfaction that my fast ... shall have repercussions outside India," Bose informed the chief warden, "for I happen to be one of the Indians known outside the frontiers of this country." See *Famous Speeches*, p. 77. After assuming command of the Japanese-backed Indian National Army (INA) in 1943, Bose claimed that he was serious about his suicide attempt. Writing to his officers on July 25, 1943, he admitted his intentions, yet one must consider the possibility that the Netaji only wanted to arouse enthusiasm for the cause. See the transcript of the INA letter in Kesar Singh Giani, *Indian Independence Movement in East Asia 2* (Lahore, 1947), pp. 37–43.

27. *Ibid.*, pp. 105–113. Also, Toye, *Tiger*, pp. 57–58; and Hari Singh Shergil, "How Netaji Escaped," *Illustrated Weekly of India*, 95 (September 8, 1974): 31. Ironically, the British decided to put Bose on trial for sedition. The trial date was set for January 26th. Bose escaped ten days before.

28. *Ibid.*

29. *Ibid.* By 1942, Bhagat Ram Talwar and some of his associates admitted to being Soviet agents while in police custody in India. Obviously, they were not very good agents, since they could not introduce Bose to any officials who could help, nor could they explain Bose's new direction. Ram Talwar said that approaching the Soviet embassy in Kabul was Bose's idea, and they could offer no explanation for the Soviet rejection. See James, *Raj*, p. 554.

30. *Ibid.* Lawrence James refers to the Italian Minister as Pietro Quanoni. See James, *Raj*, p. 551.

31. Bose, *Struggle*, pp. 415–418. This is the complete text of "Plan of Indian Revolution." The quote is from p. 415. Also see pp. 373–375, in which Bose discussed the science (or art ?) of propaganda at the 1933 Indian Political Conference in London.

32. *Ibid.* Quote from Bose, *Beacon*, p. 113.

33. *Ibid.* Also Shergil, "Escaped," 31; and [United States] War Department, Office of the Assistant Chief of Staff, G-2, MAGIC Summary No. 304, SRS 847, January 24, 1943, pp. 2–4, reel 4, frame 0262.

34. Toye, *Tiger*, p. 64; Bose, *Beacon*, pp. 116–118; and Bose, "Netaji and Nazis," pp. 321–332. Arun Coomer Bose alleges that many Nazis remained suspicious of Bose, since they knew he left Indian politics under dark circumstances, and the German ambassador in Kabul reported that he could have been an Allied spy. The Gestapo kept him under visual and wiretap surveillance.

35. *SWJN 10*, p. 81 ff; and Bose, "Intensify the Struggle" (Nagpur Address), *Famous Speeches*, p. 104. Also see Bose, *Impressions*, pp. 75–80; Bose, "Chess-board," *Living Age*, 201–207; Subhas Chandra Bose, "Europe — To-Day and To-Morrow," in *Eyes*, pp. 214–239; and Subhas Chandra Bose, "A Word about Germany," in *Crossroads*, pp. 267–268. The last item was an editorial that appeared in the *Forward Bloc* in 1940. Nehru actually supported what Bose said in June 1940. In 1941, Nehru told an audience in Allahabad that *"Nazism is but another form of impressive imperialism."* (italics mine) See "The Priority of Independence" (December 14, 1941) in the *SWJN 12*, pp. 16–28. Quote on p. 21. For similar references, see *SWJN 10*: "The Congress Offer of Cooperation" (Allahabad speech, September 20, 1939), pp. 145–148; "War Aims and Peace Aims" (editorial series for the *National Herald*, September 22–24, 1939), pp. 148–158; "The Unchanging Nature of Imperialism" (Bombay speech, October 27, 1939), pp. 210–212; "Russia and Finland" (editorial in the *National Herald*, December 5, 1939), pp. 264–267; "Prepare for All Eventualities" (Ghaziabad speech, January 9, 1940), pp. 283–284; and "[Letter] To J. Holmes Smith" (January 10, 1940), pp. 288–289. Smith was an American clergyman-educator working in India. Also see *SWJN 12*: "Non-belligerency and Not Neutrality" (Calcutta address to Congress workers, April 18, 1942), pp. 251–252.

Chapter 6: The Netaji

1. Bose, *Struggle*, pp. 419–430, 431–433. The entire texts of both the memorandum and the "Supplementary Memorandum to the German Government," dated May 3, 1941, are given.

2. *Ibid.* Quote on p. 423.

3. *Ibid.*

4. *Ibid.*

5. Bose, *Impressions*, p. 70.

6. Bose, *Struggle*, pp. 419–430, 431–433.

7. *Ibid.* Quote on pp. 420–421. Also see "Secret Message to Comrades in India," dated May 20, 1941, from Berlin, in *Struggle*, pp. 434–437. Bose once remarked to an acquaintance that the Führer reminded him of the Fakir of Ipi, but the comparison is fairly ridiculous. See Bose, "Netaji and Nazis," pp. 321–332.

8. *Ibid.*

9. *Ibid.*

10. *Ibid.* As World War II drew to a close, Jawaharlal Nehru reflected that imperialist oppression had forced patriots from colonial Asia to organize in Nazi Germany in the 1930s. Unfortunately, he did not provide names. See "The End of Domination" (Punjab Congress speech, July 13, 1945), in the *SWJN 14*, ed. S. Gopal (New Delhi, 1981), pp. 38–40.

11. Ciano, *Hidden Diary* (entry for December 15, 1938), p. 205.

12. Milan Hauner, "The Soviet Threat to Afghanistan and India 1938–1940," *Modern Asian Studies*, 15 (April 1981): pp. 287–309. The article is taken from his book, *India*

in Axis Strategy: Germany, Japan and Indian Nationalists in the Second World War German Historical Institute London Series 7 (Stuttgart: Klett-Cotta, 1981).

13. Maclean, *Approaches*, p. 47. Maclean mentioned an encounter with "Stark," a mysterious member of the Commissariat of Foreign Affairs in Georgia, USSR. During his term as a Soviet diplomat in Afghanistan, Stark became involved in revolutionary espionage in India.

14. *Ibid.*; and Hauner, "Soviet Threat," pp. 287–309.

15. *Ibid.*

16. *Ibid.* Mirza Ali Khan, the Fakir of Ipi, took offense at the British reaction to a kidnapping case concerning his tribe of Pathans. He used this incident as a rallying cause to declare an independent Pathan state, or "Pakhtunistan." *Pakhtun* is a local variation of the name "Pathan." American freelance writer Christopher Rand visited the famous Muslim rebel in his mountain headquarters sometime after the revolt. See Christopher Rand, *A Nostalgia for Camels* (Boston, 1957), pp. 86–117.

17. Bose, *Beacon*, pp. 118–126; Toye, *Tiger*, pp. 61–62; and John Toland, *Adolf Hitler* (Garden City, New York, 1976), pp. 651, 654.

18. *Ibid.* Also Goebbels, *Diaries* (entries for January 30, and March 20, 1942), pp. 60, 138.

19. *Ibid.*

20. *Ibid.* In "Secret Message to Comrades in India," Bose expected the fascists to officially commit themselves to Free India by June 1941. This, of course, never happened. See Bose, *Struggle*, pp. 434–437. The British had at least one Indian in Europe working on their side, but in a different way than the Germans used theirs. Noor Inayat Khan was an Indian-American woman writer who volunteered to be a communications spy in Occupied France. Khan, alias Jeanne-Marie Regnier and code-named MADELEINE, sent vital information to Sir William Stephenson (INTREPID), until her capture and execution in September 1944. See Stevenson, *INTREPID*, pp. 235–253.

21. Count Galeazzo Ciano, *The Ciano Diaries 1939–1943*, ed. by Hugh Gibson (Garden City, New York, 1946), (entry for June 6, 1941), p. 363. Also "The Russo-German War and Indian Struggle" in Bose, *Struggle*, pp. 438–440; and Bose, *Beacon*, pp. 118–126. Quotes from *Struggle*, p. 440; and *Diaries*, 363. Ciano's skepticism was an improvement over his earlier attitude toward the Indian question. In January 1938, after Bose expressed his concerns about Ethiopia, Ciano wrote that Indians were "flabby people, incapable of strong reactions, and that they will not get independence until other forces bring about the collapse of Great Britain. And perhaps even then the country will only get a new master." See Ciano, *Hidden Diary* (entry for January 20, 1938), pp. 65–66.

22. Hauner, "Soviet Threat," pp. 287–309; Giani, *Indian Independence 1*, p. 77; and Toye, *Tiger*, p. 68.

23. Goebbels, *Diaries* (entry for May 11, 1942), p. 211; Bose, *Struggle*, pp. 438–440; Bose, *Beacon*, pp. 118–126; and Bose, "Netaji and Nazis," pp. 321–332. Quote from *Diaries*, p. 211.

24. Bose, *Struggle*, ibid. "The Russo-German War and Indian Struggle" is the translation of Woermann's report, marked Berlin, July 17, 1941.

25. *Ibid.*

26. Bose, *Beacon*, pp. 118–126; and Toye, *Tiger*, pp. 61–62.

27. Shun Higuchi, a contributor to the "Some Reminiscences" section of Tatsuo Hayashida's study, noted that Bose held infrequent lunches in Berlin. At one, the Archbishop of Syria, the expatriate Premier of Iraq, and the Afghan ambassador joined a few Germans and Higuchi, at the time a military attaché at the Japanese embassy. See Shun Higuchi, "Movement from Outside," in Tatsuo Hayashida, *Netaji Subhas Chandra Bose: His Great Struggle and Martyrdom*, trans. by Biswanath Chatterjee (Bombay, 1970), pp. 139–140. Arun Coomer Bose suggested that Subhas Bose spoke German. While he

undoubtedly studied the language, he used translators, indicating limited mastery. He probably developed even better command of German after his 1942 marriage to his Austrian secretary. See Bose, "Netaji and Nazis," pp. 321–332.

28. Kurti, *Bose I Knew*, pp. 2–66. Quote on p. 9.

29. *Ibid*. Quote from pp. 49–50.

30. *Ibid*.

31. *Ibid*.

32. Bose, *Beacon*, p. 56; and Toye, *Tiger*, p. 75.

33. Bose, *Struggle*, pp. 441–442; and Bose, *Beacon*, p. 130. Perhaps Bose's first broadcast was anticlimactic. In May 1941, the Nazis' Irish-American collaborator, William Joyce, aka Lord Haw Haw, talked about India in one of his radio programs. He had the stunning news that Azad Hind workers had been parachuted into India from Nazi planes. This was, of course, a lie, but it excited the Bengalis and upset the Raj. After nearly a year of fading anticipation, one can understand why India's residents did not respond to the next announcement relating to Azad Hind. See James, *Raj*, p. 555.

34. Giani, *Indian Independence 1*, pp. 103–106; and John J. Stephan, *Hawaii Under the Rising Sun: Japan's Plans for Conquest After Pearl Harbor* (Honolulu, 1984), pp. 136–137. The INA commandant hoped that the joint resolution would be signed in time for the Indian Independence League convention, planned for June 1942 in Bangkok.

35. Ciano, *Hidden Diary* (entries for January 24 and February 15, 1938), pp. 66, 75; Ciano, *Diaries* (entries for February 18, April 14, May 3, May 4, May 5, and August 10, 1942), pp. 450, 473, 480, 481, 482, 513; and Goebbels, *Diaries* (entries for March 1 and May 11, 1942), pp. 107, 211. On March 5, 1942, Goebbels wrote that he planned to make Bose's program known to the public — and so binding the Nazis to it — after Bose met with Hitler. See *Diaries*, p. 111.

36. *Ibid*.

37. MAGIC Summary No. 304, January 24, 1943. US intelligence noted that, "On several previous occasions Germany has tried to persuade the Japanese to allow Bose to return to the Far East. There is some evidence, however, that the Japanese have not been very anxious to have him come, apparently preferring to place their hopes on their own candidate, Rash Behari Bose." Rash Behari Bose, alias Rash Behari Basu, was not a relative of Subhas Bose.

38. Bose, *Beacon*, pp. 60–64, 118, 135–139; James, *Raj*, p. 573; and [United States] War Department, Office of the Assistant Chief of Staff, G-2, MAGIC Summary (not numbered) SRS621, June 6, 1942, pp. 4–5, reel 1, frame 0428. The quote is taken from the MAGIC Summary. The possibility exists that Bose actually met Hitler for the first time during his 1933–1936 travels in Germany. R.C. Majumdar, chief editor of *Struggle for Freedom*, cited an obscure reference, Otto Zarek's *German Odyssey* (London, 1941). According to Majumdar, Zarek, a Jewish theater critic from Vienna, supposedly met Subhas Bose. Bose claimed to have conferred with Hitler in 1935, and, oddly enough, judged him to be very sympathetic to Free India. Bose allegedly told Zarek, "Hitler is our natural ally. And he knows it. I put before him detailed plans for an agreement between Germany and the Indian Free State which is to come into force when we gain our freedom. He is studying the project. We shall get his support when we revolt." Unless the strange wording was a factor of translation or memory, this author must note that Bose never called India the "Indian Free State." Unfortunately, my follow-up on this citation failed to turn up this quote. Bose himself briefly alluded to an earlier meeting with the Führer. In a July 1943 letter to his Indian National Army officers, Bose, by then relocated by the Japanese, assured his men of Berlin's longstanding support for their cause. See Majumdar, *Struggle*, p. 568 ff; and Giani, *Indian Independence 2*, pp. 37–43.

39. *Ibid*.

40. Bose, *Beacon*, pp. 135–139. Quote on p. 139. In his July 1943 INA letter, Bose

claimed that he did seek Hitler's advice. Germany's "experienced revolutionary" maintained that "a well-equipped army of a few thousands [*sic*] would be able to control millions of unarmed revolutionaries. He added that so long as an external power did not knock at the frontier no change could be expected in the internal situation. We should form part of this external power.... It is we, who should create a second front in India." See Giani, *Indian Independence 2*, p. 41.

41. Bose, *Impressions*, pp. 154–155; and Bose, "India Abroad" in *Eyes*, pp. 76–93.

42. *Ibid.* For years, Bose wanted a similar group to open in France. Before the Netaji's break with the Indian National Congress, Nehru described the difficulties he and Bose faced in wooing France. See "[Letter] To Charles Francois Bacon" (December 23, 1938), in *SWJN 9*, p. 223. Oddly enough, the Vichy Government refused to recognize Bose's Provisional Government of Free India in 1943.

43. Bose, *Beacon*, pp. 130–132. When the British Broadcasting Corporation referred to the Azad Hind Radio station as merely another branch of Berlin's propaganda machine, Bose's office naturally rejected the claim. The Indian station angrily responded that, "Free India Radio is the voice of freedom-loving India." See "Free India Radio: BBC Nazi Charges Denied" (March 5, 1942) in the Appendix to George Orwell, *Orwell: The War Commentaries*, ed. by W.J. West (London, 1985), p. 222. This radio commentary was originally taken from the BBC's "Summary of World Broadcasts" transcripts [SWB 962 Free India Radio. IG (ii)].

44. *Ibid.* Also Goebbels, *Diaries* (entry for March 1, 1942), p. 107. See the following Azad Hind Radio broadcasts, some personally delivered by Bose. They were reprinted in the Appendix of Orwell, *Commentaries*, but originally appeared in the BBC's "Summary of World Broadcasts" transcripts: "India's Opportunity for Freedom" (January 1, 1942) [SWB 898 Zeesen IG (i)], pp. 220–221; "India's Hour of Destiny" (by Subhas Chandra Bose, February 28, 1942) [SWB 957 Free India Radio IG (ii)], pp. 221–222; "The Formation of Greater East Asia" (by Furst Urach, March 10, 1942) [SWB 967 Frankfurt German Home Stations IA (x–xi)], pp. 222–223; "Message to Indians" (by Subhas Chandra Bose, July 20, 1942) [SWB 1099 Free India Radio IG (i)], pp. 225–228; and "Guerrilla War and Plan of Action" (by Subhas Chandra Bose, September 4, 1942) [SWB 1145 Free India Radio IG (i–iv)], pp. 230–235.

45. Goebbels, *Diaries* (entries for March 1, March 2, March 14, March 26, and April 6, 1942), pp. 107, 108, 123, 144, 161, 162. Also, Robert Edwin Herzstein, *The War that Hitler Won: The Most Infamous Propaganda Campaign in History* (New York, 1978), p. 341. Even after consulting Goebbels' diaries, Arun Coomer Bose concludes that Subhas Bose intentionally kept Germany's role secret from his countrymen. Bose suggests that the Netaji waited until the Nazis committed themselves to his cause before crediting them. This author believes that Arun Coomer Bose is just another patriotic writer trying to inflate the image of the Netaji while he was in the hands of the Nazis. See Bose, "Netaji and Nazis," pp. 321–332.

46. Orwell, *Commentaries*, pp. 11–23. The information comes from editor W.J. West's introduction.

47. *Ibid.*, (broadcasts delivered on January 17, February 14, February 21, March 14, March 21, March 28, April 4, April 18, May 2, and May 16, 1942), pp. 35–39, 50–53, 54–57, 60–64, 64–67, 67–72, 72–75, 76–80, 84–87, 92–96.

48. *Ibid.*, pp. 11–23.

49. Quote and information from "Bose: Effect of his Broadcasts" PRO F0371/31799 XC/A/048065. Also see "Japanese Propaganda: Visit of Subhas Chandra Bose to Japan," From: Mr. Wright, British Embassy, Washington, DC to Far Eastern Department [British Foreign Office], No. 2209/1/43, dated July 15, 1943, Public Records Office, London Reference: FO371/35911 XC/A/048065. In remarking upon Bose's new partnership with Japan, the British embassy noted that, "While Bose's propaganda appeals have to date

won him no substantial number of new adherents, his following in the populous and strategically located province of Bengal represents a potential menace" (p. 2). In *The War that Hitler Won*, American historian Robert Herzstein stated that, "…Hitler sadly underestimated the force of Indian nationalism, over which he had no control, only to fall into the trap of supporting an opportunist without influence…" (p. 340). In light of the second document mentioned above, Herzstein's assessment of Bose as merely an anti–British spokesman seems not entirely accurate.

Chapter 7: The Fauj

1. Bose, *Struggle*, pp. 451–459.
2. See Chapters 3 and 8.
3. Toye, *Tiger*, pp. 68–69.
4. Ganpuley, *Germany*, preface, pp. 73–79, 92; Beaumont, *Sword*, p. 179; and S.A. Ayer, *Unto Him A Witness* (Bombay, 1951), pp. 2–7. Ayer was Bose's Propaganda Minister for the provisional Government of Free India in Singapore and Burma.
5. *Ibid.* Also, Ganpuley, *Germany*, pp. 19–20; and Bose, *Beacon*, p. 126. Arun Coomer Bose suggests that Bose's friendship with the Mufti of Jerusalem led to his increased influence, but this author has found no other source to corroborate this, or even a reference to a meeting between the two. In a footnote to his important 1972 article, "Netaji and the Nazis: A Study in their Relations," Arun Coomer Bose claims that Hitler granted the Netaji full diplomatic authority after their meeting three months before. In the July 1943 INA letter, Subhas Bose complimented the Nazis for their cooperation, which included use of their communications facilities, captured Allied propaganda, and tours of military bases. See Bose, "Netaji and Nazis," pp. 321–332; and Giani, *Indian Independence 2*, p. 41.
6. Beaumont, *Sword*, p. 179.
7. Ganpuley, *Germany*, p. 20; Bose, *Beacon*, pp. 133–134; and Toye, *Tiger*, pp. 69–74.
8. Ganpuley, *Germany*, p. 96.
9. Bose, *Beacon*, pp. 133–134; and Toye, *Tiger*, pp. 69–74.
10. *Ibid*; and Ganpuley, *Germany*, pp. 70–71
11. Ganpuley, *Germany*, p. 96. Part of this quote appeared in Toye, *Tiger*, p. 72.
12. Bose, *Beacon*, pp. 133–134; Ganpuley, *Germany*, pp. 73–79, 82–83, 92; and Toye, *Tiger*, pp. 62–63, 69–74.
13. *Ibid.* Also, Beaumont, *Sword*, p. 179.
14. *Ibid.* Quote from Toye, *Tiger*, p. 70. The British apparently had trouble with their Indian troops stationed in Egypt. German and Azad Hind broadcasters reported the start of a rebellion on the El Alamein front, culminating in the assassination of a British general. London announced that this officer died on the battlefield, but according to Bose, he was murdered by an Indian soldier in the Royal Indian Army. With such stories floating around the Wehrmacht, it is little wonder that German officers questioned the use of Indian prisoners of war in their own army. See the following transcripts of Axis broadcasts, reprinted in the Appendix of Orwell, *Commentaries*: "General Gott Shot by Indian N.C.O." (August 13, 1942) [SWB 1122 German Home Service via Luxemburg IA (xxi)], 229; and "Egypt: Indian Troops 'Unreliable' " (August 26, 1942) [SWB 1136 Free India Radio IG (i)], pp. 229–230.
15. *Ibid.*
16. *Ibid.* Also, Hauner, "Soviet Threat," pp. 287–309; and Toland, *Hitler*, pp. 716, 722–728. The general consensus among historians is that the Indian Legion virtually died after El Alamein and Stalingrad, but that was not the case. According to a November 1944 MAGIC report, the 950th Indian Grenadier Regiment participated in action in France,

under the command of A.C. Nambiyar (Nambiar), a writer and Bose's longtime agent in Berlin. Nambiyar claimed few casualties and mentioned some expansion of what he called the "Indian People's Army." No follow-up on this matter was ever made by US military intelligence. In a tribute to the fallen heroes of the Asia-based Indian National Army, Kesar Singh Giani referred to Bose's Indian Legion as "affiliated" with the INA. He lauded one Mohammed Rashid, a 19-year-old soldier who singlehandedly paralyzed a convoy of American armored transports in France. See [United States] War Department, Office of the Assistant Chief of Staff, G-2, MAGIC Diplomatic Summary No. 972, SRS1494, November 22, 1944, Copy No. MI-3, pp. 2–3, reel 11, frame 0703; and Giani, *Indian Independence 2*, p. 122. After the war, Dr. Nambiyar became India's Ambassador to Germany. See Bose, "Netaji and Nazis," pp. 321–332.

17. Walter Schellenberg, *Hitler's Secret Service*, 3rd ed. (New York, 1971), (originally published as *The Labyrinth*), pp. 254–255. As indicated earlier, the Gestapo tailed Bose when he first arrived in Berlin in 1941. That the police investigated him is not surprising, considering his controversial past and German xenophobia. Bringing the RSHA into the case, however, seems to suggest serious concerns on the part of the Nazis.

18. *Ibid.*

19. Bose, *Beacon*, pp. 100–112; and Kurti, *Bose I Knew*, particularly the letters in the Appendix. Of course, Bhagat Ram Talwar and a few others who spirited Bose out of India were admitted Soviet spies, and Bose had some help from dissident CPI members during his escape. It is interesting to note that British military authorities in India occasionally mislabeled him a communist. See James, *Raj*, pp. 554, 576.

Chapter 8: Darling of the Axis

1. Subhas Chandra Bose, *On to Delhi*, ed. K.M. Tamhankar (Bombay, 1946), pp. 10–11.

2. Mahatma Gandhi, "Australia and Japan," in *CWMG (1905–1906) 5*, p. 115. This was originally published in the *Indian Opinion* on October 28, 1905. Also see his related articles, "The Rise of Japan," in *CWMG (1905–1906) 5*, pp. 57–58; and "Japan and Russia," in *CWMG (1903–1905) 4*, pp. 466–467. These, too, were published in the *Indian Opinion*.

3. Bose, *Impressions*, pp. 32–50; and Thomas A. Bailey, *A Diplomatic History of the American People*, 9th ed. (Englewood Cliffs, New Jersey, 1974), pp. 515–528, 634–654.

4. Jan Pluvier, *South-East Asia from Colonialism to Independence* (Kuala Lumpur, Malaysia, 1974), pp. 191–202; Stephan, *Hawaii*, pp. 136–137; and Bose, *Impressions*, ibid. Quote from "Attached Document: Reference Materials for Answering Questions at the Imperial Conference on September 6, 1941 Regarding 'The Essentials for Carrying out the Empire's Policies,'" in Nobutaka Ike, ed and trans., *Japan's Decision for War: Records of the 1941 Policy Conferences* (Stanford, California, 1967), pp. 152–153.

5. John Toland, *The Rising Sun: The Decline and Fall of the Japanese Empire 1936–1945* (New York, 1970), pp. 7–86; and Sabura Ienaga, *The Pacific War 1931–1945: A Critical Perspective on Japan's Role in World War II*, English ed. (New York, 1978), pp. 3–54. Jawaharlal Nehru condemned the Rising Sun as an evil in "India and the War" (Bombay speech, June 18, 1942), in *SWJN 12*, pp. 341–345; and "Real Peace As Far Away As Ever" (New Delhi press conference, January 21, 1946), in *SWJN 14*, pp. 471–473.

6. *Ibid.*

7. "Records of the 21st Liaison Conference, May 3, 1941"; and "Attached Document: 'Draft Proposal for Hastening the End of the War Against the United States, Great Britain, the Netherlands, and Chiang' for the 69th Liaison Conference, November 15, 1941," in Ike, *Japan's Decision*, pp. 24–27, 247–249. Although they took responsibility for the Asian

campaign, the Japanese still wanted Germany and Italy to "carry out measures against India" (pp. 247–249). It is also worth noting that the Japanese considered themselves fully involved in the war against the United States even before the bombing of Pearl Harbor. Also see Goebbels, *Diaries* (entries for January 22, January 30, February 22, March 13 and March 20, 1942), pp. 36, 60, 98, 123, 137–138.

8. Goebbels, *Diaries* (entries for March 20, April 12, and April 13, 1942), pp. 137, 167.

9. *Ibid.* (entry for April 25, 1942), p. 184. Ironically, Hitler also hoped that the US would keep Japanese imperialism in check. See Stevenson, *INTREPID*, p. 172.

10. Pluvier, *South-East Asia*, pp. 199–202; and Ienaga, *Pacific*, pp. 153–174.

11. Toye, *Tiger*, p. 2; Corr, *War*, pp. 53–60; Ghosh, *Army*, p. 3; and Hayashida, *Netaji*, pp. 11–13. The term "Aryan" actually refers to an ancient race that inhabited the northern half of the Indian subcontinent.

12. "Anti-British Indian Dies in Tokyo Exile" (Basu's obituary), *New York Times*, January 23, 1945, p. 10; Ghosh, *Army*, pp. 1–3; Hale, *Trouble*, p. 53; Vajpeyi, *Extremist*, pp. 193–194; and P. Kodanda Rao, *Foreign Friends of India's Freedom* (Bangalore, India, 1973), p. 185. During and immediately after World War I, Japan, as a British ally, officially condemned Indian independence, and threatened to arrest Indian revolutionaries as criminals. This situation changed with the rise of militaristic politicians in Japan.

13. "Toyama of Japan, Terrorist Leader" (obituary), *New York Times*, October 6, 1944, p. 23; Ben-Ami Shillony, "Patterns of Violence: Political Terrorism in Prewar Japan," *Asian and African Studies* 13 (undated): pp. 242–263; Corr, *War*, p. 51; and Beaumont, *Sword*, p. 177. The Black Dragon Society had close ties with European, as well as Japanese fascists. In 1937, Mussolini and Ciano met with a Black Dragon named Nakano, who conveyed to them the anti–British sentiments of the Japanese Prime Minister, Prince Konoe Fumimaro. See Ciano, *Hidden Diary* (entry for December 21, 1937), p. 47.

14. Toye, *Tiger*, pp. 1–2; Ghosh, *Army*, pp. 17–23, 47–48; and Joyce C. Lebra, "Japanese and Western Models for the Indian National Army," *Japan Interpreter* 7 (1972): 364–375.

15. *Ibid.* Also see Hayashida, *Netaji*, pp. 11–15. After the IIL established a firm alliance with Fujiwara, Giani Pritam Singh began using the letter "F" as the symbol of the League, and later, to distinguish INA positions on maps. To Singh, Fujiwara's initial stood for friendship and freedom. The F Kikan was eventually expanded to handle Chinese, Malayan and other nationalist clients.

16. *Ibid.*

17. Ayer, *Witness*, pp. 3–25; and Ghosh, *Army*, pp. 38–40.

18. Corr, *War*, p. 52; Ghosh, *Army*, pp. 48–56; and Beaumont, *Sword*, p. 177. Beaumont claims that Basu married Toyama's daughter.

19. Beaumont, *Sword*; Hayashida, *Netaji*, pp. 13–15; and Shah Nawaz Khan, ed., *The INA Heroes — Autobiographies of Maj. Gen. Shanawaz, Col. Prem K. Sahgal, and Col. Gurbax Singh Dhillon of the Azad Hind Fauj* (Lahore, 1946), pp. 16–30. Beaumont suggests that Basu actually proposed the formation of the INA, and both the Japanese government and his Indian colleagues saw profound value in the undertaking.

20. Ghosh, *Army*, pp. 25–30; Corr, *War*, pp. 67–89; and Lebra, "Models," pp. 364–375.

21. *Ibid.* Major Singh firmly denied the accusations of his early pro–Axis leanings at his court-martial after the war. In the early 1970s Singh began his memoirs, but apparently they were never published. Writer-historian Khushwant Singh researched Mohan Singh's role and attitudes. In his papers, the INA commandant said that after he was stranded, "the dormant patriotic spirit became alive. I felt that if I approached the Japanese and succeeded in obtaining their help to start a movement for India's independence, I was bound to attract a number of soldiers and was sure [to] benefit India in several ways."

See Khushwant Singh, "INA Myth and Reality," *Illustrated Weekly of India* 95 (September 8, 1974): 28–31. Quote from p. 28.

22. *Ibid.* Toye wrote that Giani Pritam Singh swayed Mohan Singh into joining the movement. See Toye, *Tiger*, p. 2.

23. *Ibid.* Also, Hayashida, *Netaji*, p. 17; and Toye, *Tiger*, p. 7.

24. *Ibid.*

25. Beaumont, *Sword*, pp. 177–178; and Toye, *Tiger*, pp. 9–13. Mohan Singh admitted that after "the Japanese failed in their efforts to brainwash a person, they seldom hesitated to smash his brains." See Singh, "INA Myth," p. 28–31. Quote from p. 29. This certainly conflicts with one of Singh's earlier remarks, in which he claimed that the POWs had so much enthusiasm for the INA, that the Japanese were amazed. See James, *Raj*, pp. 548–549. In *King Rat*, James Clavell's 1962 novel set in the Changi camp, a character named Colonel Brant suffered psychological scars after his Sikh regiment turned against him. Clavell, who was held in Changi himself, described how viciously Sikh prison guards behaved toward their former officers. See James Clavell, *King Rat*, 4th ed. (New York, 1963), p. 16. Like Clavell, the novelist Paul Scott wrote of the barbarity of World War II and its effects on the waning Raj. The protagonist of *The Birds of Paradise* (1962) endured similar treatment at the hands of Indian camp guards working for the Japanese. See Paul Scott, *The Birds of Paradise*, (London, 1990), p. 158.

26. Ayer, *Witness*, pp. 13–25; and Khan, *Heroes*, pp. 16–50, 112–117, 164. Quotes from Khan, p. 17. Sahgal particularly felt misgivings about the endeavor. Always certain that the British could never lose Singapore, when the Japanese did conquer the island, he worried that India would fall next. He knew the INA could be a tool for that purpose. Unimpressed by GEA rhetoric, he saw the exploitation of Malaya. Japanese talk of freeing Asia seemed as unrealistic as those rallies in Kuala Lumpur, where the flags of India, Malaya and the Rising Sun were crossed at the head of every glittering parade.

27. Ghosh, *Army*, pp. 27–37.

28. *Ibid.*

29. *Ibid.* Quote from p. 28.

30. Beaumont, *Sword*, pp. 177–178; and Toye, *Tiger*, pp. 9–13. According to Azad Hind bureaucrat Kesar Singh Giani, the Japanese attitude toward POWs was as follows: "Col. Iwakuro says that they are under the Japanese control, intended to be used for work. If Mohan Singh wants to pick up men for the I.N.A. from prisoners without consultation with Japanese authorities, there would be trouble." See Giani, *Indian Independence 1*, p. 103. Japanese historian Saburo Ienaga noted that INA troops were sent as far away as Rabaul, off New Guinea, and Timor, a Portuguese colony in the East Indies. See Ienaga, *Pacific*, p. 175. To further complicate matters, N. Raghwan and a Colonel Allaggapan, the Swaraj Institute's directors, accused the Japanese of sending some of their espionage students into India in December 1942, without consulting any IIL or INA officials. See Giani, *Indian Independence 1*, pp. 142–143.

31. Toye, *Tiger*; and Ghosh, *Army*, pp. 104–121. Quote from Ghosh, p. 120. Obviously, the INA and IIL were not separated, as Singh desired. Basu truly governed both organizations.

32. Bose, *Struggle*, pp. 460–461. It should be noted that Bose wrote the first letter on May 22nd, nine days after Premier Tojo publicly called for India's freedom. See Goebbels, *Diaries* (entry for May 13, 1942), p. 212.

33. Bose, *Struggle*, pp. 461–462. The second "Call From East Asia" letter was dated December 5, 1942.

34. Ayer, *Witness*, p. 3; and Giani, *Indian Independence 1*, p. 84. The relevant Bangkok Resolutions also appear in Toye, *Tiger*, p. 199. "Sjt." is an abbreviation for "Srijit," a title of respect. Three months after the Bangkok Conference, Basu again acknowledged Japan's assistance, and thanked Tokyo for sending delegates to "the recent independence rally at

Bangkok." See [United States] War Department, Office of the Assistant Chief of Staff, G-2, MAGIC Summary No. [unclear], SRS 711, September 11, 1942, pp. 14–15, reel 2, frame 0605.

35. MAGIC Summary, June 6, 1942. Also, [United States] War Department, Office of the Assistant Chief of Staff, G-2, MAGIC Summary No. 304, SRS 847, January 24, 1943, Copy No. 15, pp. 2–4, reel 4, frame 0262; [United States] War Department, Office of the Assistant Chief of Staff, G-2, MAGIC Summary, No. 305, SRS 848, January 25, 1943, Copy No. 15, pp. 5–6, reel 4, frame 0292; and [United States] War Department, Office of the Assistant Chief of Staff, G-2, MAGIC Summary No. 335, SRS 886, February 24, 1943, Copy No. 15, pp. 4–6, reel 4, frame 0638. Quote taken from the last reference, p. 4.

36. [United States] War Department, Office of the Assistant Chief of Staff, G-2, MAGIC Summary No. 411, SRS 962, May 11, 1943, Copy No. 15, pp. 10–11, reel 5, frame 0464. Also see Bose, *Beacon*, p. 144. Unknown to the Nazis, American intelligence already knew about Bose's departure from Germany. Basu's location was not a secret to the Allies either, contrary to what Tokyo believed. See "Anti-British Indian," *New York Times*, January 23, 1945, p. 10.

37. [United States] War Department, Office of the Assistant Chief of Staff, G-2, MAGIC Summary, February 24, 1943; [United States] War Department, Office of the Assistant Chief of Staff, G-2, MAGIC Summary No. 447, SRS 998, June 16, 1943, Copy No. 15, pp. 8–10, reel 6, frame 0044; and Giani, *Indian Independence 1*, pp. 134–144. Quote from MAGIC Summary, June 16, 1943, p. 10. It is possible that the US War Department's assessment of Japan's reluctance for Bose's return may be in error. According to Giani, by 1943, Basu had been labeled a "dictator" by Indian revolutionaries, who resented his heavy-handedness in filling the power void he created by removing Mohan Singh (p. 134). In April 1942, a conference between Japanese military and foreign affairs officials concluded that Bose would fit neatly into their plans for breaking the colonial government. See "Concerning the Essentials in the Treatment of Subhas Chandra Bose" (memorandum from the Liaison Conference of April 17, 1942), in Ghosh, *Army*, Appendix, p. 271. Giani and the memorandum suggest Basu's fall from grace and Imperial General Headquarters' early interest in importing the Netaji. Tatsuo Hayashida, a Japanese army officer and attaché who knew the Netaji in Berlin and followed his career, suggested that Bose's travel plans were completely engineered by Colonel Yamamoto Satoshi, who replaced Iwakuro as director of the F Kikan intelligence unit. Yamamoto, like Hayashida, had been posted to the embassy in Berlin and became personally acquainted with Bose. Yamamoto renamed F Kikan the *Hikari* Kikan (Light and Glory Agency). See Hayashida, *Netaji*, p. 24; and Giani, *Indian Independence 2*, p. 31 ff. Bose's exact travel route has always been the subject of some debate, and in particular, where he landed in Asia. See the 1999 online article, "Netaji Subhas Bose," at *http://www.sitemarvel.com/bengalonline/netaji.html*

38. MAGIC Summary, June 16, 1943, pp. 8–10. Quote from p. 9. It is mildly surprising that the Japanese used the plural "Boses" here, since the Netaji's brothers, particularly the politician Sarat, kept their activities strictly domestic. Perhaps the plural refers to Rash Behari Basu, who used the name Bose.

39. Bose, "European Chess-board," pp. 201–207; and Bose, *Eyes*, pp. 214–239.

40. Subhas Chandra Bose, "Japan's Role in the Far East," in *Eyes*, pp. 180–213. As a congressman in India, Bose supported aid to war-torn China in the 1930s.

41. Bose, "This War and its Significance," pp. 9–14; and Subhas Chandra Bose, "Observation by H.E. Netaji Subhas Chandra Bose on the Present Day Situation Made at a Press Conference," in *Blood Bath* (Lahore, 1947), pp. 22–29. Also see Giani, *Indian Independence 2*, pp. 2–6. In "This War and its Significance," a June 24, 1943 speech broadcast from Tokyo, Bose described the war as a clash of convention and the forces of change, with the revolutionary Axis holding the keys to liberation.

42. *Ibid.* The fact that large numbers of overseas Indians reportedly cooperated with the Japanese occupation forces, as well as supporting India's own growing militancy, certainly worried London. Bose's warnings to ignore any offers of self-government referred to the Cripps Mission, which is discussed later.

43. Giani, *Indian Independence 2*, pp. 7–10; and "The Guilty: Subhas Chandra Bose," *Collier's*, 114 (September 30, 1944): p. 52.

44. Orwell, *Commentaries* (broadcasts delivered on March 21, April 4, April 25, 1942, and January 9, 1943), pp. 64–67, 72–75, 80–84, 198–202.

45. *Ibid.* (broadcasts delivered on March 14, April 4, April 18, May 16 and August 8, 1942), pp. 60–64, 72–75, 76–80, 92–96, 127–131. The quote is taken from the May 16th broadcast.

46. Giani, *Indian Independence 2*, p. 9.

47. *Ibid.*, p. 7.

48. *Ibid.*, pp. 10–29. Also, Hayashida, *Netaji*, pp. 43–50; and Ayer, *Witness*, pp. 5–30. To broaden his political support, Bose began to praise Gandhi. According to *Nation* correspondent John W. Gerber, Bose even went so far as to claim that the Mahatma supported the INA in principle. This, of course, was untrue, but Azad Hind revolutionaries wanted to hear such encouragement. See John W. Gerber, "Japan's Choice for India," *Nation*, 157 (September 18, 1943): 323–325.

49. *Ibid.*

50. *Ibid.*

51. *Ibid.* Also see Subhas Chandra Bose, "The Indian National Army: Netaji's Broadcast over the I.N.A. Headquarters Broadcasting Station on the First Anniversary of the Formation of the I.N.A.," in *Blood Bath*, pp. 30–35.

52. Giani, *Indian Independence 2*, p. 22.

53. *Ibid.*, pp. 10–29; and Ghosh, *Army*, pp. 120–129. The "Indian language" probably means Hindi.

54. Bose, *Impressions*, pp. 92–93; and Bose, *Beacon*, p. 76. Needless to say, Mohan Singh's wish that the INA would function independently of the IIL was never fulfilled.

55. Subhas Chandra Bose, "Our Achievements of One Year" and "Our Programme for the Future," in *Blood Bath*, pp. 9–17, 18–21. Also see Giani, *Indian Independence 2*, pp. 30–32, 82–89; and Ayer, *Witness*, pp. 6–30. The Rani of Jhansi Regiment, named after a popular heroine of the 1850s, received a great deal of propaganda attention. See Gerber, "Japan's Choice," 323–325.

56. Giani, *Indian Independence 2*, pp. 43–61; Ayer, *Witness*; and Hayashida, *Netaji*, pp. 53–57. Hayashida described Bose as "the Modern Ulysses." Bose's Thai contemporary, Pibul, generated controversy in 1999, more than 30 years after his death. Bangkok's major English-language newspaper, the *Nation*, listed him among the top "100 Thai Artists and Entertainers of the Century." The newspaper justified putting him in this odd category because of his "individual impact on the culture." See William Barnes, "Cultural Comment as Hitler Admirer Joins Warblers and Puppeteers," *South China Morning Post* (Hong Kong), July 7, 1999, p. 10.

57. R.C. Majumdar, ed., *History of the Freedom Movement in India 3*, 2nd ed. (Calcutta, 1977), pp. 581–591; "Bose: Effect of his Broadcasts" PRO FO371/31799 XC/A/048065; and "Japanese Propaganda" PRO FO371/35911 XC/A/048065.

Chapter 9: Nobody's Darling

1. Giani, *Indian Independence 2*, pp. 62–71.

2. *Ibid.*

3. Subhas Chandra Bose, "Proclamation of the Provisional Government of Azad Hind"

appears in both Giani, *Indian Independence 2*, pp. 68–71; and Ayer, *Witness*, Appendix 2, pp. 303–306.

4. Giani, *Indian Independence 2*, pp. 62–71.

5. *Ibid.*

6. *Ibid.*

7. *Ibid*, pp. 71–80; and Ayer, *Witness*, pp. 6–25. Quote from Giani, 72.

8. *Ibid.*

9. A.M. Nair, *An Indian Freedom Fighter in Japan: Memoirs of A.M. Nair* (Bombay, 1982), pp. 239–243; "[Memorandum] Re — The Andamans and the Nicobars" (Decision made in Supreme Military H.Q. Liaison Conference, November 10, 1943); and "[Memorandum] From the Imperial Japanese Navy Department to Subhas Chandra Bose" (signed Vice-Admiral Oka Takazumo, Chief of Military Affairs, Imperial Japanese Navy, November 16, 1943). Both of these documents can be found in Ghosh, *Army*, Appendix, pp. 272, 273–274. For further information, see Bose, "Our Achievements," *Blood Bath*, pp. 9–17; and Toland, *Rising Sun*, pp. 456–460. Despite Bose's brave rejection of the GEA, he did allow himself to be photographed with the new Thai Premier, Abhai Wonges, and Burma's Dr. Ba Maw. The publicity-craving Bengali also appeared in a group portrait taken at the conference, which featured Tojo and Filipino leader Dr. José P. Laurel. Ironically, the Andamans had been the traditional penal colony during the Raj. A.M. Nair became a living legend in Asian intelligence circles, one of the few survivors of this dark period of history. In the 1930s, he studied engineering at a Japanese university. After graduation, he decided that he could best help his native India by remaining in Japan. Like his contemporary, Rash Behari Basu, Nair found a mentor in Toyama Mitsuru, godfather of the Black Dragon Society. Although Nair considered himself an Indian patriot and an active member of the Indian Independence League, he adopted Japanese ways, learned the language and married a local woman. Professionally, Nair had closer ties to the Japanese military than to his Indian colleagues. Nair served as a lieutenant colonel in the Japanese intelligence service. He monitored the puppet state of Manchukuo, sabotaged British business in China, and spied on minority tribes in the Sino-Soviet frontier region. After the war, this remarkable man took a job as manager of a "PX" or post exchange, a department store for US servicemen stationed in Tokyo. In his later years, the spry octogenarian owned an Indian restaurant in Tokyo's trendy Ginza district. See "Japan's World: Yes We Have No Indian Curry," *Asiaweek*, 13 (February 22, 1987), pp. 28–29.

10. Theodore H. White, *In Search of History*, 2nd ed., (New York, 1981), p. 179; Winston S. Churchill, *Triumph and Tragedy: The Second World War* (Boston, 1953), pp. 169–170; Archibald Percival Wavell, *Wavell: The Viceroy's Journal*, ed. by Penderel Moon (London, 1973), (entry for November 17, 1943), p. 37; Bose, *Struggle*, p. 347; Barbara W. Tuchman, *Stilwell and the American Experience in China 1911–45* (New York, 1971), pp. 247, 256–287; and Ronald Lewin, *The Chief: Field Marshal Lord Wavell Commander-in-Chief and Viceroy 1939–1947* (New York, 1980), pp. 157–158, 173–178, 187. Jiang had to support the Raj, since the Allied supply line to China originated in India. This, of course, refers to the Burma Road, which had to be closed in September 1940.

11. [United States] War Department, Office of the Assistant Chief of Staff, G-2, MAGIC Summary No. 636, SRS 1156, December 22, 1943, Copy No. 15, pp. 6–8, reel 7, frame 0839. Quote from p. 7. Also see Hayashida, *Netaji*, pp. 74–75; and Giani, *Indian Independence 2*, pp. 94–95. Jiang located his resistance government in Chungking. Jawaharlal Nehru's early papers give insight into Bose's long-standing interest and concern for China. Nehru, himself a supporter of China, noted that pro-fascist Bose conflicted with fellow congressmen who feared clashing with Japan, Italy or Germany over this issue. Through Bose's lobbying efforts, India sent monetary and even medical assistance to China. The latter, of course, was usually limited to equipment rather than personnel. See Jawaharlal Nehru, *The Discovery of India*, 2nd ed. (Garden City, New York, 1960)

(originally published in 1946), pp. 338–339; "[Letter] To Subhas Chandra Bose" (July 14, 1938), and "Spain, China and India" (interview with *Rude Pravo*, Paris, July 31, 1938), in *SWJN 9*, pp. 58–59, 91–92. Not surprisingly, at least one Chinese source credits Bose's support. Bose presided over a farewell party for Dr. D.S. Kotnis, one of the few an Indian physicians who joined a medical unit in the Chinese Red Army in 1938. See the foreword written by Dr. B.K. Basu in Sheng Xiangong, Lu Jishan and Zhang Changman, *An Indian Freedom Fighter in China: A Tribute to Dr. D. S. Kotnis*, trans. by Zhang Sen, (Beijing, 1983), iv. In 1938, Bose told Italian Foreign Minister Ciano that Indian militants might actually reject Rome's support because of its pro–Japanese stand on China. See Ciano, *Hidden Diary* (entry for January 20, 1938), pp. 65–66. Bose admired China's use of propaganda to gain world sympathy during the Manchurian crisis of 1931. See Bose, *Impressions*, p. 153. The Japanese installed two puppet governments in China proper. They paid very little attention to their Beijing regime, but worked rather closely with Wang Jingwei, their man in Nanking. Author Hayashida refers to him as "Oseiei," the Japanese transliteration for the Chinese character meaning "[Mr.] Wang."

12. Giani, *Indian Independence 2*, pp. 98–100; and Toye, *Tiger*, pp. 94–99.

13. Giani, *Indian Independence 2*, pp. 101–102. Bose also gave a special compliment to his Muslim listeners, by remarking that, "In our history we have instances of numerous kings who chose to become Faqirs for the sake of faith, justice and truth." A faqir was an Islamic pilgrim.

14. *Ibid*, pp. 101–103, 141. Quote from the photo caption between pp. 102 and 103. Also see photo between pp. 158 and 159. For more information, see Ayer, *Witness*, p. 12; and Lee Kam Hing, "Malaya: New State and Old Elites," in Robin Jeffrey, *Asia: The Winning of Independence* (New York, 1981), pp. 212–257. Note p. 226.

15. *Ibid*. Also see Toye, *Tiger*, pp. 94–99; and Wavell, *Journal* (entry for February 17, 1944), p. 56.

16. Giani, *Indian Independence 1*, p. 126.

17. Ghosh, *Army*, pp. 82–84; and Majumdar, *Struggle*, pp. 687–691.

18. Jeffrey, *Asia*, p. 15. British historian Lawrence James described an early statement from Mohan Singh, in which the unlucky commandant spoke in terms of having 89,000 troops at his disposal. Both James and this author agree that this number is so inflated as to be ridiculous. See James, *Raj*, pp. 548–549.

19. G.B. Endacott, *Hong Kong Eclipse* (Hong Kong, 1978), pp. 143, 159, 167, 175–177, 239–240, 246; and Oliver Lindsay, *At the Going Down of the Sun: Hong Kong and South-East Asia 1941–45* (London, 1982), pp. 29–30, 70, 97, 99, 110–112, 124, 146–147, 196, 200, 224, 256–257. The Japanese made some efforts to lure Indian soldiers to their side before the fall of Hong Kong. A few, mostly Sikhs, showed initial interest, while in the former Portuguese enclave of Macao, some Indian residents cooperated with Japanese agents. As a Portuguese territory, Macao was not occupied by Japan, and the situation there was never as desperate as in wartime Hong Kong. See James, *Raj*, pp. 543–544.

20. *Ibid*.

21. *Ibid*.

22. *Ibid*. One bit of popular local folklore suggests that the last tiger shot on Hong Kong Island was killed by an Indian guard working for the Japanese at Stanley Prison.

23. *Ibid*.

24. *Ibid*.

25. Ayer, *Witness*, pp. 8–15; Ghose, *Ideas*, pp. 133–136; and Giani, *Indian Independence 2*, pp. 114–132. Quote from Giani, p. 115. The US War Department intercepted a message from Bose to the German embassy in Kabul, which suggested that the INA would not be able to make an immediate putsch against Calcutta or Delhi, due to the monsoon season. The Netaji warned that Indian activists should contain themselves until the INA attacked Calcutta. The MAGIC summary referred to a report from Rangoon, confirming

Imperial General Headquarters' expectations of "active participation" by the INA. Intelligence noted that previous interceptions implied that Tokyo's major concern was still holding Burma, rather than the liberation of India. See [United States] War Department, Office of the Assistant Chief of Staff, G-2, Special Branch: M.I.D. [Military Intelligence Department], MAGIC Summary No. 687, SRS 1208, February 11, 1944, Copy No. 15, pp. 2–4, reel 8, frame 0427.

26. Giani, *Indian Independence 2*, p. 118. Bose declared March 21st Provisional Government Day in honor of this accomplishment.

27. "Axis Propaganda Barrage Badgers Britain on India," *Newsweek*, 19 (March 16, 1942): pp. 34–35.

28. Moorhouse, *Calcutta*, pp. 99–101; Beaumont, *Sword*, p. 175; Ajit Bhattacharjea, *Jayaprakash Narayan: A Political Biography* (New Delhi, 1975), p. 82; Lakshmi Narain Lal, *Jayaprakash: Rebel Extraordinary* (New Delhi, 1975), pp. 111–115; and Arun Chandra Bhuyan, *The Quit India Movement: The Second World War and Indian Nationalism* Studies in Asian History and Politics 4 (New Delhi, 1975), pp. 112–122.

29. Gopal, *How India*, pp. 434–437.

30. Bose, *Struggle*, pp. 347–349; Majumdar, *Struggle*, pp. 633–645; and Nanda, *Studies*, pp. 96–97.

31. R. Coupland, *The Cripps Mission* (London, 1942); Wavell, *Journal* (entry for July 9, 1942), 10; William L. Shirer, *Gandhi: A Memoir* (New York, 1980), pp. 211–212; Larry Collins and Dominique Lapierre, *Freedom at Midnight*, 4th ed. (New York, 1976), pp. 71–75; and Lewin, *Chief*, pp. 187–190.

32. Bose, *Struggle*, pp. 347–349. Jawaharlal Nehru still regarded Britain as India's chief enemy. He never ruled out India declaring war on Japan, but only as an independent nation. See "On the Solidarity of the Kisans [Unions]" (Allahabad speech, October 15, 1939), in *SWJN 10*, pp. 455–456. Also see "The British Must Leave India" (Bombay press conference, June 10, 1942), and "Time to Wrest Independence" (Gorakhpur speech, July 3, 1942), in *SWJN 12*, pp. 358–359, 382–383. When asked specifically about what appeared to be growing pro-fascist sentiment in India, Nehru said, "During the last three or four months, we have been fighting a definite pro–Japanese feeling in the country, which is not pro–Japanese essentially but so anti–British that it leans over to the Japanese side." See "Demand for British Withdrawal" (New Delhi press conference, July 16, 1942), in *SWJN 12*, pp. 400–404.

33. Bose, *Struggle*, 344. Nehru repeatedly denied that the Indian independence movement was traitorous in nature. See "The Evolving New Order" (Nagpur speech, January 22, 1940), in *SWJN 10*, pp. 308–310; and the following items from *SWJN 12*: "The Passion that Moves Gandhi" (Bombay press conference, June 16, 1942), pp. 367–372, and "Congress Working Committee Resolution on British Withdrawal from India" (draft of a proposal coauthored by Gandhi and Nehru, July 10, 1942), pp. 386–397.

34. Bose, *Struggle*, pp. 349–351; Shirer, *Gandhi*, p. 213; Nanda, *Studies*, p. 97; Majumdar, *Struggle*, pp. 646–648; Ghose, *Ideas*, pp. 122–130; and Francis G. Hutchins, *India's Revolution: Gandhi and the Quit India Movement* (Cambridge, Massachusetts, 1973). The entire text of the Quit India Resolution appears in Bose, *Struggle*, pp. 443–450. Under pressure from both Tokyo and Berlin, Bose was forced to *support* the Quit India Resolution in a notable radio broadcast. Goebbels and the Japanese propagandists wanted to give the impression that Bose had reached a rapprochement with Gandhi and Nehru. See James, *Raj*, p. 573.

35. An anonymous associate of Jayaprakash Narayan wrote "at night, we mistook every star for one of Subhas Babu's planes...." See Lal, *Jayaprakash*, pp. 107–108.

36. Coupland, *Cripps Mission*, p. 28; and Winston S. Churchill, *The Hinge of Fate* The Second World War 4 (Boston, 1950), p. 206. For further insight into Bose's propaganda impact, Nehru's papers proved to be of value. Nehru maintained that Japanese

propaganda might influence Malayan or Burmese nationalists, but the politically sophisticated Indians would discount any Azad Hind broadcasts. At best, such tactics might aggravate existing Indo-British tensions. See the following articles in *SWJN 12*: "India's Day of Reckoning" (article by Nehru which appeared in the March 1942 issue of *Fortune* magazine), pp. 168–177; "Note on the Indian Background" (Nehru's letter, dated May 11, 1942, to Colonel Louis Arthur Johnson, FDR's emissary), pp. 301–312; and "Visit of Chinese Leaders to India" (Nehru's statement to the *News Chronicle* of London, February 28, 1942), pp. 478–479. Also note Penderel Moon's editorial commentary in Wavell, *Journal*, 72.

    37. Bhuyan, *Quit India*, pp. 21–23, including footnotes.

    38. *Ibid.*, pp. 21–108, particularly the footnoted material.

    39. *Ibid.* Taking a more militant stand, Nehru warned Indians to resist both the Japanese invaders and Bose's INA. See the following entries in *SWJN 12*: "No Toleration of Any Aggression" (speech to Congress staff, Howrah, April 19, 1942), pp. 253–255, "Defence by One's Own Strength" (Jorhat speech, April 23, 1942), p. 262; and "Fight Hitler and Japan to the End" (Gauhati press conference, April 24, 1942), pp. 262–263.

    40. Gerber, "Japan's Choice," pp. 323–325; John W. Gerber, "India's Would-be Quisling," *Nation*, 158 (April 22, 1944): pp. 473–474; "India: Renegade's Revenge," *Time*, 43 (April 17, 1944): p. 36; Alfred Tyrnauer, "India's Would-be Fuhrer," *The Saturday Evening Post*, 216 (March 11, 1944): pp. 22, 109–110; Alfred Wagg, "Subhas Chandra Bose," the *New Republic*, 114 (April 15, 1946): pp. 499–500; and "The Guilty," *Collier's* p. 52. Surprisingly, schoolchildren were among the first Americans exposed to Subhas Bose. A fairly probing article in *Scholastic* covered Bose's early career. See "India: Britain's Problem Child," *Scholastic*, 36 (April 8, 1940): pp. 8–9.

    41. Gerber, "Quisling," pp. 473–474; and Gerber, "Japan's Choice," pp. 323–325.

    42. "Renegade's Revenge," p. 36.

    43. Wagg, "Subhas Chandra Bose," pp. 499–500.

Chapter 10: The Falling Tiger

    1. [United States] War Department, Office of the Assistant Chief of Staff, G-2, Special Branch: M.I.D. [Military Intelligence Department], MAGIC Summary No. 759, SRS 1280, April 23, 1944, Copy No. SB3, pp. 6–7, reel 9, frame 0176.

    2. Ayer, *Witness*, pp. 10–25; Majumdar, *Struggle*, pp. 623, 687–691; P.N. Khera, "Les Groupes Politiques Indiens et la Guerre," *Revue D'Histoire de la Deuxieme Guerre Mondiale*, 89 (January 1973): pp. 3–22; and Toland, *Rising Sun*, pp. 611–615. Before it became apparent that the Netaji would lose Imphal, overseas Indians renewed their enthusiasm for the INA. In the Philippines, the Japanese embassy sent word to Tokyo that the Manila chapter of the Indian Independence League had been rejuvenated, but it remained plagued by internal squabbles. See [United States] War Department, Office of the Assistant Chief of Staff, G-2, Special Branch: M.I.D. [Military Intelligence Department], MAGIC Summary No. 738, SRS 1310, May 22, 1944, Copy No. SB-3, p. 8, reel 9, frame 0558.

    3. Bose, *Blood Bath*, p. 48. Nothing Bose said ever influenced Gandhi. As always, Gandhi felt that Bose seemed blind to Japan's true intentions. Bose's collaboration, if eventually successful, would exchange one colonial master for another. The titles of Gandhi's editorials speak for themselves. See Mahatma Gandhi, "Foreign Soldiers in India" (April 26, 1942), "Are You Not Inviting the Japanese?" (May 3, 1942), and "One Thing Needful" (May 10, 1942) in *My Appeal to the British* (New York, 1942), pp. 11–12, 13, 13–15.

    4. Bose, *Blood Bath*, pp. 49–50. It is ironic that Bose should have mentioned the Andamans and Nicobars as examples of Japan's concern for Asian nationalism. After the war, the Tokyo War Crimes Tribunal carefully documented the thousands of atrocities

committed on a daily basis throughout the occupied territories. Former Japanese officers serving as witnesses testified that both island groups stayed under Japanese military control during the war, despite Tojo's show of apparent goodwill. Worse yet, most of the brutality inflicted on Indians took place in the Andamans and Nicobars. Civilians, including women, were frequently accused of being spies for the Raj, and would be punished with unbelievable torture or summary execution. The testimony suggested that some Indians chose immediate suicide when threatened with detention. See Paul S. Dull and Michael Takaaki Umemura, eds., *The Tokyo Trials: A Functional Index to the Proceedings of the International Military Tribunal for the Far East*, 2nd ed. (Ann Arbor, 1962); and *International Military Tribunal for the Far East Proceedings 1946–1948* (Washington, DC, undated), reel 10, frames 13185–13200; reel 23, frames 30195–30213; and reel 30, frames 40235–40236, 40316. In future citations, this reference will be abbreviated as *IMTFEP*.

5. Ayer, *Witness*, pp. 10–11; and Beaumont, *Sword*, p. 180. Bose may have believed in the value of psychological torture, but his Japanese masters relied on the more physical approach. When questioned at the Tokyo trials, former soldiers claimed that they were taught that Indians came from a weak race, so they would respond to pain. Beating the elbows and knees softened civilian spies and unruly POWs alike, but failing that, Japanese interrogators jabbed pins into fingers and burned private parts. See *IMTFEP*, reel 10, frames 13185–13200.

6. [United States] War Department, Office of the Assistant Chief of Staff, G-2, MAGIC Diplomatic Summary No. 932, SRS 1454, October 13, 1944, Copy No. MI-3, pp. 14–15, reel 11, frame 0218. The War Department suspected that Bose's Axis contacts in Kabul probably consulted his enemies in India. This would certainly account for his lack of accurate information regarding the Indian situation. Bose's phony agents may have been responsible for exposing many of his secret missions, particularly in 1941. Within three years, the media had complete details of Bose's escape to Germany and later clandestine activities. See [United States] War Department, Office of the Assistant Chief of Staff, G-2, MAGIC Diplomatic Summary No. 846, SRS 1368, July 19, 1944, Copy No. SB-3, pp. 7–9, reel 10, frame 0214.

7. *Ibid.*

8. [United States] War Department, Office of the Assistant Chief of Staff, G-2, MAGIC Diplomatic Summary No. 942, SRS 1464, October 23, 1944, Copy No. MI-3, pp. 11–12, reel 11, frame 0336. For additional information, see Subhas Chandra Bose, "The East Asia War Is Now Our Own War" (speech, July 4, 1944), "The Situation in East Asia" (broadcast, July 9, 1944), and "The Indian Situation" (broadcast, July 10, 1944), in *Blood Bath*, pp. 36–38, 70–81, 82–95.

9. [United States] War Department, Office of the Assistant Chief of Staff, G-2, MAGIC Diplomatic Summary No. 1104, SRS 1626, April 3, 1945, Copy No. MI-3, pp. 5–7, reel 13, frame 0161. Also see Ayer, *Witness*, pp. 13–47. Only five days before this report was filed, the Japanese ambassador in Rangoon complained of problems between Bose and Ba Maw. Ambassador Ishii told his superiors in Tokyo that he blamed the ongoing disagreements on ethnic Burmese resentment of Indian economic clout in Burma. See [United States] War Department, Office of the Assistant Chief of Staff, G-2, MAGIC Diplomatic Summary No. 1099, SRS 1621, March 29, 1945, Copy No. MI-3, p. 7, reel 12, frame 0111.

10. Richard Storry, *A History of Modern Japan* (New York, 1978), pp. 219–220; Courtney Browne, *Tojo: The Last Banzai* (New York, 1967), pp. 168–169; Majumdar, *Struggle*, pp. 687–691; and Ghosh, *Army*, p. 16. In addition to his loss of face in both the political and military arenas, Bose had personal conflicts with the Japanese. He refused to surrender a Chinese girl whose attentions led a high-ranking INA officer astray. Since the Indian became derelict in his duties, the Japanese planned to execute the girl for espi-

onage. See Ayer, *Witness*, p. 47. Professor Roger Beaumont of Texas A & M University has concluded that, "by early 1945 the INA was a military farce." See Beaumont, *Sword*, pp. 179–180.

11. Ayer, *Witness*, pp. 13–47. Ayer insisted that Bose needed to be convinced to leave Rangoon.

12. [United States] War Department, Office of the Assistant Chief of Staff, G-2, MAGIC Diplomatic Summary No. 1045, SRS 1567, February 3 (?), 1945, Copy No. MI-3, p. 10, reel 12, frame 0447; [United States] War Department, Office of the Assistant Chief of Staff, G-2, MAGIC Diplomatic Summary No. 1154, SRS 1676, May 23, 1945, Copy No. MI-3, pp. 6–7, reel 13, frame 0775; and [United States] War Department, Office of the Assistant Chief of Staff, G-2, MAGIC Diplomatic Summary No. 1172, SRS 1694, June 10, 1945, Copy No. MI-3, pp. 11–12, reel 13, frame 0944.

13. Ayer, *Witness*, pp. 40–47; MAGIC Diplomatic Summary No. 1154, May 23, 1945; and [United States] War Department, Office of the Assistant Chief of Staff, G-2, MAGIC Diplomatic Summary No. 1148, SRS 1670, May 17, 1945, Copy No. MI-3, pp. 4–5, reel 13, frame 0713. Since the Japanese Foreign Ministry only reluctantly approved Bose's move, the Netaji was forced to make a personal appeal to the Thai government.

14. Ayer, *Witness*, 41. As early as 1941, Japan took an interest in bringing the Soviets into the fold. Had Stalin joined the Axis, Tojo would have directed Japanese aggression against the British presence in India and Iran. See "Attached Document for 69th Liaison Conference, November 15, 1941" in Ike, *Japan's Decision*, pp. 247–249; and *IMTFEP*, reel 28, frames 36769–36770 (reference to a February 1941 Liaison Conference). For additional information, see Arnold Krammer, "Le Japon Entre Moscou et Berlin (1941–1945)" ("Japan Between Moscow and Berlin"), *Revue D'Histoire de la Deuxieme Guerre Mondiale*, 103 (July 1976), offprint.

15. Information and quotes from MAGIC Diplomatic Summary No. 1172, June 10, 1945; and [United States] War Department, Office of the Assistant Chief of Staff, G-2, MAGIC Diplomatic Summary No. 1197, SRS 1779 (?), July 5, 1945, Copy No. MI-3, pp. 9–10, reel 14, frame 0169. The July 5th report included Ba Maw's similar plot to subvert British influence in Burma.

16. [United States] War Department, Office of the Assistant Chief of Staff, G-2, MAGIC Diplomatic Summary No. 1188, SRS 1710, June 26, 1945, Copy No. MI-3, pp. 6–7, reel 14, frame 0084.

17. Goel, *Netaji and the CPI*. In a letter to this author, dated January 20, 1983, E.M.S. Namboodiripad, the late General Secretary of the Communist Party of India (Marxist), could not shed any further light on the Party's campaign against the Netaji.

18. Nehru, "Note on the Indian Background," in *SWJN 12*, pp. 301–312. Quote from p. 303.

19. Wavell, *Journal*, p. 55.

20. Ayer, *Witness*, pp. 8, 63–65; and Hayashida, *Netaji*.

21. [United States] War Department, Office of the Assistant Chief of Staff, G-2, MAGIC Diplomatic Summary No. 1250, SRS 1772, August 27, 1945, Copy No. MI-3, pp. 2–3, reel 14, frame 0751.

22. *Ibid.* Lawrence James' excellent study offers a few tantalizing theories about Bose's death. While the US relied on MAGIC, the British learned some details through a number of captured Japanese officers, who were interrogated in Hong Kong. James also cites a passing reference to "Agent 1189," an apparent British spy in Bose's circle. Who he was, and whether he was British or Asian, is not disclosed. "Agent 1189" was allegedly on Bose's plane, and survived to tell that Bose was heading for China to reestablish himself with "Chinese Communist" backing. See James, *Raj*, p. 575.

23. Wagg, "Subhas Chandra Bose," 499–500. The bizarre stories persist to this day.

Elvis-like reports that he survived the crash persisted among the Azad Hind believers. In 1999, a collection of these anecdotes was organized on the Internet. See "Netajigate: The After Life of Netaji Subhas Chandra Bose" at *http://www.sitemarvel.com/bengalonline/true_intro.html*

24. Goebbels, *Diaries*, p. 107; and "Anti-British Indian Dead, Inquiry Finds," *New York Times*, September 12, 1956, p. 10.

25. Bose, *Mission*, p. 238.

BIBLIOGRAPHY

Primary Sources

DOCUMENTS

International Military Tribunal for the Far East Proceedings 1946–1948 (Washington, DC, undated, available on microfilm).
The MAGIC Documents: Summaries and Transcripts of the Top Secret Diplomatic Communications of Japan, 1938–1945 (available on microfilm from University Publications of America, Inc., Washington, DC, 1980). Public Records Office, London.

PERIODICALS

New York Times
South China Morning Post (Hong Kong)

ARTICLES

"Axis Propaganda Barrage Badgers Britain on India." *Newsweek* 19 (March 16, 1942): pp. 34–35.
Bose, Subhas Chandra. "As We See It." *India In Transition* series. *The Living Age* 354 (April 1938): pp. 150–152.
_____. "European Chess-board." *The Living Age* 353 (November 1937): pp. 201–207.
Gerber, John W. "India's Would-be Quisling." *Nation* 158 (April 22, 1944): pp. 473–474.
_____. "Japan's Choice for India." *Nation* 157 (September 18, 1943): pp. 323–325.
"India: Chariot of Freedom." *Time* 31 (March 7, 1938): pp. 19–20.
"India: Renegade's Revenge." *Time* 43 (April 17, 1944): pp. 36.
"Japan's World: Yes We Have No Indian Curry." *Asiaweek* 13 (February 22, 1987): pp. 28–29.
Tyrnauer, Alfred. "India's Would-be Fuhrer." *Saturday Evening Post* 216 (March 11, 1944): pp. 22, 109–110.
Wagg, Alfred. "Subhas Chandra Bose." *New Republic* 114 (April 15, 1946): 499–500.

COLLECTED WORKS

Collected Works of Mahatma Gandhi Vol. 4 & 5. Ahmedabad: Government of India, 1961.
Selected Writings of Jawaharlal Nehru vols. 9–12, 14. Ed. S. Gopal. New Delhi: Orient Longman, 1981.

MONOGRAPHS

Ayer, S.A. *Unto Him A Witness.* Bombay: Thacker & Co., Ltd., 1951.

Banerjea, Surendranath. *A Nation in Making.* 4th ed. Calcutta: Oxford University Press, 1963.

Besant, Annie. *How India Wrought for Freedom.* New Delhi: Today and Tomorrow's Printers & Publishers, 1974. (Originally published in 1915.)

Bose, Sisir K., et al., eds. *A Beacon Across Asia.* New Delhi: Orient Longman, Ltd., 1973.

Bose, Subhas Chandra. *Blood Bath.* Lahore: Hero Publications, 1947.

______. *Crossroads.* New York: Asia Publishing House, 1962.

______. *Famous Speeches and Letters of Subhas Chandra Bose.* Ed. by Ganpat Rai. Lahore: Lion Press, 1946.

______. *Fundamental Questions of Indian Revolution.* Ed. Sisir K. Bose. Calcutta: Netaji Research Bureau, 1970.

______. *Impressions in Life.* Lahore: Hero Publications, 1947.

______. *An Indian Pilgrim: An Unfinished Autobiography and Collected Letters 1897–1921.* Calcutta: Asian Publishing House, 1965.

______. *The Indian Struggle 1920–1942.* London: Asia Publishing House, 1964.

______. *The Mission of Life.* Calcutta: Thacker, Spink & Co., Ltd., 1965.

______. *Through Congress Eyes.* Allahabad: Kitabistan, undated.

Brown, D. Mackenzie, ed. *The Nationalist Movement: Indian Political Thought from Ranade to Bhave.* Berkeley: University of California Press, 1961.

Churchill, Winston S. *The Second World War:* vol. 4, *The Hinge of Fate;* Vol. 6, *Triumph and Tragedy.* Boston: Houghton Mifflin, 1950 and 1953.

Ciano, Galeazzo Count. *The Ciano Diaries 1939–1943.* Ed. by Hugh Gibson. Garden City, New York: Doubleday & Co., Inc., 1946.

______. *Ciano's Hidden Diary 1937–1938.* Trans. by Andreas Mayor. New York: E.P. Dutton & Co., Inc., 1953.

Coupland, R. *The Cripps Mission.* London: Oxford University Press, 1942.

Curzon, George Nathaniel. *Russia in Central Asia.* New York: Barnes & Noble, Inc., 1967. (Originally published in 1889.)

Fischer, Louis. *Gandhi: His Life and Message for the World.* New York: Mentor Book, 1982. (Originally published in 1954.)

______. *The Life of Mahatma Gandhi.* New York: Harper & Row, 1983.

Gandhi, Mahatma. *My Appeal to the British.* New York: John Day Co., 1942.

______. *Swaraj in One Year,* 2nd ed. New York: AMS Press, 1972.

Ganpuley, N.G. *Netaji in Germany: A Little-Known Chapter.* Bombay: Bharatiya Vidya Bhavan, 1959.

Giani, Kesar Singh. *Indian Independence Movement in East Asia,* 2 vols. Lahore: Singh Brothers, 1947.

Goebbels, Joseph. *The Goebbels Diaries 1942–1943.* Ed. and trans. by Louis P. Lochner. Garden City, New York: Doubleday & Co., Inc., 1948.

Guha, Arun Chandra. *First Spark of Revolution: The Early Phase of India's Struggle for Independence.* New Delhi: Orient Longman, 1971.

Hayashida, Tatsuo. *Netaji Subhas Chandra Bose: His Great Struggle and Martyrdom.* Trans. and ed. by Biswanath Chatterjee. Bombay: Allied Publishers, Pty., Ltd., 1970.

Hentig, Werner Otto von. *Mein Leben: Eine Dienstreise (My Life: A Business Trip)*. Gottingen: Vandenhoeck & Ruprecht, 1963.

Hitler, Adolf. *Hitler's Secret Conversations 1941–1944*. New York: Octagon Books, 1976.

______. *Mein Kampf.* Ed. by John Chamberlain, et al. New York: Reynal & Hitchcock, 1939.

Ike, Nobutaka, ed. and trans. *Japan's Decision for War: Records of the 1941 Policy Conferences*. Stanford, California: Stanford University Press, 1967.

Khan, Shah Nawaz, ed. *The INA Heroes: Autobiographies of Maj.-Gen. Shanawaz, Col. Prem K. Sahgal, and Col. Gurbax Singh Dhillon of the Azad Hind Fauj*. Lahore: Hero Publications, 1946.

Kurti, Kitty. *Subhas Chandra Bose As I Knew Him*. Calcutta: Firma K. L. Mukhopadhyay, 1966.

Maclean, Fitzroy. *Eastern Approaches*. London: Jonathan Cape, 1949.

Nair, A.M. *An Indian Freedom Fighter in Japan: Memoirs of A.M. Nair*. Bombay: Orient Longman, 1982.

Nehru, Jawaharlal. *The Discovery of India*, 2nd ed. Garden City, New York: Anchor Books, 1960. (Originally published in 1946.)

______. *India's Freedom*. London: George Allen & Unwin, Ltd., 1962. (Originally published as *India and the World* in 1936.)

Orwell, George. *Orwell: The War Commentaries*. Ed. by W.J. West. London: BBC/Duckworth, 1985.

Rand, Christopher. *A Nostalgia for Camels*. Boston: Little, Brown & Co., 1957.

Rolland, Romain. *Mahatma Gandhi: The Man Who Became One with the Universal Being*. Trans. by Catherine D. Groth. New York: The Century Co., 1924.

Schellenberg, Walter. *Hitler's Secret Service*. 3rd ed. New York: Pyramid Books, 1971. (Originally published as *The Labyrinth*.)

Shirer, William L. *Gandhi: A Memoir*. New York: Touchstone Books, 1980.

Speer, Albert. *Inside the Third Reich*. Trans. by Richard and Clara Winston. New York: Macmillan Co., 1970.

Stevenson, William. *A Man Called INTREPID: The Secret War*. 2nd ed. New York: Ballantine Books, 1982.

Wavell, Archibald Percival. *Wavell: The Viceroy's Journal*. Ed. by Penderel Moon. London: Oxford University Press, 1973.

White, Theodore H. *In Search of History*. 2nd ed. New York: Warner Books, 1981.

Secondary Sources

ARTICLES

Bose, Arun Coomer. "Netaji and the Nazis: A Study in their Relations." *Journal of Indian History* 50 (1972): 321–332.

Gordon, Leonard A. "Radical Bengalis: Alliances and Antagonisms — A Review." *South Asian Review* 5 (1972): 341–344.

"The Guilty: Subhas Chandra Bose." *Collier's* 114 (September 30, 1944): p. 52.

Hauner, Milan. "The Soviet Threat to Afghanistan and India 1938–1940." *Modern Asian Studies* 15 (April 1981): 287–309.

"India: Britain's Problem Child." *Scholastic* 36 (April 8, 1940): pp. 8–9.

Khera, P.N. "Les Groupes Politiques Indiens et la Guerre." *Revue D'Histoire de la Deuxieme Guerre Mondiale* 89 (January 1973): pp. 3–22.

Krammer, Arnold. "Le Japon entre Moscou et Berlin 1941–1945." *Revue D'Histoire de la Deuxieme Guerre Mondiale* 103 (July 1976): offprint, pp. 1–11.

Lebra, Joyce C. "Japanese and Western Models for the Indian National Army." *Japan Interpreter* 7 (1972): 364–375.

Mahajan, Sneh. "The Defence of India and the End of Isolation: A Study in the Foreign Policy of the Conservative Government 1900–1905." *Journal of Imperial and Commonwealth History* 10 (January 1982): 168–193.

Shergil, Hari Singh. "How Netaji Escaped." *Illustrated Weekly of India* 95 (September 8, 1974): p. 31.

Shillony, Ben-Ami. "Patterns of Violence: Political Terrorism in Prewar Japan." *Asian and African Studies* (Israel) 13 (undated): 242–263.

Singh, Kushwant. "INA Myth and Reality." *Illustrated Weekly of India* 95 (September 8, 1974): pp. 28–31.

MONOGRAPHS

Appadorai, A. *Essays in Indian Politics and Foreign Policy*. New Delhi: Vikas Publications, 1971.

Bailey, Thomas A. *A Diplomatic History of the American People*. 9th ed. Englewood Cliffs, New Jersey: Prentice-Hall, Inc., 1974.

Bazaz, Prem Nath. *The Role of Bhagavad Gita in Indian History*. New Delhi: Sterling Publishers, Pty., Ltd., 1975.

Beaumont, Roger. *Sword of the Raj: The British Army in India 1747–1947*. New York: Bobbs-Merrill Co., Inc., 1977.

Bhattacharjea, Ajit. *Jayaprakash Narayan: A Political Biography*. New Delhi: Vikas Publishing, Pty., Ltd., 1975.

Bhuyan, Arun Chandra. *The Quit India Movement: The Second World War and Indian Nationalism. Studies in Asian History and Politics*, vol. 4. New Delhi: Manas Publications, 1975.

Boyd, Carl. *The Extraordinary Envoy: General Hiroshi Oshima and Diplomacy in the Third Reich 1934–1939*. Washington, DC: University Press of America, Inc., 1980.

Browne, Courtney. *Tojo: The Last Banzai*. New York: Holt Rinehart & Winston, 1967.

Chadha, Yogesh. *Gandhi: A Life*. New York: John Wiley & Sons, Inc., 1997. (Originally published as *Rediscovering Gandhi*.)

Collins, Larry, and Dominique Lapierre. *Freedom at Midnight*. 4th ed. New York: Avon Books, 1976.

Corr, Gerard H. *The War of the Springing Tigers*. London: Osprey Publishing Ltd., 1975.

Das, M.N. *India Under Morley and Minto*. London: George Allen & Unwin, Ltd., 1964.

Das, Taraknath. *India in World Politics*. New York: B.W. Huebsch, Inc., 1925.

Dull, Paul S. and Michael Takaaki Umemura, eds. *The Tokyo Trials: A Functional Index to the Proceedings of the International Military Tribunal for the Far East*. 2nd ed. Ann Arbor: University of Michigan Press, 1962.

Endacott, G.B. *Hong Kong Eclipse*. Hong Kong: University of Hong Kong Press, 1978.

Ghose, Sankar. *Indian National Congress: Its History and Heritage*. New Delhi: All-India Congress Committee, 1975.

______. *Political Ideas and Movements in India*. Bombay: Allied Publishers, 1975.

Ghosh, K.K. *The Indian National Army*. Meerut, India: Meenakshi Prakashan, 1969.

Goel, Sita Ram. *Netaji and the CPI*. Calcutta: Society for the Defence of Freedom in Asia, 1955.

Gopal, Ram. *How India Struggled for Freedom*. Bombay: Book Centre, Pty., Ltd., 1967.

Gordon, Leonard A. *Bengal: The Nationalist Movement 1876–1940*. New York: Columbia University Press, 1974.

Hale, H.W. *Political Trouble in India 1917–1937*. Allahabad: Chugh Publications, 1974.

Herzstein, Robert Edwin. *The War that Hitler Won: The Most Infamous Propaganda Campaign in History*. New York: Putnam, 1978.

Hirzowicz, Lukasz. *The Third Reich and the Arab East*. London: Routledge and Kegan Paul, 1966.

Hohne, Heinz. *Canaris*. Garden City, New York: Doubleday & Co., Inc., 1979.

Hoyland, John S. *Gopal Krishna Gokhale: His Life and Speeches*. Calcutta: YMCA Publishing House, 1933.

Hutchins, Francis G. *India's Revolution: Gandhi and the Quit India Movement*. Cambridge, Massachusetts: Harvard University Press, 1973.

Ienaga, Sabura. *The Pacific War 1931–1945: A Critical Perspective on Japan's Role in World War II,* English ed. New York: Pantheon Books, 1978.

James, Lawrence. *Raj: The Making and Unmaking of British India*. London: Little, Brown and Company, 1997.

Jeffrey, Robin, ed. *Asia: The Winning of Independence*. New York: St. Martin's Press, 1981.

Johnson, Gordon. *Provisional Politics and Indian Nationalism: Bombay and the Indian National Congress 1880–1915*. London: Cambridge University Press, 1973.

Kaura, Uma. *Muslims and Indian Nationalism: The Emergence of the Demand for India's Partition 1928–1940*. Columbia, Missouri: South Asia Books, 1977.

Keer, Dhananjay. *Mahatma Gandhi: Political Saint and Unarmed Prophet*. Bombay: Popular Prakashan, 1973.

Lal, Lakshmi Narain. *Jayaprakash: Rebel Extraordinary*. New Delhi: Indian Book Co., 1975.

Lewin, Ronald. *The Chief: Field Marshal Lord Wavell, Commander-in-Chief and Viceroy 1939–1947*. New York: Farrar Straus Giroux, 1980.

Majumdar, R.C., et al., eds. *History of the Freedom Movement in India*, vol. 3, 2nd ed. Calcutta: Firma KLM Pty., Ltd., 1977.

______, et al., eds. *Struggle for Freedom. The History and Culture of the Indian People Series*, vol. 11. Bombay: Bharatiya Vidya Bhavan, 1969.

Misra, K.P., ed. *Studies in Indian Foreign Policy*. New Delhi: Vikas Publications, 1969.

Moorhouse, Geoffrey. *Calcutta*. New York: Harcourt Brace Jovanovich, Inc., 1971.

Nanda, B.R. *Gokhale, Gandhi and the Nehrus: Studies in Indian Nationalism*. London: George Allen and Unwin, 1974.

________. *Gokhale: The Indian Moderates and the British Raj*. New Delhi: Oxford University Press, 1977.

Nath, Shaileshwar. *Terrorism in India*. New Delhi: National Publishing House, 1980.

Panikkar, K.N., ed. *National and Left Movements in India*. New Delhi: Vikas Publishing House, Pty., Ltd., 1980.

Pluvier, Jan. *South-East Asia from Colonialism to Independence*. Kuala Lumpur, Malaysia: Oxford University Press, 1974.

Rao, P. Kodanda. *Foreign Friends of India's Freedom*. Bangalore, India: PTI Book Co., 1973.

Ray, Rajat. *Urban Roots of Indian Nationalism: Pressure Groups and Conflict of Interests in Calcutta City Politics 1875–1939*. New Delhi: Vikas Publishing House, Pvt., Ltd., 1979.

Rumbold, Sir Algernon. *Watershed in India 1914–1922*. London: Althone, 1979.

Sahota, D.S. *Lala Lajpat Rai: His Life and Thought*. Dhudike, Faridkot, Punjab: Shri Balbir Singh c/o Lajpat Rai Study Centre, 1974.

Scarfe, Allen, and Wendy Scarfe. *JP — His Biography*. New Delhi: Orient Longman, Ltd., 1975.

Schectman, Joseph B. *The Mufti and the Fuehrer*. New York: Thomas Yoseloff, 1965.

Seagrave, Sterling. *The Soong Dynasty*. New York: Perennial Library/Harper & Row, Publishers, 1986.

Sheng Xiangong, Lu Jishan, and Zhang Changman. *An Indian Freedom Fighter in China: A Tribute to Dr. D.S. Kotnis*. Trans. by Zhang Sen. Beijing: Foreign Languages Press, 1983.

Shridharani, Krishnalal. *My India, My America*. Garden City, New York: Halycon House, 1943.

Singh, Pardaman. *Lord Minto and Indian Nationalism 1905–1910*. Allahabad: Chugh Publications, 1976.

Sinha, P.B. *Indian National Liberation Movement and Russia 1905–1917*. New Delhi: Sterling Publishers, Pvt., Ltd., 1975.

Spear, Percival. *A History of India*, vol. 2. Baltimore: Penguin Books, 1970.

Stephan, John J. *Hawaii Under the Rising Sun: Japan's Plans for Conquest After Pearl Harbor*. Honolulu: University of Hawaii Press, 1984.

Storry, Richard. *A History of Modern Japan*. New York: Penguin Books, 1978.

Tahmankar, D.V. *Lokamanya Tilak: Father of Indian Unrest and Maker of Modern India*. London: John Murray, Ltd., 1956.

Toland, John. *Adolf Hitler*. Garden City, New York: Doubleday & Co., Inc., 1976.

______. *The Rising Sun: The Decline and Fall of the Japanese Empire 1936–1945*. New York: Random House, 1970.

Tomlinson, B.R. *The Indian National Congress and the Raj, 1929–1942: The Penultimate Phase*. London: Macmillan Press, Ltd., 1976.

Toye, Hugh. *The Springing Tiger*. London: Cassell, 1959.

Tuchman, Barbara W. *Stilwell and the American Experience in China 1911–1945*. New York: Macmillan Co., 1971.

Vajpeyi, J.N. *The Extremist Movement in India*. Allahabad: Chugh Publications, 1974.

Williamson, Samuel R., Jr., and Peter Pastor, eds. *Essays on World War I: Origins and Prisoners-of-War*. New York: Dutton, 1983.

Wolpert, Stanley A. *Tilak and Gokhale: Revolution and Reform in the Making of Modern India*. Berkeley: University of California Press, 1962.

Yale, William. *The Near East: A Modern History. The University of Michigan History of the Modern World*. Rev. ed. Ann Arbor: University of Michigan Press, 1968.

ONLINE

http://www.sitemarvel.com/bengalonline/netaji.html

FICTION

Clavell, James. *King Rat*, 4th ed. New York: Bantam, 1963.

Scott, Paul. *The Birds of Paradise*. London: Pan Books/Heinemann, 1990. (Originally published in 1962.)

INDEX